Progression in
Primary English

⊛SAGE | 50 YEARS

SAGE was founded in 1965 by Sara Miller McCune to support the dissemination of usable knowledge by publishing innovative and high-quality research and teaching content. Today, we publish more than 750 journals, including those of more than 300 learned societies, more than 800 new books per year, and a growing range of library products including archives, data, case studies, reports, conference highlights, and video. SAGE remains majority-owned by our founder, and after Sara's lifetime will become owned by a charitable trust that secures our continued independence.

Los Angeles | London | Washington DC | New Delhi | Singapore

Progression in
Primary English

Linda Saunders

Los Angeles | London | New Delhi
Singapore | Washington DC

Los Angeles | London | New Delhi
Singapore | Washington DC

SAGE Publications Ltd
1 Oliver's Yard
55 City Road
London EC1Y 1SP

SAGE Publications Inc.
2455 Teller Road
Thousand Oaks, California 91320

SAGE Publications India Pvt Ltd
B 1/I 1 Mohan Cooperative Industrial Area
Mathura Road
New Delhi 110 044

SAGE Publications Asia-Pacific Pte Ltd
3 Church Street
#10-04 Samsung Hub
Singapore 049483

Editor: James Clark
Assistant editor: Rachael Plant
Marketing manager: Lorna Patkai
Production editor: Nicola Marshall
Proofreader: Emily Ayers
Indexer: Silvia Benvenuto
Cover design: Naomi Robinson
Typeset by: C&M Digitals (P) Ltd, Chennai, India
Printed in India at Replika Press Pvt Ltd

Library of Congress Control Number: 2014945727

British Library Cataloguing in Publication data

A catalogue record for this book is available from the British Library

ISBN 9781446282939
ISBN 9781446282946 (pbk)

MIX
Paper from
responsible sources
FSC
www.fsc.org   FSC® C016779

At SAGE we take sustainability seriously. Most of our products are printed in the UK using FSC papers and boards. When we print overseas we ensure sustainable papers are used as measured by the Egmont grading system. We undertake an annual audit to monitor our sustainability.

CONTENTS

ABOUT THE AUTHOR

Linda Saunders is a senior lecturer in primary English at St Mary's University, Strawberry Hill, Twickenham. She works on the primary PGCE and MA programmes. Prior to university work, Linda taught extensively in English primary and special schools as a class teacher, as an English and a special educational needs coordinator and as an advisory teacher for special educational needs. Following on from her doctoral thesis examining reading aliteracy, she has continued to research reading motivation.

ACKNOWLEDGEMENTS

I would like to thank my colleagues, students and former students who have advised and supported me during the process of writing this book.

Linda Saunders

SAGE would like to thank the following reviewers whose comments in the early stages of the project helped to shape this book:

Josephine Brady, Birmingham City University

Paul Gardner, University of Bedfordshire

Catherine Glavina, Warwick University

Deborah Jones, Brunel University

INTRODUCTION

Studying with Progression in Primary English

Progression in Primary English is intended to encourage you, the student teacher, to reflect on the nature of progression in primary English. The text contains four reoccurring self-study elements within each chapter. These elements are designed to encourage you to relate an area of primary English subject knowledge to your own context, build confidence with subject specific terminology and to develop the focus of your classroom observations of primary English. The whole book deliberately omits any formal kind of tick lists of attainment targets or a detailed account of a primary English curriculum. It is best studied *alongside* the specified English curriculum and attainment criteria specific to your own school circumstances. However, each of the four study elements have been formed from or informed by the statutory national curriculum in England for primary schools (DFE, 2013), current and previous national curriculum assessment criteria in England (DFE, 2011; Qualification and Curriculum Authority, 2010; The National Literacy Strategy, 2000), principles from related research and theory and from primary classroom experience.

Four study elements

1. Activities
    Short practical tasks are designed to encourage application to your own
    personal and professional school contexts, revise subject specific vocabu-
    lary and ensure that you re-examine the breadth of the primary English
    curriculum applicable in your own circumstances.

2. Pupil vignettes
    Each chapter contains fictitious examples of English work for four fictitious
    pupils, who are first outlined in Chapter 1. Although written to demonstrate
    different ages and facilities for primary English, the vignettes, with their
    fictitious samples of work, are not complete or definitive descriptions of
    English capability. *This is most important.* All children are different, learn in
    different ways and are subject to a vast range of different social, emotional,
    cultural and academic circumstances. Particular elements, such as social,
    emotional, cultural and school circumstances, have therefore been deliber-
    ately omitted. Some academic elements have been purposely included,
    where appropriate, to deepen an understanding of an important and over-
    all feature of primary English progression.
    Every chapter contains a brief overview of the vignettes' academic perfor-
    mance in one area of primary English with accompanying sets of fictitious
    work samples. You are encouraged to identify and suggest features and
    next steps for progression using these examples. Further reflection ques-
    tions are included to complement each set of work samples. Essentially, the
    vignettes provide manufactured scenarios for discussion, debate and reflec-
    tion. They stimulate further questions for deeper study. Blank versions of
    the vignette work sample charts may be used for your own classroom
    observations.

3. Observation guides
    An observation guide appears at the end of the main curriculum chapters.
    These introductory materials are intentionally very broadly based. By
    themselves they contain a minimum amount of detail with which to
    observe every aspect of primary English and must be supplemented by the
    statutory curriculum and attainment criteria specific to your own school
    circumstances.

4. Self-assessment questions
    Self-assessment questions appear at the end of every chapter. Some of the
    questions are cumulative with the intention of assisting you to build a
    picture of some of the features of primary English progression relevant to
    your own professional context. Illustrative answers are provided in the
    appendices.

The Teachers' Standards

In relation to primary English progression, elements from each of the following Teaching Standards necessary for the award of Qualified Teacher Status are addressed throughout this book (DFE, 2013).
A teacher must:

S1. Set high expectations which inspire, motivate and challenge pupils
S2. Promote good progress and outcomes by pupils
S3. Demonstrate good subject and curriculum knowledge
S4. Contribute to the design and provision of an engaging curriculum within the relevant subject area(s).
S5. Adapt teaching to respond to the strengths and needs of all pupils
S6. Make accurate and productive use of assessment
S8. Fulfil wider responsibilities

References

DFE. (2011) *Assessing Pupils' Progress (APP): Assessment guidelines*. London: DFE. Retrieved from http://webarchive.nationalarchives.gov.uk/20110809101133/http://nsonline.org.uk/node/20683.

DFE. (2013) *The National Curriculum in England: Key stage 1 and 2 framework document*. London DFE. Retrieved from www.gov.uk/government/uploads/system/uploads/attachment_data/file/335133/PRIMARY_national_curriculum_220714.pdf.

DFE. (2013) *Teachers' Standards. Guidance for school leaders, school staff and governing bodies*. London: DFE. Retrieved from www.gov.uk/government/uploads/system/uploads/attachment_data/file/301107/Teachers__Standards.pdf.

Qualification and Curriculum Authority. (2010) *The National Curriculum: Level descriptions for subjects*. Coventry.

The National Literacy Strategy. (2000) *Target statements for writing*. London: DFES.

CHAPTER 1

WHAT DO WE MEAN BY PROGRESSION IN PRIMARY ENGLISH?

Objectives

1. To understand the differences between English, literacy and language
2. To identify behaviourist, nativist and constructivist approaches to primary English progression
3. To relate key areas of cognitive and language development to primary English progression
4. To revise the principles of classroom assessment

Introduction

This book is a guide to progression in primary English but it is not a book about current educational policy or prescribed levels of attainment. Instead, this is an intensely practical volume intended for classroom use.

This book links research and theory from education, psychology and child development, to English teaching in primary classrooms. These three fields of knowledge make major contributions to our understanding of how and why children learn and develop language and literacy. Psychology offers explanations and observations of why and how humans behave. Child development study uses observation to determine children's developmental milestones. Educational research addresses pedagogy; that is, the science or profession of teaching. Within pedagogy, English progression is addressed by curriculum, learning, and assessment studies.

This book is intended for busy student teachers who wish to understand primary English progression and its relationship to primary English assessment. Existing classroom teachers may consolidate their knowledge by reading this book. To this end, recent and relevant research and theory have been selected to complement examples of primary English practice from a range of pupils and classrooms. Wherever possible emphasis has been given to classroom based research and its related theory.

Progression is part of a common primary teaching cycle: assess, plan, teach, practise, apply, and review (DfES, 2006). English is a core subject that enables pupils to access all other areas of the primary curriculum. Recognising English progression enables pupils and teachers to address the transfer of English knowledge and skills across the curriculum. An understanding of how and why progression occurs is therefore central to good primary practice.

Attainment is defined as pupils' achievement in a given area. It is measured by summative and formative assessments. Progression is different. This is defined as a cumulative process that builds on previous levels of attainment. In the classroom, progression need not necessarily be linear. Pupils progress at different rates. Progress can be consolidation, enrichment or reflection. It can focus on pupils' independence across the curriculum and in out-of-school literacies. It looks different in different age groups and it can stall or deteriorate. Managing progression in primary English involves the integration of all four modes of English: reading, writing, speaking and listening. In this book, suggested next steps for progression structure an approach to monitoring progress in each chapter. The suggested steps are not intended to be definitive but to highlight areas for discussion and exploration with pupils in your classroom and alongside statutory curriculum requirements and assessment criteria.

Observing primary English progression

It is possible to think about progression in primary English under five headings:

- Development
- Clarity
- Security
- Implicit learning
- Explicit learning

These strictly non-hierarchical headings help to categorise most types of progression in primary English that may be happening in the classroom. These are also designed to address three reoccurring theories underlying the body of knowledge in child development. The first says that children are mini adults who progress on a natural continuum towards adulthood. The second says that children are distinct beings who develop into adults through different stages that are not necessarily in one special order. The third theme debates whether children are the product of our genes (nature) or of our environment (nurture).

Development

Development in primary English progression occurs when pupils consistently demonstrate the next level of attainment.

Classroom application Classroom development in primary English can be seen when pupils attain higher assessment levels. Standardised reading tests, for example, show a snapshot of how the pupil has progressed. Teachers' class assessments of pupils' work show snapshots of progress over extended periods.

Clarity

Clarity in primary English progression occurs when pupils demonstrate fundamental shifts in their levels of understanding. This may not necessarily be a specific move to a higher level of overall attainment. It can occur when key misunderstandings are addressed or when key skills are mastered that allow access to the application and transfer of knowledge and understanding across the curriculum.

Classroom application In the classroom, clarity in primary English progression can be seen when pupils demonstrate understanding of key features. For example, pupils' use of written connectives other than 'and' often indicates a shift towards the development of varied **compound sentences** and the use of commas.

Security

Security in primary English progression occurs when pupils demonstrate spontaneous and sustained transference of knowledge or skills within the subject and across different parts of the primary curriculum.

Classroom application Classroom security in primary English progression means that pupils know when, where and how to use English knowledge and skills without being prompted to do so. The ability to transfer reading skills such as skimming, scanning and précis to personal research through reading is an example.

Implicit learning

Implicit learning in primary English progression occurs when pupils demonstrate spontaneous knowledge and skills not explicitly taught.

Classroom application Classroom provision for implicit learning in primary English means that the class teacher builds a classroom environment designed to facilitate pupils' implicit use of speaking, listening, reading and writing. The role-play areas in reception classrooms are one example. Specific grouping of children to promote particular speaking and listening skills is a further example.

Explicit learning

Explicit learning in primary English progression occurs when pupils demonstrate knowledge and skills that have been explicitly taught.

Classroom application Classroom provision for explicit learning in primary English means that the class teacher scaffolds pupils' knowledge in order to develop a toolbox of transferable English skills. The use of concept cartoons for critical reading (e.g. Naylor and Keogh, 2002) or writing frames to develop structural knowledge of written genres (Wray, 2001) are examples of scaffolding.

Activity

Identifying aspects of progression

Fill in the table to match examples of classroom observation to elements of primary English progression. The first one has been done for you.

This activity will have caused you to reflect on the range of opportunities to record primary English progression in the classroom. Consistent planning for these opportunities is part of good assessment practice.

Good teachers constantly reflect. They judge what impact their teaching has had on pupils' learning, and how this has occurred. Good teachers also need to know something of why their teaching has caused their pupils to

Table 1.1

Example of classroom observation	Development	Clarity	Security	Implicit learning	Explicit learning
Pupil uses 'look, cover, say, write, check' technique for practising own spelling	✓	✓	✓		✓
Pupil scores above chronological age in standardised spelling test					
Pupil over generalises past tense 'ed' in written work					
Pupil spontaneously writes a fable to explain the Fire of London in a history lesson					
Pupil self-corrects full stops and notices similar errors in partner's writing					

learn or not to learn. Knowing something of why learning occurs allows teachers to work beyond the level of instinct or 'what feels right' with pupils in their charge. The apparently instinctive talent of the primary teacher, with a natural flair for teaching children well, is good to see but working with knowledge of the theory and research behind pupils' learning can complement this skill. In doing so, it lessens the possibility of inaccurate subjective judgements and reduces the possibility of over generalisation about the reasons for pupils' progress. It allows a broader perspective of learning gathered from situations other than a single classroom. It allows you and established class teachers to be informed professionals who are more able to judge the validity of the many teaching plans, resources, programmes, fads, fashions and directives that will arrive on your desk during your career in primary education. Consequently, it allows you, the student teacher, to recognise and adapt your classroom practice according to the learning and social needs of pupils in your classroom.

Primary teachers are also accountable to a number of regulatory bodies such as head teachers, school governors, official inspectors, government bodies such as the Office for Standards in Education in England, and local education authorities. Teachers are accountable to parents and not least to the pupils themselves. Working with knowledge of the theory and research behind pupils' learning enhances teachers' professional dialogue with these groups of people. The result is a professional body of teachers who are able to reflect on their own classroom practice in relation to established theory and research as well as teaching experience and current educational issues.

✎ Research focus

Using long term statistics to see patterns of progression

The Progress in International Reading Literacy Study

Since 2001, the Progress in International Reading Literacy Study (PIRLS) has produced regular surveys of pupils' reading progress for pupils in the 9–10 year old age range. The 2011 survey was taken by 45 countries and 9 sub-national participants, including states of the USA. The same standardised reading assessment is used. Pupils in England score above average on the PIRLS reading score but there is a longer tail of underachievement compared to other high scoring countries. Finnish, Northern Irish and Singaporean pupils outperform English pupils. Pupils' reported reading attitudes have improved but are still not encouraging. Evaluating these data means considering them in the light of national data trends, such as Standard Attainment Test (SATS) data, taken at age 11. For example, SAT trends in England show that 11 year old girls continue to outperform boys in reading and writing (DFE 2014). Finally, a look at these data in comparison to reading progress in individual classrooms and schools allows teachers to begin to identify significant local trends and to investigate possible teaching solutions.

Chapter 1 outlines some theoretical perspectives of English progression. The first section describes three main theories of language acquisition: behaviourist, nativist and constructivist. The second section introduces four pupil vignettes. The vignettes reoccur as a core study element of the chapters in this book. Finally, the chapter summarises common forms of classroom assessment and their relationship to primary English progression.

Language, English and literacy

In order to understand English progression it is necessary to distinguish English from language and literacy. English is one of the core subjects of the national curriculum in England but because English is also the language of instruction, most primary schools will emphasise the importance of pupils' use of language across the curriculum. Language incorporates the four modes of English: reading, writing, speaking and listening. English is the term used in this book. Literacy is the capacity to read and write but what constitutes a necessary level of literacy and the social effect of or value of literacy does not have universal agreement. The use of literature in primary schools serves as a good example of this dilemma.

Activity

Discuss the following statements about the place of literature in primary schools.

- Reading non-fiction is more important than reading fiction because understanding non-fiction texts is the main type of reading required as a future adult.
- Reading fiction helps pupils to improve their creativity. Non-fiction does not do this.
- Reading classic stories is the key to good levels of reading comprehension.
- Comics have no place in the primary reading diet.
- Books that relate to films help pupils to understand a plot and should always be encouraged.
- Research using the Internet is less skilful than research using other types of text because it requires less skill in selecting appropriate sources of information.
- It is not necessary to read stories aloud to pupils beyond the age of seven because pupils beyond this age should be encouraged to read silently or aloud for themselves alone.
- Children should learn to read using real books because reading schemes depress their motivation to read for interest and pleasure.
- In these days of technology and instant access to the Internet, the reading of literature has little or no place in the formation of pupils' general knowledge, identity and personality.

This activity will have caused you to consider the role of literature in literacy development. Is literature necessary or even desirable for children while they are learning to read or is it no more than an optional addition? To what extent does reading good literature feed quality writing? Is listening to good literature read aloud necessary for literacy attainment? Answers to this type of question rely on your knowledge and experience with using children's literature. This will influence your personal beliefs about the value of it for yourself, for pupils' academic, emotional and social development in primary school, in adolescence and in pupils' future adult lives.

Theoretical perspectives of literacy acquisition

Educational theory shows us four perspectives of literacy acquisition (Unesco, 2006):

1. Functional literacy
2. Critical literacy
3. Cultural literacy
4. Personal literacy

Functional literacy is the level of literacy required for the pupil to function in everyday life. The necessary level of functional literacy will be different according to the society in which the pupil is living. For example in China, learning to speak English is seen as a central requirement for pupils in order that they can compete as future members of the worldwide market. Critical literacy is the level of literacy required for the pupil to question and interrogate text in order to detect bias, create and develop new ideas. Cultural literacy is the level of literacy required for pupils to relate to literacy within a community. Knowledge of the religious or sacred books within a community is an example of this. Personal literacy is the level of literacy required for the pupil to build personal engagement. This includes personal reading and writing repertoires as well as possessing and using an idiolect, an individual style of spoken language.

Understanding these literacy viewpoints will help you to reflect on your role as a teacher of primary English as well as to recognise potential bias in others. In turn, they allow evaluation of the purpose and method of primary English assessment in the light of the audience for whom the data are gathered. For example, the use of standardised reading tests that give a 'reading age' does not assess pupils' personal or cultural literacy. Generally, the statistical data from standardised tests is used as a benchmark or as a screening tool to measure pupils' reading comprehension against expected levels of attainment for a certain age group. Personal or cultural reading skills are not currently standardised in this way.

Theoretical perspectives of language development

Since speaking and listening underpin reading and writing, it is important to consider theories of language development. Through language, humans think and communicate things physically present and in abstract. Speaking and listening are a child's first language tools for accessing the primary English curriculum.

Psychology shows us three prominent theoretical perspectives:

1. Behaviourism
2. Nativism
3. Constructivism

Each of these is at the extreme ends of the spectrum of language acquisition theories. In practice, psychologists would generally express a combination of these points of view. They are not the only theories of language development. Others, for example, include theories based on clinical knowledge of neurological functioning.

Behaviourism

Behaviourists suggest that a child's language develops because of imitation and reward. As the child listens and repeats what he hears, he receives positive praise. His attempts at speech are rewarded, especially when repeating the words in similar situations. It is possible to observe this type of language development in young babies interacting with their caregivers. A behaviourist approach to language development like this implies that all learning occurs because of what is taught. It finds its origins in the philosophical traditions associated with John Locke. An important advocate of this type of learning was B.F. Skinner.

Classroom application   In the primary classroom, a behaviourist approach to language development is often observed, for example, when teachers model **Standard English**. Pupils are subsequently rewarded for using it when it is appropriate for their spoken and written English. One of the criticisms of this theory of language acquisition is that it does not address how children develop language that they have not heard.

Nativism

Nativists suggest that a child's language develops because of an innate capacity to communicate through speech. Probably the most famous exponent of nativist language theory is Noam Chomsky. Although chiefly a linguist with an interest in the development of grammar, Chomsky theorised that all children are born with an innate capacity for learning language. He called it a Language Acquisition Device [LAD] (Chomsky, 1965; Chomsky, 1986). Chomsky's theory helps us to understand how children develop language that they have not heard directly. It proposes that children are active and experimental learners in the process of learning language because it is inborn. In particular, Chomsky's theories help us to view language development as part of the child's immediate social and cultural community. In the primary classroom, this theory of language development is observed when pupils generalise grammatical rules and approximate the pronunciation of words. So-called 'errors' (Herriot, 1971) are made when pupils apply standard rules of grammar to non-standard examples. For example, the child who speaks and writes about feets and tooths is applying the 'add an s' plural rule to its exceptions. Further examples are heard in the immature language of young children. For example, in our young family 'ammy' replaced 'hammer' and 'otterbe' replaced 'hot water bottle'.

Classroom application Class teachers need to be sensitive to the presence of immature language as part of English language progression. It is also important that pupils be given many opportunities to explore and experiment with language, particularly in the early years of schooling. This is why the reception class in school is full of opportunities for structured play and especially role-play activity. One of the criticisms of nativist theories of language development is that they do not fully address the contexts in which the meaning and structure of conversation takes place.

Constructivism

Constructivists suggest that language develops as the child actively builds language strategies and knowledge of language, rather than because it is taught or because it is naturally innate. A branch of constructivism is called social constructivism. This aspect of constructivism theorises that children develop language because of social influences. In this way, they become sensitive to the signs and symbols of language that are unique to that culture. The different interpretations of non-verbal body language in different cultures are an example of this idea. For instance, eye contact with the speaker is not universally appropriate. Likewise, nodding your head as affirmation is not universally understood. The inability of non-native speakers to speak a new language with a perfect accent or to understand its dialects is a verbal example.

Two major theorists of significance in any discussion of social constructivism are Vygotsky and Bruner. Bruner disputes Chomsky's theory of the LAD. Instead, he argues that language evolves because of the interaction between the caregiver and the child in specific situations, not in a haphazard way. Through this interaction, children develop an understanding of the structure and meaning of language. Joint problem solving occurs (Bruner, 2006). Bruner discussed the concept of scaffolding to describe the idea of structuring the child's learning activity in order to facilitate growth.

Classroom application   In the primary classroom, the development of children's ability to take turns is a prime example of joint problem solving behaviour. Bruner was a disciple of Vygotsky. A brief look at Vygotsky's ideas clearly shows where Bruner's theories have come from. Again, social and cultural contexts underpin his whole work. Vygotsky placed emphasis on the development of language to solve problems or to make meaning.

> '...the most significant moment in the course of intellectual development ...occurs when speech and practical activity ... converge'. (Vygotsky, 1978: 24)

In his research with children, he saw language develop from language that accompanies a task to language used to plan before an activity begins. In the primary classroom, language development like this can be seen in the differences between how children prepare their work. The youngest children tend to describe their work after it is done. Older children tend to be more able to use plans and to pre-plan accordingly. Vygotsky suggested that therefore the adults' role was to scaffold language development according to the child's zone of proximal development (ZPD). In essence, such a zone was the child's likely field of understanding. In the classroom, good differentiation of pupils' work allows this to happen. This is much more than providing varying amounts of work but instead involves careful grading so that pupils can access learning at the right level to succeed with the right level of motivating interest and challenge.

Vygotsky quoted further examples of young children, often around the age of six, who spoke to themselves while carrying out a new activity. He called this inner speech or private speech. He placed problem-solving language like this alongside that of the child's descriptive language of the world around them.

One final essential theorist is important to this brief outline of language theorists: Jean Piaget. His ideas are often contrasted with those of Vygotsky. Great debate surrounds which of these ideas are more valid and why. In essence, Piaget seems to have provided less evidence to explain the relationship between language and thought. Further discussion of Piaget's contribution to our understanding of language development appears in Chapter 2.

✎ Research focus

Culture and language development in the USA

The work of Shirley Brice-Heath is significant in understanding the influence of culture and society on English and language progression. Her work described and analysed the lived experiences of an American minority community over many years. Amongst a wealth of narrative description, her longitudinal case studies revealed the effect of social upheaval caused by economic change. In particular, the case studies tracked how increased social isolation reduced the children's opportunities for language development. New types of housing and a move away from the old community reduced children's opportunities for guided learning, observation and role play that had previously been available when they were living within a more stable and tighter social community (Brice-Heath, 1990).

Brice-Heath's findings illustrate the importance of a wider social and cultural community in the development of children's language and English skills. In the classroom this means acknowledging and building on pupils' social and cultural contexts as well as consciously building school and classroom communities full of reading, writing, speaking and listening.

Introducing the vignette pupils

This section of the chapter introduces four pen portraits of primary pupils. The pupils are fictitious composites of primary pupils with particular primary English needs. These character sketches are designed to illustrate what progression in primary English may look like in a primary classroom.

The pen portraits are not exclusive or complete descriptions of all primary pupils with similar characteristics. This is most important. Any such claim is invidious. Indeed, certain key elements of English progression, such as fictitious details of pupils' social backgrounds, have been deliberately omitted in order to prevent such conclusions from being made. All children are naturally different. Instead, you are encouraged to use these pen portraits as a *starting point* for discussion and debate. Use these portraits to compare, contrast, reject, question and add to in order to develop your understanding of pupils in your classroom and under your instruction. They are designed *only as a basis* from which to develop your understanding of the nature of progression in primary English. The pen portraits are a recurring study element for the chapters of this book.

Pupil 1: a pupil with literacy difficulties

Speaking and listening

John is 7 years old. John enjoys make-believe play as part of a small group. He enjoys telling adults about his favourite activities and his family. He speaks freely with his friends. John can take turns and carry out simple instructions. He can take simple verbal messages to another classroom. He is less able to ask for help if he does not understand, often relying on direction from other children or from the class teacher. John is not confident to speak in front of the class but he will answer questions directly addressed to him.

Reading

John has a standardised reading age of 6 years. The standardised test shows that his ability to read fluently is less than what is expected of pupils of his age. John tends to read slowly, spending a lot of time **decoding** the written words. Before and after reading, John can make basic predictions using the book. He can recall the main features of what he has read by using the pictures in the book along with some of the written text on the same page. He also uses the pictures to draw simple inferences, often in answer to a 'why did this happen?' type of question. John is using a popular reading scheme that favours a mix of phonetic and **high frequency words** for teaching pupils to read. He is using books at the Orange Book Band level (Bickler et al., 2003). John's favourite stories are about animals and monsters.

Writing and spelling

John can write sentences but tends to 'write as he speaks'. He likes to write about events that are familiar or important to him. He can use some capital letters. He tends to forget full stops when working independently. John makes good phonetic attempts to spell. He receives daily phonics work in a small group. Vowel **phonemes** are a current focus. He can read, spell and write most early high frequency words. John struggles to hold a pencil properly. He has difficulty tracing and colouring within the lines but his ability to draw free hand pictures that look more realistic has improved. His current standardised spelling age is 5.5 years. He receives weekly support to build his touch typing skills.

Pupil 2: a pupil with English as an additional language

Speaking and listening

Analyn is 9 years old. She speaks fluent Tagalog. Her parents speak Tagalog and some English. They have told Analyn's class teacher that Tagalog is the

(Continued)

(Continued)

main language spoken at home. Her parents say that Analyn is not literate in her home language. Analyn and her family have lived in the UK for two years. Analyn's confidence to use English at school is growing. She can hold conversations with her peers and will frequently switch between Tagalog and English, depending on who she is talking with. Her English vocabulary to describe objects and people has increased. She struggles to know and understand some subject terminology and the language to use to understand particular concepts in school. Maths problem solving and science lessons are especially challenging. She can struggle to understand some English idiomatic phrases such as 'to pull your socks up'. Analyn receives additional support from a teacher skilled in working with pupils for whom English is an additional language.

Reading

Analyn can read English fluently but her level of comprehension is below that of her ability to decode written English. Analyn is currently reading books at an easier level than her ability to decode in order that she may build her English comprehension skills. Many of these are sophisticated picture books and non-fiction as well as everyday literature such as catalogues, cookbooks, timetables, magazines and brochures. She chooses familiar texts to re-read in her free time at school.

Writing and spelling

Analyn is able to write simple accounts of what she has done. She has begun to write simple stories, often based on stories she has heard in the classroom. She needs support from an adult who speaks Tagalog and English to orally rehearse her writing. Analyn holds her pencil or pen correctly. She uses a cursive, joined up script. Analyn can memorise the spellings of whole words and use some phonic skills. She uses an English picture dictionary. Her current standardised spelling score is 8.0 years.

Pupil 3: an able pupil in primary English

Speaking and listening

Peter is 5 years old. He is the oldest boy in his class. Peter is confident to speak in small and larger groups of children with some awareness of the purpose and audience for his speech. He can speak clearly about his passion, dinosaurs, as well as his family and school life in general. Peter leads small groups, tending to dominate the conversation if the subject is of interest to him. He is sometimes impatient for his turn to speak. Peter asks many more questions of adults and peers than he answers. These, often good questions, strengthen and generalise his own understanding of the current topic; however, Peter will often only answer direct questions. Peter has a small circle of friends with whom he especially enjoys active outdoor play activities and games.

Reading

Peter has a standardised reading age of 7.5 years, more than two years in advance of his chronological age. He has an established reading repertoire that includes fiction and non-fiction. His favourite authors are Dick King-Smith and Antony Browne. Peter consistently uses a combination of **reading strategies** to decode unfamiliar words. These include the use of **phonics** and reading whole words. He will often substitute words with a similar meaning; he reads for meaning, not just to decode. For example, he will re-read sentences to work out the context of an unknown word. He will use previous knowledge of similar texts to predict, infer, recall and summarise themes across parts of a book but his inference is not always accurate because he has misread.

Writing

Peter enjoys writing. He chooses to use writing as a natural form of communication during his free play activities. For example, he will write emails, postcards, letters and captions for his artwork. He can write stories and accounts of what he has done. The writing is logically structured, usually in chronological order. Borrowed words or phrases from stories he has read are evident. He uses a wide range of adjectives. Full stops and capital letters are mostly accurate. He makes a good attempt at using commas in a list, and exclamation marks. Peter mainly uses **simple sentences**. Letters are evenly printed with his left hand.

Pupil 4: a pupil within expected levels of primary English

Speaking and listening

Japonica is 10 years and three months old. Her assessments show that she is performing some of the skills within the expected levels of English attainment for her age. Japonica is a shy child who is unconfident to speak out in a large

(Continued)

(Continued)

group and to answer questions. Role-play is difficult for Japonica but she works well as part of a team. She is considerate of others in a group, often allowing them to speak first and prefers to build on the ideas of others rather than offer her own opinions and ideas first. Nevertheless, she is methodical in her approach to carrying out instructions and can keep a group focused on a task by her example just as much as by her requests. She has a good awareness of the purpose and audience for her speech. For example, she re-phrases the same question for different audiences.

Reading

Japonica has a standardised reading age of 10 years. She can read fluently and is able to comprehend what she has read. Japonica can skim and scan the text to answer literal and inferential questions. She knows the basic structures of common fiction and non-fiction genres. Although she can identify the author's main purpose in writing, she does not easily recognise how an author has used particular methods to engage the reader. Consequently, evaluating what she has read is hard for her. Japonica reads for pleasure but has a limited reading repertoire and few real reading preferences other than the easier books by Jacqueline Wilson. However, Japonica does enjoy listening to stories, and viewing stories on film. She can use a search engine to find information on the Internet but does not fully understand how to evaluate the information she has found. In the library, Japonica mainly borrows non-fiction books and those related to film or television. She is not skilled at using books or magazines for her own research.

Writing and spelling

Japonica enjoys writing. She especially likes writing extended stories and non-fiction writing projects from other areas of the curriculum. Her writing has a clear beginning, middle and end. Paragraphs are used with prompts to do so at the planning stage. She adds adventurous vocabulary and a mix of sentence structures. Japonica generally needs to balance her ideas as a whole. Her standardised spelling score is 9.4 years. She has an exploratory approach to spelling, using a combination of skills to work out spelling for herself. Dictionaries are used, but the spellchecker while word processing is a more popular tool. Japonica's use of a range of punctuation is not consistent.

Assessment

This section briefly revises the main types of English assessment currently found in primary classrooms. Understanding the different types of assessment will enable you to recognise, evaluate, select and design an appropriate assessment for particular aspects of primary English progression.

Teachers have a professional responsibility to improve pupils' English capability. Assessment begins and ends this process but high stakes statutory assessment has added a controversial dimension, including the risk of teaching to the test. For this reason, it is important to understand the nature, purpose and audience for whom English assessments are undertaken.

There are three basic types of assessment:

1. Formative
2. Summative
3. Diagnostic

Formative assessment is ongoing. This is assessment for learning. It is primarily the role of the classroom teacher. Examples for primary English are marking, targeted questions for particular pupils and pupils' self-assessment of their progress in comparison to their class teacher. Class teachers, parents and regulating authorities, where comparisons are made with summative test data, require formative assessment data. Formative assessment may include, for example, a series of assessed pieces of written work from the class teacher. This provides a cumulative picture of a pupils' attainment. It will complement results from a summative writing test. An analysis of formative data can indicate strengths and areas of weakness across a group or a whole class. It can also show strengths and weakness in the teaching that preceded the formative assessments.

Summative assessment is periodic. This is assessment of learning, a snap-shot of English ability. It can be initiated by class teachers, a head teacher, or by external regulatory bodies such as the government. It is not always stand-ardised. Examples of summative primary English assessment are commercial standardised reading tests that give a level of attainment comparative to the pupils' chronological age. The measurement of pupils' performance in this way is important for establishing and recording the attainment of expected levels of progress. It is also a way of analysing the impact of classroom instruction at a local and national level. Summative data is required by regulating authorities, parents and by pupils. Summative assessments can also serve to screen pupils for future ability groups in the classroom. An analysis of summative data can indicate strengths and areas of weakness across a whole class and areas of strength and weakness in the teaching that preceded the testing.

Diagnostic assessment is usually periodic. It is a specific needs analysis of an aspect of pupils' English needs. Examples of diagnostic English assessments are non-word reading tests. These tests look at pupils' current knowledge of pho-nemes. Diagnostic assessments of handwriting that determine specific issues such as difficulties with writing speed are a further example. Some tests identify pupils at risk of specific learning difficulties in preparation for more formal assessment by the educational psychologist. Screening tests for dyslexia are an example of these types of tool. Sometimes ongoing, highly structured classroom observations will contribute to a later formal diagnosis for a particular English need by an external professional. This is why it is necessary to record good classroom observations of pupils not making steady English progress. An analysis of diagnostic data can indicate strengths and areas of English weakness for individual pupils or areas of concern in the teaching that preceded them.

Activity

Assessment

Match the English assessments to their audience type and purpose. One has been completed for you.

Table 1.2

Example of assessment	Type of assessment	Audience	Purpose
Weekly class spelling test from a scheme of work			
Standardised reading test	Summative	Pupil, parent, teacher, regulatory bodies	To assess pupils' expected level of reading comprehension, fluency and decoding
Class teachers' portfolios of annotated samples of written work across the ability spectrum			
Classroom assistant's observations of pupils' team working skills			

Undertaking this activity will have caused you to consider the value of each type of assessment for English progression in your classroom practice. Sometimes you will have no choice about what English assessment you are required to administer but using assessment critically means reflecting on a number of questions about how it may be used. Each of the forthcoming chapters contains practical examples of how to address each of the following questions.

- How does assessment link to classroom practice in order to improve pupils' English attainment?
- What sets of data are most valuable for daily classroom practice?
- Is there a place for integrating some summative and formative assessments?
- How, why and should you create a better assessment?
- What type of assessment is best for certain parts of English progression?
- Is it necessary to assess all aspects of English?
- Are there aspects of English progression that you cannot or should not assess?

Summary of chapter

This chapter introduced the arguments for using research and theory from education, psychology and child development. It has outlined key theorists and research associated with language acquisition and progression. It has introduced what primary English progression can look like in the classroom. Fictitious pen portraits that will be a cumulative reference point in the remainder of this book were introduced. It has revised the main forms of assessment for primary English. Throughout your future teaching career, you will be accountable for pupils' progress. Using key principles from established research and theory will enhance your professional dialogue and your ability to evaluate what, when, how and why pupils make progress in primary English.

? **Self-assessment**

1. Provide at least two reasons why behaviourism and nativism cannot be complete explanations of how children acquire language.
2. List three examples of different types of primary English assessment.
3. List one classroom example of English progression characterised by two of the following: development, clarity, security, implicit or explicit learning.

Annotated further reading

Child, D. (2011) *Psychology and the Teacher* (8th edn). London: Continuum International Publishing.
This classic text provides the class teacher with a substantial overview of psychological theory and practice.

Further resources

www.nfer.ac.uk The National Foundation for Educational Research provides current research, theory and discussion of statutory assessment procedures.

www.literacytrust.org.uk/ This organisation provides a wealth of literature, resources and research in secondary and primary literacy and research.

http://timssandpirls.bc.edu/ This site gives the international PIRLS reading data from 2001 to 2011.

References

Bickler, S., Baker, S., and Hosbaum, A. (2003) *Book Bands for Guided Reading* (3rd edn). London: Institute of Education.

Brice-Heath, S. (1990) 'The children of Trackton's children: Spoken and written language in social change', in J. W. Stigler, R. Shweder and G. Herdt (eds), *Cultural Psychology.* Cambridge: Cambridge University Press. pp. 498–519.

Bruner, J. S. (2006) *In Search of Pedagogy* (Vol. 2). London: Routledge.

Chomsky, N. (1965) *Aspects of the Theory of Syntax*. Cambridge, MA: MIT Press.

Chomsky, N. (1986) *Knowledge of Language: Its Nature, Origin, and Use*. New York: Praeger Publishers.

DfES (2006) *Primary National Strategy: Primary Framework for Literacy and Mathematics*. London: DfES.

DFE (2014) *National curriculum assessments at key stage 2 in England (Provisional)*. London: National Statistics. Retrieved from www.gov.uk/government/uploads/system/uploads/attachment_data/file/347653/SFR30_2014_Text.pdf.

Herriot, P. (1971) *Language and Teaching: A Psychological View*. London: Methuen.

National Primary Strategy (2006) *Excellence and Enjoyment: Learning and Teaching in the Primary Years* (Ref: 0521–2004). London: Department for Education and Science.

Naylor, S., and Keogh, B. (2002) *Concept Cartoons in Science Education*. Crewe: Millgate House Publishers.

Skinner, B. F. (1957) *Verbal Learning*. New York: Appleton-Century-Crofts.

Unesco (2006) *Understandings of Literacy*. www.unesco.org/education/GMR2006/full/chapt6_eng.pdf.

Vygotsky, L. S. (1978) *Mind in Society: The Development of Higher Psychological Processes*. Cambridge, MA: Harvard University Press.

Wray, D. (2001) *Developing Factual Writing: An Approach through Scaffolding*. Paper presented at the European Reading Conference, Dublin.

CHAPTER 2

SPEAKING AND LISTENING

Objectives

1. To exemplify language for thought and language for communication
2. To identify key features of speaking and listening progression in primary English
3. To relate speaking and listening progression to daily primary practice
4. To evaluate the process of assessment for speaking and listening in the primary classroom

Introduction

This chapter is the first of eight core chapters that address curriculum and pedagogy necessary for understanding primary English progression. In order to facilitate ease of access for busy student teachers, these chapters all have the same structure. Each chapter has three sections. In all sections the assess, plan, teach, practise, apply and review process is addressed (DfES, 2006). The pupil vignettes from Chapter 1 are used to exemplify the content. The first section summarises theorists and current research. The second section relates current and seminal research relevant to progression in the primary classroom. The third section evaluates common summative and formative examples of classroom assessment.

Language acquisition

In order to understand progression in speaking and listening in the primary classroom it is necessary to consider the components of language itself. Speaking and listening describes language that is understood and spoken. Human language is made up of four key components.

1. **Phonemes** are the smallest units of sound. Examples are consonant digraphs, vowels and the separate phonemes in consonant **blends**.
2. **Morphemes** are the smallest units of meaning. Examples are **suffixes**, **prefixes** and some whole words.
3. Syntax or grammar governs the way in which words combine to make meaning. Examples are the construction of simple, **complex** or **compound** sentences and the use of plurals and tenses.
4. Pragmatic rules govern how we use language as a form of communication, verbally or non-verbally. Understanding these rules requires some kind of choice plus effective listening skills. Examples are turn-taking, the ability to hold an effective conversation or speaking to have a specific effect on the listener such as to persuade. Part of pragmatics is meta-linguistics, or the ability to use language to talk about language. Understanding jokes and other types of word play are examples of meta-linguistic skills.

Table 2.1 presents a categorisation of speaking and listening in our vignette pupils. It allows us to track some of the features of attainment and suggested next steps for progression. In these examples, we can see that learning pragmatic rules of language is a key component of pupils' attainment across the primary age range. This is not surprising since competent speakers and listeners of any age know how to use language to communicate effectively in many circumstances. These examples also show the importance of vocabulary development and the formulation of questions. Vocabulary and question skills are examples of the relationship between pupils' language and thought.

Table 2.1   Summary of speaking and listening in the pupil vignettes

Pupil	Age	Attainment level	Language component	Features of progression	Suggested next steps for progression
Japonica	10	Within expected levels	Pragmatic rules of language	Empathetic in a group, phrases questions with awareness of different audience	Formulating critical questions Confident oral presentations
Analyn	9	EAL pupil at the earlier stages of English language acquisition	Pragmatic rules of language Syntax Morphemes	Understands social routines in the classroom, code switches (mixes English and Tagalog) accurately, naming vocabulary increasing	Vocabulary comprehension and confidence in small group discussion, including simple idiomatic phrases in conversation
John	7	Below expected levels	Pragmatic rules of language Syntax	Answers direct questions, retells personal events, takes turns in conversation and in a group	Vocabulary comprehension, asking for help if unsure
Peter	5	Above expected levels	Pragmatic rules of language	Extensive vocabulary, phrases focused questions with awareness of audience, takes turns	Empathy in small group work Confidently answering open questions

Developing vocabulary

The breadth of pupils' understood and spoken vocabulary is a key component to overall progression in speaking and listening. Vocabulary is the largest part of language. By the time pupils enter primary school they will have normally mastered the infant stages of speech and language development. Pupils will have passed through the processes of babbling, gestural language to ask for things from adults and building a basic vocabulary for understanding and expression. From five years onwards, children normally continue to develop their knowledge of grammar, vocabulary and pronunciation for their first language. Children's language grows to enable them to categorise vocabulary. For example, from 6 to 12 years of age anything from 5,000 to 10,000 words are added to children's vocabulary per annum (Anglin, 1993, 1995; Skwarchuk and Anglin, 2002).

Research focus

The predictive significance of language development in infancy

Pupils' early language ability appears to predict their cognitive and academic attainment at school age. Evidence comes from long-term studies of the breadth of infants' vocabulary compared with records of their attainment later in primary school. In this example, Hohm and her colleagues tracked German infants from 10 months until they were 11 years old. The investigation confirmed the predictive significance of early language skills in thinking and academic attainment ten years later (Hohm et al., 2007).

Possessing an extensive vocabulary is a key to pupils' ability to describe, think and understand the world around them. It helps pupils to create shades of meaning. For example, familiarity with a wide vocabulary is one measure of pupils' general knowledge that lasts across a lifetime (Stanovich et al., 1995). This is part of pupils' progression in conceptual development. Concepts develop because the pupil is increasingly able to use vocabulary to categorise and connect the essence of larger and larger bodies of information. Such vocabulary includes verbal and non-verbal examples as well as a whole range of signs, symbols and images. Familiarity with large numbers of concepts enables the development of logical reasoning and higher order comprehension skills such as inference, deduction and empathy. Principal theorists of concept formation were Piaget, Vygotsky and Bruner. These giants in the field of cognitive and language development present contrasting but complementary ideas about the relationship between language and thought.

Activity

Synonyms

Add ten words that have the same or a similar meaning to each word in the list below. Classify these lists into named categories.

Under
Road
Blue
Happily
Swoop

This activity will have caused you to consider the richness of the English language. It may also have caused you to consider how, why and when children process vocabulary, the relationship between vocabulary that is spoken and that which is understood and children whose vocabulary acquisition is impaired or those with English as a second language. Your answers to these questions rely on your knowledge and experience of observing and listening to pupils' language in the context of their academic, emotional and social development in the primary school.

Classroom application Pupils' vocabulary develops from a number of different sources. These include the pupils' home, social and cultural community and their schooling. These environments allow the pupil to use language and to understand how it is used in a variety of different contexts. In this way, pupils' vocabulary and concepts develop alongside thinking skills.

In the classroom, this means providing explicitly planned and taught opportunities to develop pupils' spoken and understood vocabulary, as well as opportunities to practise, apply and monitor its development. Thus, learning drives the planned activity, not vice versa. For example, weekly spelling lists often use current topic or subject specific vocabulary as well as morpheme and phonic based words. Other well-tested teaching methods of categorising and extending pupils' vocabulary include subject specific dictionaries, cloze procedure (fill in the gap), group prediction and group sequencing of ideas. Information technology provides a range of graphical learning programmes that enable pupils to retrieve, extend and categorise information in diagrammatic forms. Mind mapping techniques apply here. Lastly, basic vocabulary-building research skills include indexing, glossary and contents usage plus confident use of the thesaurus and dictionary in paper and digital formats.

Multimodal and audio resources provide a range of materials for developing vocabulary. These include open source material such as Audacity software for recording. Audio and interactive talking books online are freely accessible from many publishers.

Implicit vocabulary development is fostered by providing a classroom environment where speaking and listening can thrive. In a vocabulary rich environment, current, interactive and vibrant classroom displays of new concepts and new words are always evident. Drama, role play, judicious groupings for classroom discussion and using talk as a basis for writing are all examples of conditions that allow vocabulary to grow.

Theories of language and thought

Psychologists are divided in their interpretation of the relationship between language and thought. Three possible views seem to exist:

1. Language determines thinking
2. Thinking determines language development
3. Thinking and language develop separately but both contribute to communication and concept development.

Evaluating the evidence for each of these points of view allows us to consider the place of speaking and listening within the assess, plan, teach, practise, apply and review framework. (DfES, 2006)

Language determines thinking

In essence, this theory of language and thought says that language determines human thought. It is generally attributed to Edward Sapir and Benjamin Lee Wolf. In its purest form, the hypothesis is questionable. If language determines thought, people speaking different languages understand the same concept in different ways. Some linguistic examples bear this out, such as those languages that have multiple words to describe one particular noun. The occurrence of idioms unique to a language is another. Typically, both aspects are challenging for foreign speakers who may only understand a literal translation without knowing about the social and cultural influences. One of the criticisms of this theory of language and thought is that it does not address why or how an idiolect or an individual style of spoken language develops that can remain misunderstood to foreign and to native speakers alike. For example, the LOL mobile telephone text abbreviation stands for 'laugh out loud' but an older generation may interpret it as 'lots of love', with disastrous consequences! In this context, the environment dictates the expression of the language. Recognition and categorisation of LOL depends on the users' past experiences and cultural awareness of the social nuances of texting.

Classroom application In the classroom, evidence for language determining thinking can be observed when children experiment with written and spoken vocabulary. Overzealous or misplaced use of new vocabulary appears. Sometimes particular words and phrases become fashionable. Popular books, film and television can be the root for such classroom trends. It is the teachers' responsibility to introduce new vocabulary and concepts within a relevant context. Perhaps a pertinent example of this is in the introduction of learning objectives at the beginning of a lesson. If the purpose of the learning objective is to introduce a shared understanding between the teacher and the pupil then it is important that the pupil can understand it too. Since pupils' self-assessment against lesson objectives is important to primary English progression, sensibly composed learning objectives can enable success.

Thinking determines language development

In essence, this theory of language and thought says that thought precedes language because knowledge of concepts is expressed in other ways. Piaget advocated this hypothesis. For him language was a single part of precise stages of child development, common to every culture. Children can speak language that they do not understand. Using it properly means understanding its purpose and function in a variety of circumstances. Observations of young children and infants at play clearly demonstrate understanding of a range of concepts without the need for language.

  Activity

Observing play

Match the observations of play with the concept in the opposite column.

(Continued)

(Continued)

Table 2.2

Observation of play	Possible concept
Child chooses different shapes to fit into corresponding holes	Friction
Using a funnel	Objects exist even though you cannot see them
Pushing toy cars on different surfaces	The properties of some shapes
Searching for a hidden toy under a cloth	The flow of water can be diverted

This activity will have caused you to consider the role of exploratory and problem solving play in the primary classroom and its contribution to the progression of speaking and listening. Is play a natural part of all learning? Should play be part of every primary classroom, not just in the early years? What other types of play are useful in developing children's speaking and listening? How can the class teacher contribute to pupils' play in order to extend speaking and listening skills without destroying pupils' spontaneity, personal interests and choices? Answers to this type of question rely on your knowledge and experience of observing children's play. This will influence your personal beliefs about the value of play in developing speaking and listening, and the ways in which play can function as a means through which to assess pupils' progress.

Thinking and language develop separately but both contribute to communication and concept development

In essence, this theory of language and thought emphasises the joint functions of human language, to communicate and to structure thinking. Vygotsky advocated this hypothesis. He proposed that by the age of two the child had assimilated sufficient vocabulary and sufficient knowledge of the elements of social communication. This included non-verbal rules like eye contact and facial expression as well as basic social and cultural norms (Vygotsky, 1962). As the child grew, language for developing concepts and language for social communication became more and more connected and advanced.

Classroom application   In the primary classroom, evidence for thinking and language as complementary routes is observed when children work in groups to problem solve and to prepare joint pieces of work. Close observation of group work reveals pupils taking on different group roles consciously or unconsciously. These roles depend on the pupils' capability as well as their self-confidence working in the group. Work outside of the classroom helps language to develop further. Varied opportunities for interaction allow pupils to practise, apply and review new vocabulary, new concepts and new social ways of interacting within a safe and nurturing environment. It is the class teachers' responsibility to structure the environment to accommodate these factors and to explain the relevance of what is happening at the pupil's level of understanding. Further discussion of group work appears in section two.

✎ Research focus

Interaction in speaking and listening

In 2009, Professor John Hattie at Auckland University published an outstanding analysis of educational research called *Visible Learning* (Hattie, 2009). Hattie carried out a systematic examination of what caused effective learning. The top four indicators for effective learning, pupils' self-assessment, teaching based on principles from Piaget, teachers' formative assessment and microteaching, all require interaction through speaking and listening. Hattie's findings have significant implications for the development of pragmatic language skills in the classroom, in conjunction with appropriate formative assessment techniques for speaking and listening.

Developing an ability to communicate

Constructivist principles state that language and learning are active social processes in which children use their current knowledge to understand and formulate new ideas and concepts. Pragmatic rules are part of this. They govern how we use language as a form of communication, verbally or non-verbally. Four headings are useful to describe how pupils communicate with each other (Bloom and Lahey, 1978):

1. The speaker selects their information to provide a context for the listener
2. The speaker and the listener have a shared knowledge with which to infer
3. The speaker can adjust talk for different audiences
4. The speaker and the listener follow the unspoken rules of conversation

Classroom application Pupils need a reason to communicate in the classroom. It is the teacher's responsibility to provide a classroom environment where meaningful communication is positive and worthwhile. For this reason, trying not to ignore, anticipate or repeat pupils' comments, questions or answers is good practice. Pupils will stop useful speaking and listening if they feel that their contributions are unnecessary, unwanted or ignored. There are many ways to address language for thought and communication in the classroom. Further reading is recommended at the end of this chapter; other approaches are addressed in section two.

Speaking and listening progression in the primary classroom

This section of the chapter puts the theories of language, thought and communication into a classroom context. Using current research and the pupil vignettes from Chapter 1, it describes and evaluates evidence to support understanding of progression in speaking and listening in the primary classroom.

Social circumstances often represent unseen and unspoken cultural literacy traditions that effect pupils' English attainment. Research presents a large body of evidence to suggest social and cultural trends that class teachers need to be aware of in order to understand and address primary English progression.

Research focus

An environment for primary English progression

Parental involvement in their children's language and literacy development has positive effects on pupils' long-term progress. Flouri and Buchan's psychological research studied the effects of early parental involvement on their child's language and school achievement. The fathers' and mothers' involvement in the schooling of 7-year-olds predicted educational attainment at 20 years of age (Flouri and Buchanan, 2004). Lutz-Klauda's analysis of adolescent reading engagement and parental support shows similar patterns of behaviour for older pupils (Lutz-Klauda, 2009). However, parental involvement in school tends to reduce as children mature. The child tends to mediate the parent's influence. Children who are more able tend to attract higher levels of parental involvement (Desforges and Abouchaar, 2003).

Each of these pieces of research illustrates the importance of early language development to the development of reading and writing. Progression in English is central to overall academic progress. Class teachers therefore need to be aware of the changing influences of home, community, school, peers and the media throughout the primary years and beyond. In practice, this means incorporating pupils' social and cultural language experiences into a classroom ethos that fosters and supports the development of pupils' overall primary English skills.

In the classroom, a three-pronged approach to developing pupils' speaking and listening skills is useful as a basis for understanding progression:

1. Vocabulary development: this area includes conceptual development
2. Group working skills: this area includes discussion and drama work
3. Question and answer skills: this area includes listening and responding to different audiences and conceptual development

These categories are not exclusive to all aspects of pupils' speaking and listening attainment but are intended to be a convenient starting point for assessment, planning and teaching.

Vocabulary development

The bulk of research in this area addresses the importance of building pupils' vocabulary in order to facilitate the development of conceptual thinking. This includes the development of spoken grammar and its relationship to written English. General knowledge and pupils' reading repertoire are related to understanding and using an extensive vocabulary.

Activity

Vocabulary in speaking and listening

Look at the three transcripts from the pupil vignettes. Record the features and suggested next steps for progression in vocabulary in speaking and listening. The first one has been done for you.

(Continued)

(Continued)

Table 2.3

Pupil	Transcript of independent retelling of Red Riding Hood	Features of progression	Suggested next steps for progression
Japonica	*This is from the wolf's point of view. Once upon a time, a poor wolf suffered in his lair. He mithered and mithered, 'I'm hungry, it has been such a hard winter.' ....What do you think miss? Will this grab the listener's attention?*	Uses standard and non-standard English anecdotes and nuances to entertain and persuade, gives evidence for point of view	Use of descriptive vocabulary in extended sentences
John	*The big bad wolf didn't like the girl called Red Riding Hood so he tricked her and then she was scared and ran away so the axe man cut down the tree and the wolf died.*		
Peter	*Red Riding Hood, huh, I've heard that one ages ago. It's about a little girl in a red cape who is taking food to her Gran but the wolf has put the Gran in the cupboard. The wolf wants to eat so he pretends he's Gran in the bed but luckily the woodcutter saves Red Riding Hood.*		

〰️ **Reflection questions**

- Identify a common strength and weakness in vocabulary use for each pupil.
- Identify a common strategy to boost vocabulary development for each pupil.

This activity will have caused you to consider vocabulary connections between the four modes of English: reading, writing, speaking and listening. Most pupils need a wide oral vocabulary before they can become effective readers and writers. Research suggests that the development of pupils' vocabulary significantly affects pupil progress in all aspects of primary English (Echols et al, 1996; Nagey and Anderson, 1984).

🖐 Research focus

Vocabulary growth and reading habits

There is a relationship between early comprehension skills and vocabulary growth. A long-term study of 8–16 year olds found that pupils with strong reading habits and good reading comprehension scores had better levels of vocabulary as they matured (Cain and Oakhill, 2011).

Print and speech are different types of communication. Pupils learn not to write in the way in which they speak. Texts they read are not normally written like speech, but a broad and balanced vocabulary is necessary for effective communication as pupils mature to adulthood. Cain and Oakhill's work looks toward the pupils' future. It highlights the necessity of supporting and building literacy-based leisure pursuits such as reading for pleasure. This must include a full range of multi-modal texts and skills.

Grammar is the analysis of words and sentences to make meaning. 'Grammar is the skeleton which makes everything hang together. Without grammar, we are left with a jumble of words and word-parts and nothing makes sense' (Crystal, 2000: 6).

Pupils' awareness of grammar develops at an early age. In infancy, children will have progressed from stringing two words together to making inflections. Inflections are aspects such as using 's' to denote a plural and 'ed' to mark tenses. As part of normal progression, young children use inflections too broadly. Examples are 'comed' or 'sleeped' instead of 'came' and 'slept'. Here, young children are applying their own rules, not imitating adults' talk in a behaviourist manner. Nativist and constructivist theories of language acquisition have been discussed in Chapter 1.

While there is limited research evidence to suggest a direct relationship between separate grammar teaching and improved writing (Andrews et al., 2006), there are obvious connections between vocabulary and grammatical speech. In order to be able to communicate effectively with a wide range of other people, pupils need to be able to choose the most effective vocabulary and sentence structures for different circumstances. Successful communication will also involve pupils choosing appropriate standard and non-standard English forms.

Classroom application   In the classroom, a useful method of monitoring pupils' vocabulary and grammatical development is to attend to the length and then the complexity of pupils spoken and understood sentences, and also to look at how often pupils ask and answer questions. One technique is to model longer answers or questions, providing pupils with oral sentence stems from which to build their responses. For example the pupil can build a cause and effect answer from the stem: I saw... change because...'. Similar approaches apply to teachers monitoring the length and complexity of oral instructions that pupils understand. A further technique is a systematic plan to expect questions and answers from targeted pupils. Discreet use of Q and A cue cards to remind pupils to respond can be of practical help. The advent of new digital software to record language in situ has made speech recording easy. Teachers normally automatically plan their own differentiated questions for most lessons.

Group working skills

The bulk of research in this area addresses the development of different types of talk and pragmatic rules for communication. Group working skills include pupils' awareness of the role of the speaker and the listeners, and the context and purpose for using language to address the task.

Activity

Group work in speaking and listening

Look at the three classroom observations from the pupil vignettes. Record the features of and suggested next steps for progression in group working for speaking and listening. The second one has been done for you.

Table 2.4

Pupil	Observation of mixed ability science group	Feature of group working progression	Suggested next steps for progression
Japonica	*Japonica listens carefully in her group. She agrees with what is said by smiling or repeating the point, she takes control of the equipment and written work. She does not contribute by herself. She asks questions about timekeeping.*		
John	*John takes proper turns to speak in this group. He speaks mainly to one other pupil. He will answer and ask direct questions. He can predict what he thinks will happen but is restless after ten minutes of waiting to speak or having to listen to everyone in the group.*	Turn taking Understands direct questions Prediction	Sharing thoughts with the group Summarising the main points for group
Peter	*Initially, Peter dominates this group. He has clear ideas about how to extend the topic and sets out to instruct his peers about how they should carry out his ideas. One other has similar thoughts. For a while, the two boys work as an exclusive pair, firming up and extending Peter's original idea. Others chat and then follow their directions, asking for clarification towards the finish.*		

Reflection questions

- What happens if the group structures are changed? How and why will ability groups, friendship groups, group size and groups with common interests change pupils' language?
- What is the role of the classroom teacher in shaping group discussion?

This activity will have caused you to consider the nature of interaction in small groups. Social constructivist ideas can form a useful framework for understanding how language develops from group work.

The first aspect to consider in group interaction concerns the quality of the language itself. The work of Neil Mercer is of relevance here. He discusses three types of talk (Mercer, 1995). Cumulative talk consolidates the responses of others. Disputational talk disagrees or challenges other speakers. Exploratory talk extends ideas from most group members. The vignettes show examples of each kind of talk. Japonica uses cumulative talk. She risks shallow learning because questions, creative language and thinking have no starting point. Peter uses talk that is more exploratory when he is working with a partner. A plan of action is agreed and the group carry it out. Obviously, next steps for Peter would show group decision making. John shows some elements of disputational talk, probably because he does not fully understand, but he is able to work successfully in a pair. Bruner's and Vygotsky's work on scaffolding as part of social interaction is of significance here. Scaffolding proposes that adults or persons who are more experienced teach pupils through graded steps towards a known concept or solution. As the pupil learns, less and less scaffolding is required.

Classroom application In the field of educational research, Robin Alexander has developed constructivist ideas into the principles of dialogic teaching (Alexander, 2008). Scaffolded dialogue contains interactions that encourage diverse thinking, open-ended questions, elaborated answers, informative feedback and extended contributions that build concepts. The thinking skills work of Robert Fisher and the Philosophy for Children movement are also relevant to small group work.

The applications of multimedia to group discussions are many and various. They represent social constructivist approaches to learning. For example, the convenience of using digital cameras and audio recording through devices such as iPads allow for spoken language and performance to be routinely recorded and captured as easily as writing. Online discussion tools such as Skype and more sophisticated educational versions like Voice Thread permit discussion with a wider audience and outside of the school day. Blogs and Google docs are written examples of ways to continue the online discussion.

Question and answer skills

The bulk of research in this area addresses the development of thinking skills and conceptual development. Four main aspects of progression in speaking and listening can be monitored through pupils' questioning and answering skills:

- Comprehension that includes higher order skills
- Ability to manipulate language for effect

- Ability to summarise
- Ability to evaluate spoken language

These are also features of progression in pupils' involvement in their learning. Involvement promotes motivated, self-regulated learning. Self-regulated learning promotes new knowledge, discussion, exploratory talk, better comprehension, self-evaluation and deeper thinking (Black and Wiliam, 1998). However, various classroom studies show that the amount of pupil questioning is often low and limited to answering narrow questions. It is therefore appropriate for teachers to take periodic audits in their lessons of the balance of oral contributions between teacher and pupil as well as between pupils' ability, age and gender.

Activity

Look at the three transcripts from the pupil vignettes. Record the features of and suggested next steps for progression in question and answer skills. The last one has been done for you.

Table 2.5

Pupil	Transcript of oral responses in guided reading group addressing the motives of a main character	Feature of progression	Suggested next steps for progression
Japonica	T: *Are there any heroes in this play?* J: *Titania, well is she the hero, I mean really... a true one. What do you think? She survives kissing a donkey, magic potions, Puck and still keeps her husband at the end! I think Shakespeare wants us to learn from fairies and the fools in this play, they are cleverer. Oberon, a hero? I don't think so!*		
John	T: *Who is Max?* J: *Max sails away on a boat (flicks through book). I think it's because he is having a dream about monsters on an island. It's spooky to look at the pictures. Max is king of the monsters, the wild things.*		

(Continued)

(Continued)

Pupil	Transcript of oral responses in guided reading group addressing the motives of a main character	Feature of progression	Suggested next steps for progression
Peter	T: *What about the main character?* P: *Emily? Now, she's by Dick King Smith, I like those books. That Emily is a spider she has ninety-nine brothers and sisters. Her legs are very special and they help her in the spider sports. She had ten legs!*	Listens and answers appropriately, summarises relevant points from across the story.	Evaluate language

〰 Reflection questions

- What literal, inferential and evaluative levels of comprehension do these pupils show?
- What two questions would you ask each pupil in order to extend and then to assess his or her answers?

This activity will have caused you to consider the role of the teacher in asking questions that extend pupils' thinking and expression. Pupils have also to be involved in formulating questions and answers to foster progression. Rephrasing questions and answers is part of this process. It assists pupils in recognising the gaps in their understanding as well as practising their questioning skills. The bulk of research in this area addresses the field of meta-cognition, exploring social, constructivist principles of language acquisition. Meta-cognition is the ability to identify and articulate personal thinking and learning processes. For example when a native of Peterhead in Scotland explains his use of the verb *shopping* instead of the dialect word *messages*, for a Londoner, he is demonstrating meta-cognitive skills. Meta-cognitive skills promote self-regulation.

✎ **Research focus**

Using sentence stems to support pupils' online questioning

A Taiwanese study looked at the effectiveness of using question stems to help pupils' formulation of science questions for primary school children. Providing pupils with detailed sentence stems increased the number, value and kind of questions that pupils asked online. This finding is an example of teachers' scaffolding learning in order to promote higher order thinking. The researchers note, however, that pupils needed a basic level of knowledge in order to use detailed question stems. Their note highlights the necessity of pupils' summary skills. It is hard to think about questions without a store of knowledge to begin with (Hu and Chiou, 2012).

Progression can also be monitored through looking at the type and quality of questions that pupils use. Closed, open and rhetorical questions begin this process. Then, factual, comprehensive and integrated questions allow pupils to synthesise and apply their cross-curricular knowledge to each question and answer (King, 1994). In this way, literal, inferential and evaluative questions and answers progress.

🖾 **Activity**

Types of questions

Classify the examples of questions asked by the pupils in the vignettes into closed, open, factual, comprehensive or integrated examples.

Japonica: Do you think that Shakespearian people believed in fairies for medical or for religious reasons?

John: What colour were the Wild Things?

Peter: Why do spiders make webs so big?

Classroom application In the classroom, systematic planning of question types and group work is necessary such as through the use of the Interactive Whiteboard as a joint teacher-pupil tool for recording questions and answers during and after the lesson. Certain types of questions are useful for monitoring progression. Contradictory questions do this. They allow pupils to detect errors or misconceptions in their own understanding. Other daily techniques include providing alternatives to questions. Both approaches promote strategies for pupils' meta-cognitive talk. The following examples are adapted from Fisher and the DfEE (Department for Education and Employment, 1999; Fisher, 2005).

- Invite and offer personal experiences. This allows pupils to recognise empathy.
- Wait longer for answers. This allows personal thinking time or with a partner.
- Offer a suggestion, offer information or make observations. This allows pupils to build on their own knowledge.
- Justify personal views. This encourages the importance of evidence.
- Tell me more. This allows pupils to elaborate their answers.
- Withhold judgement. This encourages more pupils to answer.

The assessment of speaking and listening

This section evaluates common summative and formative examples of classroom assessment. It does not address diagnostic speech and language assessment since this is the responsibility of trained clinicians. However, systematic and thorough observations of pupils' speaking and listening skills can contribute to formal requests for assessments of speech and language delay. The section combines summative and formative assessment of individual pupils' needs.

Summative assessment

Speech therapists and educational psychologists often complete summative assessment of speaking and listening. Pupils undertaking these assessments will normally have been referred to investigate possible speech and language delay observed in the classroom, at home or in both settings. Typically, these professionals carry out standardised assessments of pupils' verbal and non-verbal reasoning skills. The assessments can include measures of vocabulary, memory, grammar and the meaning of sentences as well as understanding oral instructions of varying complexity. They may also include specific assessment of pupils' pragmatic skills: how the pupil understands social communication. Lastly, physical speech difficulties such as stuttering are part of this referral process. Many speech and language difficulties can occur in primary school pupils and it is important for teachers to be alert to the possibility of specific clinical needs. Concerned student and existing teachers will consult the school's special educational needs coordinator for advice.

Formative assessment

A formative assessment of pupils' speaking and listening can highlight strengths and weaknesses in your own teaching. Your future planning will be shaped by what you find. Shared formative assessment also encourages pupils to become involved in their own learning. Formative assessment of speaking and listening can illustrate pupils' language, what they know and how they learn.

One of the dangers of externally imposed summative assessments is that teachers teach to the test. However, any lack of statutory assessment for speaking and listening should not stop teachers from using formative techniques. Unfortunately many commercially produced assessments for regular speaking and listening skills are cumbersome, time consuming or unrelated to the general primary curriculum. Commercial packages can also drive the curriculum and separate it from pupils' learning. To be workable, a consistent and informative choice of assessment tool is needed. It should cater for broadly defined needs. Exceptional individual needs can then be identified for possible intervention later on.

An alternative to commercial assessment is to plan your own schedule based on your curriculum, your classroom context and your pupils' cultural and social setting. Within this, differentiated planning indicates points of progression for groups of pupils, when and how their speaking and listening is to be taught, monitored and assessed.

Observation forms the basis of formative assessment of speaking and listening. This can be focused observation for particular learning objectives or general observation for generic features of progression such as question use, vocabulary or group working skills. It provides both a record of what is said and understood, plus insight into the classroom context for speaking and listening. It is both an observation record of pupils' language and thinking skills and an illustration of their understanding of a new concept.

There are two main types of observation: continuous notes of everything that occurs or observations based on prescribed criteria. The latter can be taken at specific timed intervals or for set periods. Not every piece of conversation can or should be recorded. Classroom support assistants can assist with observation schedules. The appendix of this book contains an example of a generic observation recording sheet for speaking and listening in the primary classroom.

As with all samples of work used to monitor progression, several observations are needed in order to give breadth to any judgements that are made. In practice, this means recording similar examples of the same features of speaking and listening in a number of different situations across a period. The number of observations will differ according to pupils' age. Younger pupils, for example, will need more speaking and listening assessment observations because it is their main form of English and language expression. Older pupils will require more opportunities to use speaking and listening in formal situations such as for debate and interview.

Observations of pupils in social situations are also important, as are observations of pupils with unfamiliar adults, such as the supply or cover teacher. As with writing and reading, competent skills drive pupils' progression. This is just as important as the products of speaking and listening, such as role-play, presentation and debate. Pupils' presentations are part of formative assessment. The use of multi-media resources such as PowerPoint and Prezi are useful in addition to the use of digital cameras and audio recording. Making and using film and audio recordings are integral parts of the assessment of speaking and listening skills.

Formative assessment is also a measure of the quality of the classroom experience as well as a measure of pupils' capability. For this reason, simple daily techniques for formative assessment of speaking and listening will help you to monitor pupils' progress and check the quality of speaking and listening opportunities in your classroom. Simple techniques include varying question types, using alternatives to questions, pupils' oral summaries at various stages of a lesson, pupils orally re-presenting new knowledge in a different form (genre exchange), asking and answering true or false questions.

Table 2.6 presents the first entry for a matrix of primary English progression. This matrix is a cumulative element to the first eight chapters of this book. They're not a diagnostic measure of progression. As noted in the introduction, they have been formed from or informed by the statutory national curriculum in England (DFE, 2013), current and previous national curriculum assessment criteria in England (DFE, 2011; Qualification and Curriculum Authority, 2010), principles from related research and theory and knowledge of the primary classroom. Speaking and listening develop at different rates in different pupils and in different circumstances. Use this grid as a guide for classroom observation.

The gradual increase in vocabulary adds to pupils' grammatical confidence and the ability to choose the different types of language for different purposes, audiences and effects. Knowledge from growing reading repertoires and exploration of ideas in group situations allows the pupil to consolidate, justify and extend personal opinion. Eventually pupils are able to detect finer and finer nuances of communication such as bias, persuasion, humour and sarcasm. Developing vocabulary contributes to pupils' ability to describe and manipulate ideas and concepts with words and sentences rather than by using objects or non-verbal gestures alone. General knowledge can grow.

Table 2.6 Observing progression in speaking and listening

	Vocabulary development	Questions, answers and contributions	Group work	Examples of links with other 4 modes of English
Lower primary years	Uses conversational vocabulary for social and personal needs, tries out new vocabulary in imaginative and exploratory play Expands some sentences, often on request Mostly grammatical speech	Uses and understands direct questions and answers Speaks at length about familiar topics Takes messages and follows simple instructions Retells familiar events or stories in order	Takes turns Eye contact Uses gesture and tone of voice Predicts, recalls and sequences States ideas, uses cumulative talk, may talk alongside peer Some spasmodic listening	Listens to whole stories read aloud, makes relevant comment, re-reads familiar stories
Middle primary years	Uses vocabulary for effect Tries out new vocabulary in extended sentences, some inappropriate use of vocabulary Minor grammatical errors	Beginning to use extended sentences automatically Beginning to distinguish Standard English and non-Standard English usage Delivers a clear explanation and account	Takes turns, allows others to contribute, uses general knowledge to build contributions of others Empathy with speaker Active listener, debates Confident short presentation	Borrows fashionable phrases or words from media, peer group etc Comments on purpose of text Developing reading repertoire, literal, inferential and evaluative comprehension
Upper primary years	Chooses vocabulary for purpose, audience and effect Uses longer sentences for audience and effect Uses anecdotes and language play such as puns, for audience and effect Secure grammar in speech	Deliberately chooses Standard and non-Standard English for audience and purpose Can give extended answers or descriptions of new or unfamiliar topics, uses evidence to support personal opinions Speaks from different perspectives	Confident use of exploratory talk in group situation Secure empathy with speaker Evaluates language for audience, purpose and effect Active and sustained listening Confident range of presentation styles	Note taking from listening and viewing multimedia sources Established reading repertoire, literal, inferential and evaluative comprehension skills within and across texts and multi-media themes and examples

Summary of chapter

This chapter has described the elements of language acquisition. It has outlined the theoretical arguments for the connections between language and thought, vocabulary and group work in a classroom context. Pupil vignettes were used to illustrate the application of theory. It expanded these ideas in relation to current research and the four modes of English. It looked at the assessment of speaking and listening in the primary school. This chapter has emphasised your role as a classroom teacher in promoting consistency, continuity and progression in pupils' speaking and listening opportunities while they are in your care. In order for pupils to progress, their feelings of ownership and responsibility for their learning should also be accommodated. Productive speaking and listening begins this process.

? **Self-assessment**

1. List the four components of language.
2. Provide at least three reasons why the pragmatic use of language is emphasised in the primary classroom.
3. List and justify three items that you consider important features or a suggested next step for progression in speaking and listening. Choose items for the oldest, mid-range and youngest pupils in the primary school.

Annotated further reading

Baumann J., Ware, D. and Edwards, C. (2007) "Bumping into spicy, tasty words that catch your tongue': A formative experiment on vocabulary instruction', *The Reading Teacher*, 61: 108–122. This article describes practical details of a vocabulary instruction and enrichment programme.

Bowkett, S. (2007) *Jumpstart Creativity*, Abingdon: Routledge. This book contains a wealth of practical ideas to boost speaking and listening in the primary classroom.

Fisher, R. (1996) *Stories for Thinking*, Oxford: Nash Pollock. This book contains a series of thought-provoking stories with a range of structured questions suitable for group discussion.

Fisher, R. (2006) *Starters for Thinking*, Oxford: Nash Pollock. A whole range of similarly themed thinking skills books is available from this publisher.

Further resources

Inspiration software provides visual learning tools based on the principles of mind mapping. Available at: www.inspiration.com

Audacity software is available at http://audacity.sourceforge.net/about/

Photo books contribute to real contexts for speaking and listening.

Further details of Robin Alexander's dialogic talk are obtainable from www.robinalexander.org.uk/dialogic-teaching

The philosophy for children movement is an independent organisation that promotes the development of thinking in children and adults. www.philosophyforchildren.co.uk/index.php/1214

References

Alexander, R. (2008) *Towards Dialogic Teaching: Rethinking Classroom Talk* (4th edn). York: Dialogos.

Andrews, R. C., Torgesson, S., Beverton, A., Freeman, T., Locke, G., Low, G., et al. (2006) The effect of grammar teaching on writing development. *British Educational Research Journal*, 32, 39–55.

Anglin, J. M. (1993) Vocabulary development: A morphological analysis. *Monographs of the Society for Research in Child Development*, 58 (238).

Anglin, J. M. (1995) Word learning and the growth of potential knowledge vocabulary. Paper presented at the Society for Research in Child Development, Indianapolis, IN.

Black, P. and Wiliam, D. (1998) *Inside the Black Box: Raising Standards through Classroom Assessment*. London: King's College.

Bloom, L. and Lahey, M. (1978) *Language Development and Language Disorders*. New Jersey: John Wiley & Sons, Inc.

Cain, K. and Oakhill, J. (2011) Matthew Effects in young readers: Reading comprehension and reading experience aid vocabulary development. *Journal of Learning Disabilities*, 44, 431–443.

Crystal, D. (2000) *Discover Grammar* (5th edn). Harlow: Longman.

Department for Education and Employment (1999) *National Literacy Strategy: Teaching and Learning Strategies*. London: DfEE.

Desforges, C. and Abouchaar, A. (2003) *The Impact of Parental Involvement, Parental Support and Family Education on Pupil Achievements and Adjustments: A Literature Review*. London: Department for Education and Skills.

DFE (2011) *Assessing Pupils' Progress (APP): Assessment Guidelines*. London: DFE. Retrieved from http://webarchive.nationalarchives.gov.uk/20110809101133/http://nsonline.org.uk/node/20683.

DFE (2013) *The National Curriculum in England: Key Stage 1 and 2 Framework Document*. London: DFE. Retrieved from www.gov.uk/government/uploads/system/ uploads/attachment_data/file/335133/PRIMARY_national_curriculum_220714.pdf.

DfES (2006) *Primary National Strategy: Primary Framework for Literacy and Mathematics*. London: DfES.

Echols, L. D., West, R. F. and Stanovich, K. E. (1996) Using children's literacy activities to predict growth in verbal cognitive skills: A longitudinal investigation. *Journal of Educational Psychology*, 88, 296–304.

Fisher, R. (2005) *Teaching Children to Think* (2nd edn). London: Continuum.

Flouri, E. and Buchanan, A. (2004) Early father's and mother's involvement and child's later educational outcomes. *British Journal of Educational Psychology*, 74, 141–153.

Hattie, J. (2009) *Visible Learning*. Abingdon: Routledge.

Hohm, E., Jennen-Steinmetz, C. and Laucht, M. (2007) Language development at ten months: Predictive of language outcome and school achievement ten years later? *European Child and Adolescent Psychiatry*, 16, 149–156. doi:10.1007/s00787–006–0567-y.

Hu, H. and Chiou, G. (2012) The types, frequency and quality of elementary pupils' questions in a online environment. *The Turkish Online Journal of Educational Technology*, 11, 325–335.

King, A. (1994) Guiding knowledge construction in the classroom: Effects of teaching children how to question and how to explain. *American Educational Research Journal*, 31, 338–368.

Lutz-Klauda, S. (2009) The role of parents in adolescents' reading motivation. *Educational Psychology Review*, 21, 325–363.

Mercer, N. (1995) *The Guided Construction of Knowledge: Talk Amongst Teachers and Learners*. Clevedon: Multilingual Matters.

Nagey, W. E. and Anderson, R. C. (1984) How many words are there in printed English? *Reading and Research Quarterly*, 19, 304–330.

National Primary Strategy (2006) *Excellence and Enjoyment: Learning and Teaching in the Primary Years* (Ref: 0521–2004). London: Department for Education and Science.

Qualification and Curriculum Authority (2010) *The National Curriculum: Level Descriptions for Subjects*. Coventry.

Skwarchuk, S. and Anglin, J. M. (2002) Children's acquisition of the English cardinal number words. *Journal of Educational Psychology*, 97, 107–125.

Stanovich, K. E., West, R. F. and Harrison, M. (1995) Knowledge, growth and maintenance across a life span: The effects of print exposure. *Developmental Psychology*, 31, 811–826.

Vygotsky, L. S. (1962) *Thought and Language*. Cambridge, MA: MIT Press.

CHAPTER 3

ENGLISH AS AN ADDITIONAL LANGUAGE

Objectives

1. To exemplify language for thought and language for communication in pupils with English as a second language
2. To identify features of progression in acquiring English as a second language
3. To relate progression in acquiring English as a second language to daily classroom practice
4. To evaluate common forms of assessment for pupils with English as a second language

Introduction

Pupils with English as an additional language (EAL) are a feature of many primary classrooms in the United Kingdom. These pupils have specific patterns of progression in acquiring English that are both similar to and different from native English speakers. EAL pupils are not a uniform group. Like monolingual pupils, some may have learning difficulties and some may be very able pupils. All EAL pupils come to school with different language experiences. Consequently, they will travel through different stages of learning English in school. EAL pupils are not necessarily fluent in more than one language; some may be at the early stages, some may be fluent and some may also be literate in more than one language.

It is the class teacher's responsibility to assess their pupils' stage of English language acquisition and their level of academic attainment within secure and happy classrooms that reflect, accommodate and celebrate cultural diversity. The purpose of this short chapter is to provide an introductory context for monitoring the language progression of pupils with English as an additional language. It may be read in conjunction with references to the recurring classroom vignettes featuring Analyn, an EAL pupil, as they occur in other chapters.

Communicating in a new language involves three main areas of competence (Council of Europe, 2001).

1. Linguistics includes the phonics, vocabulary and grammar of the new language. It necessarily involves the development of language and vocabulary for thought and conceptual development.
2. Pragmatics covers how we use language as a form of communication, verbally or non-verbally. It includes areas such as turn-taking, listening skills and structuring language to have an effect on the receiver.
3. Sociolinguistics covers the social conventions associated with the use of language in different societies and cultures. It examines areas such as the use of language across social classes, gender and different social communities. It includes idiolect, or personal language repertoire, dialect and accent, Standard and non-Standard English. For example, in English, pupils will need to understand the social and cultural significance of local colloquial expressions and traditional constructions such as idioms and proverbs.

Activity

Language in context

Complete the table below. Rate your proficiency in using the languages that you speak to each context. Link the contexts to one or more language competencies.

Table 3.1

Language in context	First language	Second language	Third language	Fourth language	Language competency: Linguistics (L) Pragmatics (P) Sociolinguistics (SL)
Pronunciation					
Understanding the television					

Language in context	First language	Second language	Third language	Fourth language	Language competency: Linguistics (L) Pragmatics (P) Sociolinguistics (SL)
Reading a novel					
Writing a letter to a friend					
Conversation with peers					
Spoken grammar					
Written grammar					
Sending a text message					
Using a dictionary					
Telling or understanding a joke					
Understanding the rules of politeness and manners					
Asking directions					

This activity will have caused you to consider the complexities of applying and learning a second language in everyday life. You will have noticed that none of the examples of using and applying language relies on one competency. EAL pupils orchestrate a range of language skills in order to communicate through reading, writing, speaking and listening.

In school, EAL pupils have two challenges for learning in a new language: understanding the language for communication and understanding the language of each curriculum subject. These challenges incorporate the use of language for conceptual development and thought within linguistics, pragmatics and sociolinguistics.

Learning English as an additional language

The research and theory that underlies our knowledge of how pupils acquire a second language is large and complex. Further recommended reading appears at the end of this chapter. Previous chapters have outlined constructivist and social constructivist approaches to language progression. Social constructivist learning is embedded in a real context that enables pupils to take an active role in their own learning. Social constructivist perspectives highlight the importance of social and cultural interactions and the development of pupils' personal identity. This is vital for all pupils and especially so for pupils whose cultural and social backgrounds may be unfamiliar to their current school community. Research suggests that EAL pupils have a common underlying language proficiency that forms a basis for learning any new language (Cummins, 2001). For example, pupils who naturally insert vocabulary and phrases from different languages, called code switching, demonstrate an ability to manipulate and transfer separate languages. Nevertheless, teachers need to provide opportunities for learning and practising new language linked to each new task in school.

Table 3.2 presents further detail of the English attainment for our vignette pupil with English as a second language, Analyn. The table is intended as a starting point for discussion in relation to your current experience of pupils with English as an additional language. Analyn's first language comes from the Philippines. Analyn speaks Tagalog at home with her parents who also speak some English. The family has lived in the UK for two years. Analyn cannot read or write Tagalog.

〰️ **Reflection questions**

- For Analyn, what are the benefits of using both Tagalog and English in the classroom?
- How may Analyn's love of story add to her English language for core curriculum subjects?
- How would you increase Analyn's opportunities to speak English on a daily basis within the regular classroom routine?

Progression in acquiring English as a second language

In this section, two areas of progression are addressed: language for thought and language for communication. These areas deliberately mirror those of monolingual pupils outlined in Chapter 2, allowing some reflection on the differences between each group of pupils. Linguistic, pragmatic and sociolinguistic language competencies are examined under both headings. Research comes from the fields of linguistics and educational research. Evaluating the evidence allows us to consider its place within the assess, plan, teach, practise, apply and review framework (DfES, 2006).

Language for thought

At the heart of social constructivist principles of learning is the use of talk. As discussed in Chapter 2, vocabulary, group-working skills, question and answering

Table 3.2 A summary of English language attainment in Analyn

Selected examples of Analyn's English language in context	Linguistics	Pragmatics	Sociolinguistics	Features of progression	Suggested next steps for progression
Switches languages between English and Tagalog with Philippine peers	Uses Tagalog grammar and vocabulary, inserts English vocabulary where there is no Tagalog equivalent	Confident use of first language in school	Communicates with all peers and familiar adults	Uses Tagalog with native speakers, using English vocabulary in regular conversation	Teach some Tagalog vocabulary to native English speaking peers
Developing English naming vocabulary for social communication and curriculum subjects, uses picture cues, follows routines	Mainly nouns and verbs, some categorisation and synonyms	Uses non-verbal and visual cues when verbal language fails	Requests classroom objects from peers, follows classroom routines	Uses curriculum subject and Tagalog/English picture dictionaries, strengths in maths and science terminology and some associated concepts	Develop conceptual vocabulary for curriculum subjects, develop adverbs, prediction
Decodes print mainly phonically, increases reading fluency with familiar text, sequences using pictures	Segments and blends all types of phoneme orally and in print	Enjoys repetition in stories she knows Re-reads familiar stories	Follows directive signs and symbols in school community	Strong segmentation and blending skills	Develop reading back and on to decode unfamiliar words
Answers literal comprehension questions, retells familiar stories in sequence orally, re-reads and chooses favourite books	Scans text and pictures, beginning to develop reading repertoire	Early discussion of text and stories she has heard	Shares audio stories with peers, searches for familiar text, enjoys repetition in story	Effective literal comprehension, uses picture and caption evidence from single sections in text	Prediction of unfamiliar stories and text

(Continued)

Table 3.2 (Continued)

Selected examples of Analyn's English language in context	Linguistics	Pragmatics	Sociolinguistics	Features of progression	Suggested next steps for progression
Writes captions for pictures, labels diagrams with given English vocabulary	Selects vocabulary from personal and commercial picture dictionaries	Shares dictionaries, re-reads work aloud	Makes her own dictionaries of mainly nouns and verbs using shopping catalogues	Copies English words accurately	Write varied simple sentences
Completes written cloze sentences from multiple choice and picture cue	Selects missing nouns and verbs	Shares own written work	Reads own written work aloud	Reads for meaning in English	Complete cloze based tasks with familiar stories or events
Communicates personal needs and requests, positive interactions and communication with friends	Some English grammatical errors	Turn-taking	Uses common social phrases for asking questions	Initiates conversation, asks for help	Develop repertoire of English phrases

skills are key curriculum elements of this process. It is the same for pupils learning English in school. Using talk assists EAL pupils to make cross-curricular links. It allows cognitive and academic language proficiency (CALP) to grow through practice and application. This term comes from the eminent researcher, Jim Cummins (Cummins, 2001). Typically, proficiency in CALP increases as pupils are able to manage abstract ideas and use subject-specific vocabulary in the broadest and deepest contexts. Examples are the language for explora-tory discussion, prediction and categorisation, as well as understanding language devices such as similes and the grammatical and morphemic con-struction of sentences and words. Cummins' studies found that CALP generally took at least seven years to become established in second language learners.

✎ Research focus

Progression in reading comprehension in pupils learning English as an additional language

An English study looked at 78 primary pupils over two years (Burgoyne et al. 2011). Half were EAL pupils and half were native English speakers. Both groups read fluently and accurately but monolingual pupils had greater reading comprehension. Pupils with English as an additional language had weaker vocabulary skills, suggesting an impact on comprehension. The authors note the need to further explore inferential and literal questions. The results of this study illustrate the importance of vocabulary development in its widest and deepest sense. This is more than learning a list of topic-specific words but involves assisting pupils to develop the connections within and between them. Useful classroom techniques include generating and rejecting synonyms and mind mapping target words.

Part of CALP is the development in EAL pupils' reading and writing skills. Like monolingual pupils, pupils need a range of **reading strategies**, including phonics. Rapid word recognition is important and phonics is an efficient way to achieve this. It is also possible to decode using pupils' knowledge of gram-mar, sight words and through the meaning of the text. Good decoding skills will not necessarily automatically result in adequate reading comprehension beyond decoding. This is particularly so for EAL pupils, who may not initially have sufficient knowledge of grammar and vocabulary in the new language in order to comprehend text beyond the literal. Chapter 4 outlines the process of reading acquisition in detail.

✍ Research focus

Phonic progression in monolingual and bilingual pupils

A recent study in the Netherlands found that there was no difference in the phonemic awareness of young monolingual pupils or those with an additional language. (Janssen and Bosman, 2013). Similar research in the USA found that bilingual Spanish and English pre-school children developed separate phonological skills specific to either language with only rhyme having a different developmental progression (Lopez, 2012). Rhyme is part of **phonological awareness**.

The studies highlight the importance of using a variety of strategies in reading for meaning and the importance of utilising pupils' first language skills.

Writing in a second language is a further example of CALP. Common indicators of attainment in writing centre on the pupils' ability to write coherently and to use cohesive writing techniques such as pronouns and tenses correctly. A coherent piece of writing makes overall sense because the different themes within it fit together. This requires knowledge of the genre as well as the audience and purpose of the writing itself. These are pragmatic as well as linguistic skills because they consider the readers' perspective.

Classroom application In the primary classroom, understanding progression in language for thought in EAL learners includes:

- providing extensive opportunities for genre development;
- providing explicit opportunities for learning connectives, modal verbs, adverbs, and prepositional phrases (Cameron and Bessener, 2004);
- providing explicit opportunities to access written language in a range of layouts, including multi-media sources;
- building on pupils' prior language experiences;
- putting the new language in a real context;
- using visual aids;
- building vocabulary;
- building EAL pupils' ability to articulate their thought processes;
- monitoring EAL pupils' acquisition of key terminology to access the subject and the phrases and vocabulary necessary to interpret the subject

itself. This means that the class teacher has mapped the language content of each subject alongside regular curriculum planning.

Language for communication

Language for communication is usefully summarised by Cummins as Basic Interpersonal Communication Skills (BICS) (Cummins, 2001). BICS incorporates social and functional language that is part of an everyday context. Greetings, conversation, asking directions and following routines are examples. Usually, because it is less abstract, BICS language is learnt faster than the CALP. Cummins found that BICS generally took up to two years to become established.

A distinction between language for thought and language for communication can assist teachers in separating EAL pupils from those with special educational needs or learning difficulties. Progression in acquiring English is assessed and monitored across a range of relevant contexts. Cummins states that BICS and CALP are on a continuum, used according to how well the pupil understands the context in which the language is used. These are immediate day-to-day situations and specific situations (Halliday, 1975). EAL pupils may use their first language in school while they are learning English.

Classroom application   In the primary classroom, pupil progression in language for communication among EAL learners includes:

- teachers allowing for a 'silent period' for new arrivals;
- pupils following school routines and social expectations;
- pupils making choices;
- pupils using visual aids;
- pupils putting the new language in a real context;
- pupils choosing to work and communicate with native speakers.

The progression of English as an additional language in the primary classroom

This section of the chapter puts the research and theory of progression in English as an additional language into a primary classroom context. Some of the pedagogy associated with teaching EAL pupils echoes existing research into reading comprehension, meta-language and meta-cognitive skills. It is also necessary to understand underlying social and cultural issues of identity.

Activity

Observing linguistic, pragmatic, sociolinguistic and academic language in the classroom

Look at the extracts from the class teacher's observations of Analyn in her first two terms in school. Decide if they refer to linguistic, pragmatic, sociolinguistic or academic needs or achievements. The first one has been done for you.

- Analyn cannot read the instruction sheet for making pop-up greetings cards for Mother's Day. The instructions are listed without illustrations. *Analyn needs pictures to understand the written vocabulary in the instructions. This is a linguistic need. Analyn may also need an explanation of the social and cultural significance of Mother's Day in the United Kingdom.*
- In the playground, Analyn has argued with her friends. The support assistant asks her why she has fallen out with them. Analyn does not understand what it means *to fall out.*
- Analyn has difficulty answering open questions in a maths class using fractions to solve real problems. She has good fraction calculation skills.
- Analyn is observed playing a listening, questioning and describing barrier game in class. They are using pictures of food. Analyn can list types of food but not descriptions or varieties of each food.

This activity will have caused you to separate the needs of EAL pupils' language needs in more detail. Your judgement of the progression of English in EAL pupils may be affected by one or more of these factors. A further dimension to classroom application is the use of the funds of knowledge (Moll et al., 1992) that pupils bring to school from home. Such practice enhances engagement through using language and cultural diversity. Cummins describes a quadrant of learning goals for EAL pupils who face the dual challenges of managing cognitive demand and understanding the context for language (Hornberger and Baker, 2001). According to Cummins, English progression in EAL pupils means that pupils move from understanding language and learning fixed in a comprehensible context to understanding language and learning out of context. Then it allows increasingly independent abstraction, discussion, exploration, criticality and interpretation. For example, Analyn's teacher uses the reciprocal reading technique to develop her prediction skills during guided reading (Palincsar and Brown, 1984). Using this technique, Analyn is instructed to predict, question, clarify and summarise what she has read at strategic points during her reading. This approach allows her to monitor her understanding while she reads. Further discussion of reciprocal reading appears in Chapter 5.

Classroom application   Monitoring the progression of EAL pupils in the classroom can be usefully summarised under five headings (South, 1999):

1. Activating the pupils' prior knowledge
2. Working in a context relevant to the EAL pupil
3. Actively encouraging the pupil to speak with understanding
4. Making grammatical elements explicit for a purpose
5. Developing learners' independence

As with monolingual pupils, each of these areas can be addressed through the development of group working skills, vocabulary development, including conceptual development, and question and answer skills. Separating the differences between written and spoken language underlie these techniques. The techniques add to the class teacher's planning, which details the language content necessary for EAL pupils. They allow pupils to practise, apply and review their new language skills.

The assessment of English as an additional language

This section examines the assessment of English as an additional language in the light of standardised testing and formative assessment. Assessment for pupils with English as an additional language covers assessment of pupils' attainment in BICS and CALP and assessment of their academic attainment through reading, writing, speaking and listening across the curriculum.

It is important to distinguish between assessment and progression of BICS and CALP. The pupils' current and previous experience and knowledge of English will necessarily affect both, particularly when pupils are asked to take statutory curriculum assessments not designed for EAL learners. Poor results in such assessments may not necessarily reflect pupils' true ability, as would have been shown if the test had been presented in the pupil's first language. The class teacher, while monitoring daily progression, must make similar judgements. For example, using translated reading comprehension exercises can allow the pupil to demonstrate greater levels of inference. Using an interpreter and amanuensis can show pupils' academic performance in their first language. Using picture cues can assist English language comprehension.

Summative assessment

In the United Kingdom, there is currently no nationally agreed summative assessment to gauge pupils' acquisition of English (Conteh, 2012). It is generally understood that such an assessment is not beneficial to class teachers or pupils because of the diversity of language experience and knowledge of the community of EAL learners. Valid and useful summative assessment is therefore difficult to design.

Formative assessment

A range of formative observational assessment tools for English language acquisition exists. References for the NALDIC and older Hester scales appear at the end of this chapter.

As well as measuring capability, formative assessment can highlight the strengths and weaknesses in your own planning and teaching. Daily, routine, formative assessment techniques will help you to monitor pupils' progress and check the quality of EAL provision in your classroom.

There are four areas for the assessment of pupils' language for communication and language for thought. Competence in these areas will be different according to whether the pupil is at an elementary, intermediate or advanced level of learning English.

Listening: this area covers progression in understanding verbal and non-verbal language and instructions through to following conversations, questions, answers and attending to oral presentations.

Speaking: this area covers pupils' expression of English. Areas include making basic needs known, imitating spoken English, developing longer phrases in relevant and broader contexts and developing vocabulary.

Reading: this area includes pupils' knowledge of print, decoding and comprehension skills such as prediction, sequencing and recall. Knowledge of genres is a key area. Some pupils may read their first language.

Writing: this area includes pupils' spelling, grammar and genre writing skills. Some pupils may write in their first language.

Activity

Plotting progression in English as a second language

The NALDIC descriptors distinguish between common descriptors, 'frequently observed and relatively stable' and less common descriptors 'which are likely to be emerging' (Scott and Leung, 2009: 2). Sort the following examples of Analyn's language attainment into common and less common descriptors. Justify your choice. Analyn is working within the elementary stages of learning English.

Table 3.3

Example of Analyn's language	Common descriptor	Less common descriptor	Justification for choice
Retells familiar stories in sequence			
Follows classroom routines using non-verbal cues and visual timetable displayed in the classroom			
Growing vocabulary: asks for lunch and snack options by name			
Chooses to use Tagalog with other native speakers in class			
Sometimes switches between English and Tagalog when English vocabulary is lacking			

This activity will have caused you to consider patterns of progression in EAL pupils. It is unlikely that pupils will develop English in a linear fashion (Scott and Leung, 2009). Progression is more likely to be spread out over a long period and be related to the pupils' current and prior English usage and their overall experience of language diversity.

Summary of chapter

This chapter has provided an introductory context for monitoring the language progression of pupils with English as an additional language. It has used a single vignette pupil to illustrate the dual challenges for pupils using English as an additional language: developing language for basic communication and language for academic learning. It presented these principles in relation to the four modes of English (reading, writing, speaking and listening) and to assessment. This chapter has emphasised your role as a classroom teacher in building on the previous language skills and knowledge of EAL pupils. Identifying the language demands of the curriculum in order to build a cumulative, contextually and vocabulary rich approach for EAL learners follows this process.

> **?** **Self-assessment**
>
> 1. List and justify three items that you consider important features or a suggested next step for progression in learning English as a second language for communication and learning. Choose items for elementary, intermediate and advanced English language learning pupils in the primary school. Look at the NALDIC and older Hester descriptors to help you.

Annotated further reading

Conteh, J. (2012) *Teaching Bilingual and EAL Learners in Primary Schools*. London: Sage. This book provides a very practical guide to EAL teaching.

Leung, C., and Creese, A. (eds) (2010) *English as an Additional Language: Approaches to Teaching Linguistic Minority Students*. London: Sage
This book contains a breadth of international perspectives of EAL pedagogy from leading experts in the field.

Hornberger, N. H. and Baker, C. (eds) (2001) *An Introductory Reader to the Writings of Jim Cummins*. Clevedon: Multilingual Matters.
This book provides an introduction to the principles of Cummins' work.

Further resources

The National Association for Language Development in the Curriculum [NALDIC] is the national subject association for English as an additional language in the United Kingdom. Their website can be accessed at www.naldic. org.uk/

NALDIC formative assessment descriptors are available at www.naldic.org.uk/ Resources/NALDIC/Teaching%20and%20Learning/NALDICdescriptorsKS1.pdf

Formative assessment descriptors from Hilary Hester at the CLPE are available at www.clpe.org.uk/search?q=hester&yt0.x=19&yt0.y=24&yt0=submit

References

Burgoyne, K., Whiteley, H. E. and Hutchinson, J. M. (2011) The development of comprehension and reading-related skills in children learning English as an additional language and their monolingual, English speaking peers. *British Journal of Educational Psychology*, 81, 344–354.

Cameron, L. and Bessener, S. (2004) Writing in English as an additional language at KS2: DfES research report 586. London.

Conteh, J. (2012) *Teaching Bilingual and EAL Learners in Primary Schools*. London: Sage.

Council of Europe (2001) *Common European Framework of Reference for Languages: Learning, Teaching, Assessment*. Cambridge: Cambridge University Press.

Cummins, J. (2001) *Negotiating Identities: Education for Empowerment in a Diverse Society* (2nd edn). Ontario, CA: California Association for Bilingual Education.

DfES (2006) *Primary National Strategy: Primary Framework for Literacy and Mathematics*. London: DfES.

Halliday, M. A. K. (1975) *Learning How to Mean: Explorations in the Development of Language*. London: Arnold.

Hatcher, P. J., Hulme, C. and Snowling, M. J. (2004) Explicit phoneme training combined with phonic reading instruction helps young children at risk of reading failure. *Journal of Child Psychology and Psychiatry*, 45, 338–358.

Hornberger, N. H. and Baker, C. (eds) (2001) *An Introductory Reader to the Writings of Jim Cummins*. Clevedon: Multilingual Matters.

Janssen, M. and Bosman, A. M. T. (2013) Phoneme awareness, vocabulary and word decoding in monolingual and bilingual Dutch children. *Journal of Research in Reading*, 36, 1–13.

Lopez, L. M. (2012) Assessing the phonological skills of bilingual children from preschool through kindergarten: Developmental progression and cross-language transfer. *Journal of Research in Childhood Education*, 26, 371–391.

Moll, L. C., Amanti C., Neff, D. and Gonzalez, N. (1992) Funds of knowledge for teaching: Using a qualitative approach to connect homes and classrooms. *Theory into Practice*, 31, 132–141.

Palincsar, A. and Brown, A. (1984) Reciprocal teaching of comprehension-fostering and comprehension-monitoring activities. *Cognition and Instruction*, 1, 117–175.

Scott, C. and Leung, C. (2009) *EAL Formative Assessment Key Stages 1 and 2*. Available at www.naldic.org.uk/

South, H. (ed.) (1999) *The Distinctiveness of English as an Additional Language: A Cross-curriculum Discipline* (Working Paper 5). London: NALDIC.

CHAPTER 4

READING ACQUISITION

Objectives

1. To identify key features of progression in reading acquisition
2. To examine key models of the reading process
3. To relate progression in reading acquisition to daily classroom practice
4. To evaluate common forms of reading assessment

Introduction

This is the first of three chapters that address reading progression in the primary classroom. It examines the process of how children learn to read. Learning to read is different from being a reader. Being a reader requires motivation and a reason to read as well as an environment that enables reading to thrive. Learning to read is only the first step in a life-long process.

It is important to note here that not all children learn to read in the same way. Although children should read print automatically and comprehend what they are reading, exactly how and why they achieve this will be subtly different for every child. Sadly, some children will still leave school without having learnt to read, despite the best efforts of everyone involved. As long as this situation persists, reading research will grow and teachers will continue to search for the best methods for helping every child to become a reader for life.

Much of the history of reading research and theory has focused on the reading process rather than the process of becoming a reader. Reasons for this imbalance are discussed in this chapter. While a large amount of research has examined how pupils recognise words and comprehend text, there has been less interest in examining pupils' motivational contributions to the reading process. Both are necessary. This chapter introduces three significant approaches to reading acquisition: psycholinguistic, socio-cultural and cognitive (Lambirth, 2011). Each is relevant to understanding progression in reading acquisition and its link to classroom teaching.

Activity

How did you learn to read?

- Can you remember listening to stories sharing rhymes, songs and books with an adult?
- Can you remember your first reading books?
- Can you recall your favourite books from childhood?
- Did you read before starting school?
- How did you progress as a reader in school?
- Are you a regular reader now?
- Do you read for pleasure as well as for work purposes?

Answers to these questions will have caused you to consider the process of learning to read and of becoming an established adult reader. You may have recalled your early attempts and experiences of reading. Perhaps you recall listening to and sharing books with an adult. Re-reading books, learning stories and rhymes by heart and developing favourites are part of this. Perhaps you recalled how you learnt to read. Did you learn whole words, perhaps taking them home to learn by heart? Did you learn to **blend** and **segment phonemes** in the process of learning to read with **phonics**? Answers to these questions will largely depend on the approach adopted when you learnt to read and the balance of different types of **reading strategies** to decode and comprehend text unique to your own reading ability.

The Simple View of Reading

Precisely how reading occurs is a complex process. The Simple View of Reading [SVR] framework (Gough and Tumner, 1986) categorises its processes into two components: word recognition and language comprehension. It links pupils' ability to comprehend reading to their ability to **decode** print and their ability to understand written and spoken language. In reading 'Gough and Tumner further make clear that word recognition is necessary but not sufficient for reading because the ability to pronounce printed words does not guarantee understanding of the text so represented. Furthermore, linguistic comprehension is likewise necessary, but not sufficient for reading: if you cannot recognise the words that comprise the written text you cannot recover the **lexical** information necessary for the application of the processes that lead to comprehension' (Rose, 2006: 76).

A key feature of the SVR is the importance placed on the use of phonics to decode print. Phonic acquisition typically encompasses **synthetic**, **analytic** and **orthographic** approaches to decoding. These are discussed in more detail in the second section of this chapter. While providing a framework, the SVR does not contain details of reading processes including **fluency**, **orthographic** or **phonological awareness** references. Neither does it reference a range of comprehension skills. It does not capture the integrated nature of knowledge and skills necessary to learn to read including pupils' familiarity with the texts and the book as an object in itself. However, in the classroom, the SVR may be used as a starting point for observing pupils' reading behaviours according to these dimensions of reading: language comprehension and word recognition.

In England the Primary National Strategy (2006) plotted four dimensions of pupils' reading acquisition using Gough and Tumner's work:

1. Pupils with good reading comprehension and good decoding skills
2. Pupils with poor reading comprehension and good decoding skills
3. Pupils with good reading comprehension and poor decoding skills
4. Pupils with poor reading comprehension and poor decoding skills

Activity

Using the SVR as a classroom tool

Look at the dimensions of the SVR above. Can you say where the four vignette pupils in this book would be placed on these reading dimensions? What other aspects of reading acquisition will their class teachers need to observe?

Table 4.1 presents a categorisation of the reading behaviours of our vignette pupils. The table allows us to track some of the features and next steps for progression in reading acquisition that can occur across the primary years of schooling. In these examples, there are definite patterns in the process of learning to read. Firstly, every vignette pupil seeks to make meaning from the reading text. Secondly, every vignette pupil uses a range of strategies to decode print.

Table 4.1 Summary of reading acquisition in the pupil vignettes

Pupil	Age	Attainment level	Key strategies for decoding print	Features of progression	Suggested next steps for progression
Japonica	10	Within expected levels	Seeks meaning from all text Decodes print fluently, using whole words, phonic cues, structure, spelling patterns, and sentence structures Uses pictures	Uses a range of reading strategies Uses phonics to decode if words are unfamiliar Uses knowledge of similar types of text to predict meaning Identifies and predicts meaning of unfamiliar vocabulary using text type Inferential comprehension of ideas across a chapter	Use of increasingly detailed evidence to support inference Note taking Established personal reading repertoire
Analyn	9	EAL pupil at the earlier stages of English language acquisition	Decodes print using phonic cues, fluent reader of familiar text, uses picture cues, sequences picture stories, matches written captions to pictures	Literal comprehension, recalls and sequences familiar stories orally, simple naming vocabulary, re-reads favourite books	Intonation while reading, prediction, simple inference such as cause and effect, using text and pictures from one page, use wider range of reading strategies, develop number of familiar sight words

(Continued)

Table 4.1 (Continued)

Pupil	Age	Attainment level	Key strategies for decoding print	Features of progression	Suggested next steps for progression
John	7	Below expected levels	Enjoys favourite books and themes, decodes print, reads high frequency words, uses picture cues, recalls main features of story, segments and blends phonemes	Uses phonics as primary decoding strategy, reads initial and final sounds confidently, makes predictions before and after reading, recalls main features of what he has read, intonation when characters speak	Increased fluency, re-read texts to build confidence, use whole range of reading strategies, secure reading of medial vowels
Peter	5	Above expected levels	Use range of strategies to decode and derive meaning from text: reads on and back, uses knowledge of grammar to guess unfamiliar words, uses picture cues, uses knowledge of structures in similar texts to guess unknown words	Established reading favourites including authors, summarises, infers and recalls main ideas, can talk about characters and events in the story, reads punctuation	Infer using greater details in the text, begin to use non-fiction to find information in unfamiliar text, including digital forms

Thirdly, every vignette pupil uses some knowledge of other books and genres to decipher the written word and to comprehend the text that they have read.

The reading process

The process of learning to read is a complex mix of theory, philosophy and research-based evidence.

The Simple View of Reading and the phonetic principles that underlie it are an example of a cognitive approach to learning to read. Cognitive theories suggest that pupils move through stages of reading acquisition and that the features of reading can be observed and measured. Not all philosophies or theories of reading have a cognitive perspective. Three main approaches examined by Andrew Lambirth (2011) are summarised here. The first stems from a **psycholinguistic** perspective, an example of a top-down model of reading acquisition. Top-down models emphasise the importance of what the reader brings to the reading process from language such as knowledge of story structure, grammar and vocabulary. The second stems from **cognitive** perspectives. These are bottom-up models of reading acquisition (Chall, 1983). Bottom-up models address reading as discrete stages of information processing, beginning with letter and word recognition, proceeding to sentence and text comprehension. The third approach stems from socio-cultural conceptions of the place of reading in a culture and society.

Psycholinguistic approaches to learning to read

Psycholinguistic approaches to learning to read emphasise the place of reading as part of language. They assume that all pieces of reading, like speech, have an understandable meaning. Readers predict the meaning of unknown words based on previous conceptual knowledge and their store of vocabulary to express it. An important advocate of the psycholinguistic model was Kenneth Goodman. Goodman proposed that pupils can decipher meaning from print by linking three sets of reading cues (Goodman, 1967). He suggested that each provided insight into pupils' thinking processes while reading.

- *Semantic* cues enable pupils to predict the meaning of the word because of the knowledge they bring to reading. Sometimes this relates to familiarity with similar texts as well as pupils' general knowledge and experience.
- *Syntactic* cues enable pupils to predict the meaning of a word based on pupils' knowledge of language and grammar.
- *Grapho-phonic* cues enable pupils to predict the meaning of a word based on knowledge of phonemes, **graphemes** and the visual appearance of words.

Psycholinguistic models of reading assist teachers in ensuring that learning to read is part of a rich, language-based curriculum where pupils are actively engaged in real contexts for reading, writing, speaking and listening. **Whole Language theory** grew from psycholinguistic models. The Whole Language philosophy of reading acquisition extends psycholinguistic ideas by suggesting that reading occurs naturally, like language, in literacy rich environments (Tracey and Morrow, 2012). Critics question the value of Whole Language approaches for pupils with limited access to books and spoken language at home (Nicholson, 2008).

Cognitive approaches to learning to read

Cognitive approaches to learning to read emphasise the process of decoding the print on the page in order to make meaning. A phonics-based approach is frequently recommended with grammatical and semantic cues from the text coming later. Pupils progress at different rates. Cognitive models assist teachers in ensuring that pupils can automatically decode words at an early stage of reading. Studies of eye movements while reading, **fluency** and **automaticity** in reading, and brain imaging studies in cognitive neuroscience are also part of the evidence to support this approach.

An example of cognitive approaches to reading is illustrated by Ehri's staged model which proposes four stages in the process of learning to read (Ehri, 1995). (Other similar models exist, such as Chall, 1996; Frith, 1985).

1. The pre-alphabetic phase describes pupils' use of symbols, logos and print before the alphabet has been mastered.
2. The partial alphabetic phase describes pupils who read using some letters in a word, often the first and last.
3. The full alphabetic phase describes pupils who can make **grapheme-phoneme correspondences** and have established a bank of familiar sight words.
4. The consolidated alphabetic phase describes pupils who are confident with recurring letter patterns like **onsets, rimes** and **morphemes**.

Cognitive models of reading assist teachers in understanding how thinking takes place when the pupil is reading and how the process of reading becomes automatic. This is a complex area because of the range of cognitive and perceptual skills that interact with reading skills, such as working memory, eye movements, auditory and visual discrimination.

Interactive models of the reading process suggest that pupils process syntactic, lexical and semantic information in a non-linear fashion (Tracey and Morrow, 2012). The interactive compensatory model (Stanovich, 1984) suggests that pupils automatically use their strongest reading strategy.

Socio-cultural approaches to learning to read

Socio-cultural approaches to learning to read see reading as the product of pupils' social and cultural communities, where the nature and value of English and literacy is developed by the members of that community. Reading is a social act. Progression in reading from a socio-cultural approach is bound to the child's circumstances and to their environment at home and in school (Gee, 2004). Younger readers are necessarily developing reading acquisition skills and establishing their reading choices, only some of which will be for sustained personal and recreational purposes outside of school.

Socio-cultural models of reading assist teachers in understanding how reading relates to the four modes of English across the curriculum and outside of school. They encourage teachers to choose real and relevant reading material for the cultural backgrounds in their own classes, such as in the content of reading schemes and in the use of digital texts to support reading progress. Teaching techniques such as guided, shared reading and paired reading acknowledge this perspective because they build reading through social interaction. Digital applications such as Google Docs, Wiki-spaces and the construction of classroom websites do the same.

✎ Research focus

Teaching for progression: A balanced approach

In 2008 a North American study produced an analysis of the most effective teaching strategies for older readers with special needs (Roberts et al., 2008). The study found that word study, reading fluency, vocabulary instruction, comprehension and reading motivation all made significant and lasting contributions to reading attainment. However, this has not applied to younger underachieving readers where the teaching of phonemic awareness, phonics, vocabulary, fluency and comprehension taught separately had previously been part of mandatory policy (Gamse et al., 2008). The first official evaluation of the USA *Reading First* legislation found that blanket and separate teaching of these reading skills did not significantly improve pupils' reading comprehension.

This research highlights reading instruction as a balance of approaches for interacting with text. In order to do this effectively teachers need a clear understanding of differentiation and the implications of short-term intervention programmes that are not necessarily effective for all pupils. This means monitoring progression during pupils' implicit opportunities for reading as well as during explicit instruction.

The progression of reading acquisition in the primary classroom

This section of the chapter puts reading process theories into a classroom context. Using current research and the pupil vignettes from Chapter 1 it describes and evaluates evidence to support understanding of progression in reading acquisition in the primary classroom. It is possible to see progression through the processes and the products of learning to read. The processes are the mechanisms of reading text, language and reading comprehension and word recognition. The products of learning to read include established personal reading habits, wide reading repertoires, spelling skills and a wide vocabulary. In this chapter, the progression of word recognition is examined. Chapters 5 and 6 contain details of progression in reading comprehension and reading engagement.

✍ Research focus

Long-term trends in reading progression

In 2011, the National Literacy Trust published a further survey of reading attainment in the United Kingdom (Clark et al., 2011). Over 18,000 students aged from 8–17 were surveyed. Information was gathered on reading attitude, ownership of books and how often students read. Each factor was linked to attainment. For example, 97 per cent of students who enjoyed reading were at or above the expected level of attainment. Overall, students who did not enjoy reading were 11 times more likely to be below the expected level of attainment than those who liked to read. This research illustrates the importance of providing a school and classroom community rich with literature and language alongside carefully differentiated teaching. Predicting the factors that affect reading achievement are essential in order to begin to address the socio-cultural statistics associated with non-readers (Jama and Dugdale, 2011).

Much of the educational and psychological research into children's reading development has focused on the predictors of long-term reading achievement. The purpose of these studies is to find out the essential aspects of learning to read successfully and to develop teaching and assessment that includes them. Common findings have emerged. In the classroom, a four-pronged approach to developing pupils' reading acquisition is useful as a basis for understanding primary English progression.

1. Phonics
2. Orthography
3. Vocabulary
4. Comprehension

Evaluating the evidence for each of the four aspects allows us to consider their place within the assess, plan, teach, practise, apply and review framework (DfES, 2006).

Phonics

The bulk of research in this area covers the development of **phonological awareness**, phonemic awareness, alphabet knowledge and short-term memory. All are important for fluent word reading (Goswami and Bryant, 1990).

✍ Activity

Look at the four running records of independent reading from the pupil vignettes. Record features and suggested next steps for progression in phonics. Sections are completed for you. An explanation of **running records** and **miscue analysis** appears in the glossary.

Table 4.2

Pupil	Extract from teacher's running records of pupils reading aloud	Features of progression in phonics and phonological awareness	Suggested next steps for progression
Japonica Extract from Midsummer Night's Dream Act 2 Scene 1	I know a bank where the wild thyme// (pronounced thime) // (Substitutes grows for blows)//, where ox—lips (hesitates and splits the word)// and the nodding violet//(substitutes violets) (omits plural s) // grows)//,quite over- (substitutes copied for canopied)// with luscious wood-bine, with sweet (omits musk) // rose and with (reads phonetically eg-lan-tine). //	Know y acting as a vowel (thyme) and split vowel digraph Check suffixes (plural)	
John Extract from Sendak: Where the Wild Things Are	'Now stop!' Max said and (Uses phonics to sound out s-e-n-t) // the wild things off to bed// (sounds out w-i-th-ou-t)// without //(omits their) // supper.//	Segments and blends single letters, and consonant digraph (th), uses syllables (somewhere/one)	

(Continued)

(Continued)

Pupil	Extract from teacher's running records of pupils reading aloud	Features of progression in phonics and phonological awareness	Suggested next steps for progression
	And Max the king of all the wild things was// (Reverses letter order says saw) // sounds out l-o-n-e-l-y says y)// and wanted to be (omits where) some// (Re-reads word and splits to substitute some-where for someone) // love// (hesitates and re-reads to self-correct loved) // him (uses phonics to sound out b-e-s-t // of all		
Analyn Extract from: *DK Ultimate Sticker Book: Puppy* 2006	A sleepy// (reads sleep, omits y) // family// (sounds out f-a-m-i-l omits y) // resting //(reads rest, omits ing) // after a busy, //(reads bus, omits y) // day. Six week old puppies//(reads pup, omits ies) // tired (reads tried) after a run	Phonological awareness: identify rhyming words ending in y
Peter Extract from: King-Smith: *Emily's Legs* p. 4	Father spider didn't notice // (omits notice).// For one thing he didn't like children. For another he was // (substitutes also for always) // too // (hesitates at busy re–reads sentence, omits busy and reads also too bad sitting// (omits quite)// still..		

⁓ Reflection questions

- What is the significance of high or low levels of self-correction?
- Why does Analyn use so few phonic strategies to decode the text?
- What phonic progression is shown by the similarities and differences between the word substitutions for each pupil?

In the field of educational research, there has been much controversy as to how phonics should be taught for maximum effect. In particular, the merits of discrete, synthetic or analytical phonics teaching for long-term reading progress has been a focus for concern (Dombey, 2010; Ellis, 2007). In essence, **synthetic phonics** approaches teach pupils to segment phonemes in unfamiliar words and blend them for reading. Analytic approaches also teach pupils to read using **analogy**. For example, pupils look for spelling, onset and rime sound patterns within whole words such as spr/ing, and generate other words with similar patterns. Analogies are only possible if pupils know the alphabet, letter-sound correspondences and have an ability to hear at least the first letter in a word.

The first step in phonic development is phonological awareness. Phonological awareness includes syllables, rhythm, rhymes, alliteration, oral blending, segmentation, visual discrimination, and auditory discrimination of everyday sound. The second aspect to consider is phonemic awareness. This involves orally blending, segmenting and writing 44 English phonemes and the 26 letters of the alphabet.

Analyn is not able to predict unknown words using the rhythm of the text. Peter substitutes *also* for always based on the initial sound. His substitution also makes sense. John uses most phonics. He segments and blends phonemes to read unfamiliar words. Japonica's phonic strategies show the links between phonics and spelling. She misreads the plural suffix s and misreads thyme as thime. She reads 'y' acting as a vowel, but fails to read the alternative pronunciation of 'th'.

Classroom application   In the classroom, progression in phonic acquisition is observed in 1:1 reading sessions, guided reading and during direct phonics instruction. The progressive sequence of phonics teaching usually depends upon the commercial programme in place. The following summarises the sequence found in the 'Letters and Sounds' materials from England (Department for Education and Skills, 2007).

1. Phonological awareness: syllables, rhymes, oral blending and segmentation, visual and auditory discrimination
2. Spelling regular words: VC CVC and two-syllable words
3. Complete alphabet, two-syllable words, sounds represented by more than one letter
4. Adjacent consonants and polysyllabic words
5. Recognition and recall of final sets of common grapheme-phoneme correspondences and alternative pronunciations
6. Transition and consolidation stage for linking reading and spelling

Orthography

Orthography enables pupils to use information from the spelling system in order to decode words. Orthographic knowledge is necessary to address pupils' rapid recognition of key sight vocabulary and to manage phonemes written in different ways. Like phonemic awareness, orthographic skills also appear to promote pupils' reading fluency. For example, some pupils use their knowledge of common letter patterns before phonemic knowledge is fully formed (Bourassa and Treiman, 2010). The bulk of research in this area has looked at the links between reading, writing and spelling. This includes pupils' ability to recognise words via knowledge of syllables, **suffixes**, **prefixes** and spelling rules.

Activity

Look at the four extracts from group reading tests of independent reading, from the pupil vignettes. Record the features and suggested next steps for progression in orthography. The last one has been done for you.

Table 4.3

Pupil	Extract from multiple choice answers in a whole class reading test	Features of progression	Suggested next steps for progression
Japonica	*The reading book was ____by all of the children in class* read, reed, **red**, reading		
John	*The ___was fat and full of fish* **cot**, cut, cup, kit, cat		
Analyn	*Cats want to____* swim, sleep, **squash**, smile		
Peter	*Today the men ____the apples to sell in kilogram bags* **way**, weigh, whey, they	Uses correct initial letter *w* Reads for meaning	Know that a sound can have different phonemes but sound the same

Reflection questions

- In what order do pupils generally focus on letters in a word: first and last, last and first or first, middle and last?
- How does the reading context help pupils to complement their knowledge of spelling?
- What common strategies could boost pupils' phonic and spelling progression simultaneously?

Classroom application In the classroom, the main implication from orthographic research is for teachers to teach spelling at the same time that pupils are taught to read. Educational research has documented the benefits of pupils' experimental spelling because it follows a process of phonetically plausible attempts through to correct spelling (Gentry, 1987). Exploratory spelling is also encouraged as part of pupils' vocabulary development. A structured spelling programme is complementary to this process. Chapter 9 addresses spelling development and its relationship to reading acquisition.

Vocabulary

The bulk of research in this area has looked at the relationship between early vocabulary acquisition and long-term achievement in reading comprehension. Vocabulary acquisition is also associated with reading practice and the amount of pupils' independent reading (Aarnoutee and Van Leeuwe, 1998).

Activity

Look at the four transcripts of book discussion in the pupil vignettes following their running records. Record the features and suggested next steps for progression in vocabulary development. The third one has been done for you.

Table 4.4

Pupil	Transcript of book discussion with teacher after reading aloud	Features of progression	Suggested next steps for progression
Japonica Extract from *Midsummer Night's Dream* Act 2, Scene 1	T: *What unusual words did you find?* J: *Tons, wood-bine, My grandad smokes them, eglantine, oxlips, how can those things be in a wood? I mean violet too that's a colour isn't it?*		
John Extract from Sendak: *Where the Wild Things Are*	T: *Lovely reading, John, can you find me exciting words in this book?*		

(Continued)

(Continued)

Pupil	Transcript of book discussion with teacher after reading aloud	Features of progression	Suggested next steps for progression
	J: *Well I know that Max was king of the wild things, they are monsters, all green and scary with big teeth, look, like this on this page, and Max was scared, he ate tea at the end, on the last picture, see?*		
Analyn Extract from: *DK Ultimate Sticker Book: Puppy* 2006	T: *Lovely, Analyn, can you tell me any more dog words, like bark, dogs make a noise when they bark.* A: *Food, running, neck thing, jump, pat, ball, walk with me on a string*	Names vocabulary associated with dogs generally	Develop synonyms and vocabulary directly describing the noun
Peter Extract from: King-Smith, *Emily's Legs*, p.4	T: *What unusual words did you find?* P: *None really, the spider was just waiting and had a lot of babies*		

〜〜 Reflection questions

- Why does Peter not comment on the difficult words that he failed to read?
- How and why does context affect the development of vocabulary skills?

✎ Research focus

Vocabulary growth as a predictor of reading comprehension

A large Dutch study tracked the development of reading vocabulary and reading comprehension of over 2,000 pupils aged from 5 to 10 years old (Verhoeven et al., 2011).The study found that as children develop their vocabulary, their reading improves. In particular, successful early reading skills promote vocabulary development after the age of seven years. Understanding and using a wide vocabulary supported reading comprehension.

Classroom application In the classroom, vocabulary building comes before, during and after pupils learn to read. If pupils are to exploit their natural store of words, classrooms need to be full of vocabulary building opportunities as part of a rich and engaging environment. Literature is a rich source for pupils' vocabulary development. The choice of reading schemes needs consideration particularly if restricted vocabulary or only phonetically regular books are used without access to 'authentic' books elsewhere.

In the classroom, vocabulary development may be usefully approached through consistent routines that address personal reading repertoires, spelling, word games and topic vocabulary. The aim is to develop an interest in words and to understand their potential for knowledge building. For example, weekly spelling lists may contain a mixture of phonically-based words, key sight words and current topic based words. Ten minutes of daily word and spelling games tend to be more useful in developing vocabulary than a single weekly 30-minute session. Dictionary and thesaurus skills are included. A focus on generating and categorising relevant vocabulary within and between subjects can help pupils to make cross-curricular links between conceptual areas of development. For example, using mind-mapping techniques before, during and after teaching can illustrate pupils' vocabulary growth. Personal dictionaries and vocabulary books can contain this work.

Comprehension

When reading progression moves from 'learning to read to reading to learn' (Rose, 2006: 27), semantic skills come into focus. This area covers the use of grammar, inferences, drawing on different sources of information and how these sources combine to add to pupils' reading strategies. Chapter 5 addresses reading comprehension.

Activity

Reading strategies

Classify the following examples of reading strategies. Some sections have been completed for you.

Table 4.5

Strategy	Phonics	Comprehension	Vocabulary	Orthographic
Use pictures in the book		✓	✓	
Blend and segment phonemes in words				

(Continued)

(Continued)

Strategy	Phonics	Comprehension	Vocabulary	Orthographic
Guess using context plus the first and last letter	✓	✓		✓
Make syllables				
Look for smaller words, suffixes or prefixes within bigger words				
Re-read a sentence		✓	✓	
Use onset and rime	✓			
Read out loud, using the punctuation accurately				
Find related words within longer words				
Skip the word and read to the end of the sentence to predict meaning				
Look for similar words on the classroom walls, or in a dictionary or a thesaurus				

The assessment of reading acquisition

This section evaluates common summative and formative examples of classroom reading assessment. It does not address diagnostic reading assessment of specific reading difficulties. This is the responsibility of the educational psychologist. There are four aspects to assessments of reading acquisition: understanding oral language, understanding the concept of print, fluency, and strategies for decoding and comprehending text. An understanding of the purpose and audience for reading enriches them all.

Summative assessment

Summative reading assessments provide pupils' data on reading accuracy and comprehension skills. Some assessments also provide reading fluency data. There are three types of summative reading assessment.

Standardised norm-referenced reading assessment

These written or online group-reading tests are developed using statistical trials to indicate expected levels of attainment. The tests provide information about pupils' progress within and across year groups and schools. They can provide teachers with a reading age and often contain details of trends in pupils' reading attainment. All ask pupils to read a text silently and answer questions. Multiple-choice questions, cloze procedures (fill in the gap) or longer written answer questions are included. Some assessments provide follow-on diagnostic screening tests. The dangers of teaching to statutory test criteria exist, particularly when these test results are part of external monitoring of teaching standards as well as pupil progress.

Criterion-referenced reading assessment

These reading assessments list skills that pupils must achieve. Easily administered, these checklists do not always provide sufficient information to inform teachers and can lead to a narrow focus on skills teaching rather than reading development as a whole.

Individual reading assessment

An individual reading test is generally diagnostic and designed to provide detail for pupils who inexplicably exceed or fail to meet expected levels of attainment. Fluency, accuracy and comprehension are assessed. Teachers can see and hear precise reading strategies as the pupil reads aloud. Commercial examples generally contain further explanatory notes with which to standardise and interpret the results.

Formative assessment

Like speaking and listening, formative assessment of pupils' reading strategies can highlight strengths and weaknesses in your own teaching. Your future planning will be shaped by what you find. Shared formative reading assessment also encourages pupils to become involved in their own reading progress. There are five basic types of formative reading assessment:

1. Pupil's **concepts about print** (Clay, 2000)
2. Running records and miscue analysis
3. Structured questioning to gauge comprehension
4. Observations
5. Cloze procedure

Explanations and sample frameworks appear in the glossary and appendices.

After the child has secured concepts about print and progressed to reading texts, each formative assessment is used at all stages of the primary school and at all levels of attainment. Using each type shows pupils' progression across the curriculum, how pupils' reading skills are transferred and pupils' progression as active readers.

✎ Research focus

The emotional response of the reader

The seminal work of Louise Rosenblatt considers the emotional response of the reader (Rosenblatt, 2004). Her reader response theory describes reader stance: how readers respond to text at an emotional level. Efferent reading stances concentrate on what happens after reading. They seek a tangible product, such as the latest political updates, a recipe for biscuits or an answer to a science problem. Aesthetic reading stances enable the reader to experience the text during reading, such as through the thrills and tensions of an exciting novel. Emotional responses to text like this are important steps for progression because they are indications of pupils' interest. Interest rewards the reader with behaviours that encourage more reading, as when pupils search for peculiarity or uniqueness in what they have chosen to read (Parker and Lepper, 1992). The pupils who race to browse books such as *The Guinness Book of Records* exemplify this type of reading interest. How far is reader response an indication of pupils' actual reading progression? It is known that reading practice and large amounts of reading lead to greater attainment (Stanovich, 1986). A reader's response to text is part of this but it may also depend on the range of texts that the pupil chooses to read.

Classroom application   Rosenblatt's work has implications for the assessment and progression of pupils' reading repertoire based on traditional forms of testing. Is it necessary to set formal assessment criteria for developing pupils' reading repertoire? How much do teachers really know about pupils' personal responses to text? How would such knowledge influence the quality, range and type of text used in the classroom? In response, teachers may develop pupils' reading repertoire by building in daily, authentic opportunities to choose real texts for real purposes. Pupils may choose texts to be read aloud by the teacher as a class novel or storybook. Rotated pupils may be responsible for stocking the class library. Teachers and pupils may develop joint records of what is read for pleasure and pupils' response to the chosen texts. Teachers may assess pupils' self-selection strategies and library skills. Finally, teachers may assess pupils' reading stamina. Chapters 5 and 6 contain further details of monitoring progression in pupils' personal response to text as they learn to read.

Non-word reading assessment

Non-word reading assessments consist of a series of non-words that the pupil is required to read aloud. The non-words contain examples of English phonemes

Table 4.6 Observing progression in reading acquisition

	Phonics	Vocabulary	Orthography	Examples of comprehension	Examples of links with other four-modes of English
Lower primary years	Segments, blends and uses analogy, plausible phonetic predictions, reads syllables, uses alphabet	Knows common sight words, uses picture cues, orally retells and recalls what has been read in detail, discusses word meaning, uses sentence structure to aid decoding	Uses classroom environment to assist with unknown words, uses visual cues, may over-use common letter patterns	Expects text to make sense, reads with expression using punctuation and pictures as a cue, asks questions, retells and recalls what has been read in the correct sequence, re-uses story patterns while retelling and inventing, predicts, finds specific parts of text, has reading favourites	Exploratory spelling, plausible phonetic attempts often without vowels, vocabulary building through reading and listening to stories, knowledge of narrative structure.
Middle primary years	Uses a mixture of syllables and phonics to decode unfamiliar words	Established sight vocabulary, uses picture cues and sentence construction, identifies some key words, generates some alternative vocabulary	Uses suffixes and prefixes to predict unknown words in context, recognises some spelling irregularities	Reads fluently, uses punctuation, established re-reading to work out and predict, infers, beginning to evaluate consistently using knowledge of text and personal reading, key words, index, contents, subheading and glossary use	Established written sight vocabulary, applies orthographic knowledge to reading and writing, reads independently, using a range of skills
Upper primary years	Uses phonic skill mainly for unfamiliar words out of context and for new topic vocabulary	Confidently uses key vocabulary to skim and scan text for research and evidence gathering	Consistently uses suffix and prefix, and **homophone** knowledge to predict unknown words in and out of context	Reads fluently in a range of situations, established reading choices and habits, skims and scans, secure inference using evidence, summarises, looks for key words and clues to text structure, index, contents, subheading and glossary use secure, reads like writer	Established orthographic knowledge and interest in the etymology of words, dictionary and thesaurus skill secured, uses spell-check as last option

and therefore provide data on the pupils' ability to decode phonemes out of context. The merits of this assessment need to be considered in the light of interactive models of the reading process. If pupils actively employ a range of strategies to read for meaning there is a limit to the level at which pupils will be able to understand a non-word reading test. However, non-word reading assessments are useful for screening pupils to detect specific phoneme difficulties.

Table 4.6 presents the next entry for a matrix of primary English progression. It shows progression in reading acquisition across the primary years. Use this grid as a guide for classroom observation, running records, structured questioning to gauge comprehension and guided reading sessions.

Summary of chapter

This chapter has described the elements of reading acquisition. It has outlined three theoretical perspectives for the process of learning to read in relation to language progression and being a reader. Pupil vignettes were used to illustrate the application of theory. It expanded these ideas in relation to current research and the four modes of English. It has evaluated the main types of reading assessment. This chapter has emphasised your role as a classroom teacher in finding efficient and effective ways to teach each individual pupil to read in order that they may become readers for life.

? **Self-assessment**

1. Compare and contrast the elements of psycholinguistic, cognitive and socio-cultural approaches to reading.
2. List the advantages and disadvantages of summative and formative assessments for monitoring daily reading progression.
3. List and justify three items that you consider important features of progression or a suggested next step in learning to read. Choose items for the oldest, mid-range and youngest pupils in the primary school.

Annotated further reading

Tracey, D. and Mandell-Morrow, L. (2012) *Lenses on Reading: An Introduction to Theories and Models* (2nd edn). New York: Guilford Press. This revised edition provides a clear critique of reading theory. The book is scattered with relevant classroom applications and pupil vignettes.

Rose, J. (2006) *Independent Review of Early Reading: Final Report*. London: Department for Education and Science. This report contains details of the research base for the Simple View of Reading.

Further resources

The United Kingdom Literacy Association produces a useful series of mini books that address reading acquisition, including miscue analysis and the teaching of reading.

The Australian My Read organisation provides a range of resources for developing reading in the 8–13 year old age group. It is developed by the Australian Association for the Teaching of English. For further information go to www.myread.org/

There are a number of online interactive reading clubs to support pupils' reading acquisition. Bug Club is one example, at www.bugclub.co.uk/. It contains a large number of resources and e-books that can be used in partnership with parents.

References

Aarnoutee, C., and Van Leeuwe, J. (1998) Relations between reading vocabulary, reading for pleasure and reading frequency. *Educational Research and Evaluation*, 4, 143–166.

Bourassa, D. and Treiman, R. (2010) Linguistic foundations of spelling development. In D. Wyse, R. Andrews and J. Hoffman (Eds), *The Routledge International Handbook of English Language and Literacy Teaching*. Abingdon: Routledge.

Chall, J. S. (1983) *Learning to Read: The Great Debate*. New York: McGraw-Hill.

Chall, J. S. (1996) *Stages of Reading Development* (2nd edn). Fort Worth, TX: Harcourt Brace.

Clark, C., Woodley, J. and Lewis, F. (2011) *The Gift of Reading in 2011: Children's and Young People's Access to Books and Attitudes Towards Reading*. London: National Literacy Trust.

Clay, M. (2000) *An Observation Survey of Early Literacy Achievement*. Auckland: Heinemann.

DfES (2006) *Primary National Strategy: Primary Framework for Literacy and Mathematics*. London: DfES.

Department for Education and Skills (2007) *Letters and Sounds: Principles and Practice of High Quality Phonics. Ref 00282–2007BKT-EN*. London: Department of Education and Skills.

Dombey, H. (2010) *Teaching Reading: What the Evidence Says*. Leicester: United Kingdom Literacy Association.

Ehri, L. C. (1995) Phases of development in learning to read by sight. *Journal of Research in Reading*, 18, 116–125.

Ellis, S. (2007) Policy and research: Lessons from the Clackmannanshire synthetic phonics initiative. *Journal of Early Childhood Literacy*, 7, 281–297.

Frith, U. (1985) Beneath the surface of developmental dyslexia. In J. Patterson, J. C. Marshal and M. Coltheart (Eds), *Surface Dyslexia*. pp. 301–330.

Gamse, B. C., Bloom, H. S., Kemple, J. J. and Jacobs, R. T. (2008) *Read First Impact Study: Interim Report*. Washington, DC: National Centre for Education and Regional Assistance, Institute of Education Sciences, US Dept of Education.

Gee, J. P. (2004) Reading as situated language: A socio-cognitive perspective. In R. Ruddell and N. Unrau (Eds), *Theoretical Models and Processes of Reading* (5th edn). Newark, NJ: International Reading Association. pp. 116–132.

Gentry, R. (1987) *Spel...is a Four Letter Word*. New York: Scholastic.

Goodman, K. S. (1967) Reading: A psycholingusitic guessing game. *Journal of the Reading Specialist*, 4, 126–135.

Goswami, U. and Bryant, P. (1990) *Phonological Skills and Learning to Read*. Hillsdale, NJ: Lawrence Erlbaum.

Gough, P. B. and Tumner, W. E. (1986) Decoding, reading and reading disability. *Remedial and Special Education*, 7, 6–10.

Hulme, C. and Snowling, M. J. (2013). Learning to read: What we know and what we need to understand better. *Child Development Perspectives*, 7, 1–5. doi:10.111/odep.12005

Jama, D. and Dugdale, G. (2011) *Literacy: State of the Nation. A Picture of Literacy in the UK Today*. London: National Literacy Trust.

Lambirth, A. (2011) Reading. In R. Cox (Ed.), *Primary English Teaching: An introduction to language, literacy and learning* London: Sage. (pp 23–36).

Nicholson, T. (2008) Lagging behind in the reading stakes. *Opinions on Education*, (115), 1–2. Available at: www.educationforum.org.nz (accessed June 2009)

Parker, L. E. and Lepper, M. R. (1992) Effects of fantasy context on children's learning and motivation: Making learning more fun. *Journal of Personality and Social Psychology*, 62, 625–633.

Primary National Strategy (2006) *Primary National Strategy*. Available at: www.educationengland.org.uk/documents/pdfs/2006-primary-national-strategy.pdf

Roberts, G., Torgessen, S., Boardman, A. and Scammaca, N. (2008) Evidence-based strategies for reading instruction of older students with learning disabilities. *Learning Disabilities: Research and Practice*, 23, 63–69.

Rose, J. (2006) *Independent Review of Early Reading: Final Report*. London: Department for Education and Science.

Rosenblatt, L. M. (2004). The transactional theory of reading and writing. In R. Ruddell and N. Unrau (Eds), *Theoretical Models and Processes of Reading* (Vol. 5,). Newark, NJ: International Reading Association. pp. 1363–1398.

Stanovich, K. E. (1984) The interactive-compensatory model of reading: A confluence of developmental, experimental and educational psychology. *Remedial and Special Education*, 5, 11–19.

Stanovich, K. E. (1986) Matthew effects in reading: Some consequences of individual differences in the acquisition of literacy. *Reading Research Quarterly*, 4 (21), 360–407.

Tracey, D.H. and Morrow, L.M. (2012) *Lenses on Reading: An Introduction to Theories and Models* (2nd edn). New York and London: Guilford Press.

Verhoeven, L., van Leeuwe, J. and Vermeer, A. (2011) Vocabulary growth and reading development across the elementary years. *Scientific Studies of Reading*, 15, 8–25. doi:10.108/10888438.2011.536125

CHAPTER 5

READING COMPREHENSION

Objectives

1. To identify key features of progression in reading comprehension
2. To examine literal, inferential and evaluative comprehension
3. To relate progression in reading comprehension to daily classroom practice
4. To evaluate common forms of reading comprehension assessment

Introduction

The purpose of reading is to gain meaning from print. Reading for meaning is the ability to comprehend and engage with print. Pupils' use of multimodal text and illustration are part of the reading comprehension process. Effective reading comprehension is the key to becoming an active and enthused reader since effective comprehension is the ultimate reward for reading. By discovering new, unexpected and multiple layers of meaning, both within and across texts, readers are prompted to choose to read for their own purposes and for their own pleasure. In this way, independent reading, fuelled by rewarding comprehension, becomes a self-regulated act. Pupils' reading engagement can grow. Self-regulation is meta-cognition, knowledge of what influences your thinking processes. It lies at the heart of teaching reading comprehension both for learning and for personal reading pleasure.

Activity

What does reading comprehension mean to you?

In one minute, compile a list of words that you associate with reading comprehension and those that you associate with reading for pleasure.

This exercise will have caused you to consider the process of reading comprehension. Traditional approaches to practising and assessing reading comprehension in school have involved pupils reading short pieces of text and answering a series of graded questions. Children may also be encouraged to demonstrate understanding of their reading book through answering a series of oral questions after reading aloud to the teacher. These approaches generally assume sub-skills of comprehension and therefore that these skills may be taught in an established, progressive order. This approach to teaching reading comprehension springs from the earlier work of reading researchers. More recently, researchers have shown that effective reading comprehension involves a combination of pupils' prior knowledge and the place of reading and literature within a social and cultural context (Duke et al., 2011). It is from this background that pupils' engagement, comprehension, analysis and reflection of new and unfamiliar texts can begin to develop.

Reading for pleasure involves developing a personal reading repertoire. It links to reading comprehension because as the repertoire grows, pupils' knowledge of literature and social reading practices come to the fore. Initially, because writing is not merely speech written down, early readers may also need to be taught concepts about print (Clay, 1999). Knowing how to follow the direction of the print and how to read punctuation are examples. Next, familiarity with narrative structure, through hearing and sharing stories before and after learning to read, serves to strengthen pupils' building of reading repertoires and their knowledge of language patterns and text structures. For example, knowing the language of traditional fairy tales can assist pupils to predict similar language patterns in newer versions. Early readers tend to build their comprehension skills from narrative texts that have a clear, linear progression. Eventually pupils' wider reading repertoires include a balance of fiction and non-fiction. These texts provide a framework for pupils' reading and writing of different genres and vocabulary development while adding to their general knowledge and an enjoyment of reading.

The process of reading comprehension

At the basic, literal level, the progression of reading comprehension generally correlates with the progression of language comprehension. In this instance, language comprehension encompasses listening comprehension skills (Gough and Tumner, 1986). Once young readers have some rapid word recognition skills, the meanings of words and sentences can begin to expand. As with any new skill, practise and experience of reading is crucial for progression. The more pupils read, the more they have the chance to practise word recognition, reading fluency and reading comprehension skills. Pupils who practise reading widely develop greater levels of comprehension as well as larger vocabularies and increased spelling skills (Cunningham and Stanovich, 1990; Stanovich, 1986).

The skills of reading comprehension can be summarised under four headings (Pearson, 2009):

1. Making inferences
2. Drawing on different sources of information
3. Using the grammar of sentences and genres to comprehend
4. Using specific strategies to check for understanding

Table 5.1 presents a categorisation of the reading comprehension behaviours of our vignette pupils and allows us to track some of the features and suggested next steps for progression in reading comprehension that can occur across the primary years of schooling. In these examples, there are definite patterns in the process of developing reading comprehension. Firstly, every vignette pupil seeks to make meaning from the reading text. Secondly, every vignette pupil is able to predict and recall aspects of their reading. Thirdly, every vignette pupil uses some knowledge of other books or genres to decipher words and to comprehend themes in the text that they have read. Fourthly, every vignette pupil shows and requires further vocabulary development.

Progression in reading comprehension

Although understanding speech is different from understanding the printed word, some of our knowledge of the growth of language and thought can help us to understand how reading comprehension develops. Research comes from the fields of psychology and educational research. Evaluating the evidence allows us to consider its place within the 'assess, plan, teach, practise, apply and review' framework (DfES, 2006).

The processes of reading comprehension can be summarised under two broad headings: vocabulary and comprehension through interpretation. There are a number of separate elements under each heading. These elements combine to

Table 5.1 Summary of reading comprehension in the pupil vignettes

Pupil	Age	Attainment Level	Key strategies for reading comprehension	Feature of progression	Suggested next steps for progression
Japonica	10	Within expected levels	Seeks meaning from all text, skims and scans text for key words, reads punctuation, re-reads to decipher new words in the context of the sentence, identifies authors' intent but lacks skill in backing up her ideas with evidence from the text	Demonstrates literal and inferential comprehension, interprets multi-modal sources, uses search engine, uses knowledge of genre structures to make connections between similar types of text	Use more evidence from the text to reinforce point of view, extract key words for note taking, informed selection of various texts for own research, established personal reading repertoire
Analyn	9	EAL pupil at the earlier stages of English language acquisition	Uses picture cues, sequences picture stories, matches written captions to pictures	Answers literal comprehension, questions, able to recall and order familiar stories orally, simple naming vocabulary, re-reads favourite books for personal pleasure	Building spoken and read vocabulary, building oral prediction, recall skills and story sequencing skills
John	7	Below expected levels	Uses phonics as the main strategy for decoding print, inserts some words based on word shape, with some inaccuracy, enjoys favourite books and themes, uses picture cues, recalls simple inferences from the text, own experience and pictures mainly based on cause and effect	Makes predictions before and after reading, recalls what he has read, reads speech marks and exclamation marks, uses intonation and reads most full stops	Recall correct sequences, re-read to decipher words and word meaning over whole text, increase use of pictures and reading ahead to predict
Peter	5	Above expected levels	Mixed reading strategies to derive meaning, re-reads, reads ahead, uses picture cues, uses knowledge of features in similar sentences, words and texts to work out meaning	Established personal reading repertoire, including favourite authors, summary skills, inference and recall of main themes	Infer using details in the text, begin to talk about unfamiliar text, using pictures and reference to text, connect to other fiction and introduce skills for non-fiction

produce a constructivist model of learning to comprehend text. Constructivist approaches to literacy learning understand that the pupil is actively engaged in the learning process, often by testing out hypotheses. Prediction, inference, recall and summary are part of active engagement as well as judgement of text with the use of suitable evidence.

Cognitive psychologists describe reading comprehension as the process of making a mental representation of the text. Sequentially this will be the words, the sentences and the overall message of the text with any accompanying illustrations. As soon as pupils have a mental picture of what they have read, they begin the process of integrating it into their existing body of knowledge. Learning occurs. Pupils' knowledge grows when the integration is complete (Kintsch, 2004).

Comprehension through interpretation

There are two basic levels of comprehension through interpretation. The first level uses the information in the text itself. The second level uses pupils' prior knowledge (Duke et al., 2011). Accurately reading the text involves literal comprehension. This means that the pupil has understood and remembered the main ideas in the text in order to be able to summarise it. Skimming and scanning of the text to find written evidence is necessary. Part of this process involves pupils using their implicit knowledge of grammatical sentence structure (Duke et al., 2011). Known as textual **cohesion**, this knowledge of consistency applies across sentences, paragraphs and whole texts. Less skilled comprehenders struggle to demonstrate these cues orally (Cain, 2003).

The second level of comprehension through interpretation involves the use of information from pupils' prior knowledge in order to read between the lines of the text that is being read. Inference is the ability to read between the lines, to hypothesise and to form opinions about what has been read.

Inferential skills rely on pupils' general knowledge, vocabulary, prior knowledge of the genre, the language patterns in the text and the ability to make connections between them. Inferential comprehension may involve a personal response to the text that can incorporate an evaluation of its success for the reader or for other criteria. Pupils need to understand the audience, purpose and context of what they have read.

All pupils have the potential to infer but younger readers are less likely to do so of their own accord. Knowing when and how to use inferences while reading seem to be important factors in their progression (Cain and Oakhill, 1999).

Activity

Formulating comprehension questions

Look at the examples of reading comprehension questions based on the traditional tale of *The Elves and the Shoemaker*. Classify them as literal, inferential or evaluative comprehension questions. The third one has been done for you.

Table 5.2

Question	Answer	Literal	Inferential	Evaluative
How many elves were in the story?	Two			
Why were the shoemaker and his wife poor?	On page 3 and 4 it says that the shoemaker and his wife had bills to pay and little money, they have patched clothes in the pictures too			
Explain the morals of the story	The moral is never look a gift horse in the mouth. Always give thanks as the shoemaker did when he made clothes for the elves			✓
Why was the shoemaker worried about shoes being made overnight at first?	He was worried because he did not know how they had appeared, or if they had been stolen or made illegally			

This activity will have caused you to consider the layers of meaning that are possible, even from a relatively simple story. Certain features of reading comprehension seem to be important for progression. These include rapid word recognition, understanding the structure of stories, recognising grammatical and general inconsistent meanings in a text and short-term memory for what has been read (Cain, 2003; Cain et al., 2004).

Classroom application   In the classroom, formulating questions like this is a useful tool for formative reading assessment. Teachers or pupils may write these questions in order to separate layers of meaning. Bloom's and Barrett's taxonomies are traditional resources that provide frameworks for structuring reading comprehension questions (Barrett, 1972; Bloom, 1956). The revised Bloom's Taxonomy sets out to align it more closely to the teaching cycle (Krathwohl, 2002).

Vocabulary

Increased vocabulary assists reading comprehension. If a word is not part of a pupil's spoken or mental dictionary of vocabulary it will not be immediately understood in print. Developing readers learn to integrate and add new words into their spoken vocabulary and into their existing mental structures of ideas. Specific vocabulary teaching can improve pupils' reading vocabulary, but spontaneous, repeated and varied opportunities for developing pupils' vocabulary can all contribute to wider vocabulary knowledge (National Reading Panel, 2000).

Research focus

Oral language and reading comprehension

Recent research has begun to isolate the specific details of pupils with very poor reading comprehension (Clarke et al., 2010). In a randomised controlled study, 8–9 year old children received either additional oral language work, additional text comprehension work or a combination of the two. In comparison to the control group, all groups improved their reading comprehension. The oral language group made the most long-term reading comprehension gains. Both the oral language and combination groups made reading gains in comprehension related to improving their vocabulary. These findings suggest that poor oral language, including vocabulary, may be a factor in poor reading comprehension.

Classroom application   In the classroom, developing vocabulary is a cross-curricular practice. This approach enables the pupil to see the links between different subjects and to make conceptual connections. Categorising and generating vocabulary is one technique to begin to make those connections. For example, the use of graphic organisers such as Venn diagrams both generates and shows the relationships between different vocabulary lists. Teachers have also to be aware of pupils' out of school experiences of vocabulary, reading and literacy. The quality of pupils' language and reading environment at home can be more influential than pupils' socio-economic status (Organisation for Economic Cooperation and Development, 2000; Roulstone et al., 2011).

The progression of reading comprehension in the primary classroom

This section puts reading comprehension research into a classroom context. Using research and the pupil vignettes from Chapter 1 it describes and evaluates evidence to support understanding of progression in reading comprehension in the primary classroom.

Much of the educational and psychological research into reading comprehension has focused on pupils' learning processes. In the classroom, two strands are useful as a basis for understanding progression in reading comprehension at the primary level. They describe cognitive strategies and social practices to enhance pupils' understanding and engagement with text.

1. Meta-cognitive reading strategies
2. Reading engagement

In this section, the progression of meta-cognitive reading strategies is examined. Chapter 6 contains details of progression in reading engagement.

Meta-cognitive reading strategies

The teaching of reading comprehension incorporates the teaching of specific reading strategies. Once mastered, pupils develop conscious usage of these strategies before, during and after reading. Reading strategies are not isolated from other aspects of the reading curriculum. They are part of 'learning to read and reading to learn' (Rose, 2006 p.27). Properly taught, they can become an instinctive part of pupils' independent reading and reading for pleasure.

Meta-cognitive reading strategies, or learning how to learn from text, equip pupils with standard tools with which to actively read text. Like wide vocabulary skills, they enable pupils to make links between what is read, what is known and what needs to be known. These are the characteristics of good readers. Good readers can self-correct; tackle unfamiliar vocabulary; monitor and adapt their reading according to their understanding; summarise; understand authors' intentions; predict; set reading goals; evaluate; read selectively; compare and contrast; question; and recognise how to read genres differently (Duke and Pearson, 2002). Progression through these skills tends to be recursive rather than linear. It is seen when pupils use them independently with a wide range of texts.

One of the most important features of all meta-cognitive instruction is how pupils transfer skills from one situation to another. Various factors are important for a positive transfer. Broadly, general intelligence affects pupils' ability to learn meta-cognitive reading strategies. An ability to see opportunities for their transfer to other texts is also important Consistent teaching is required with elements of rote learning. For example, pupils need to know the routines for tackling unfamiliar words in a text automatically (Child, 2011).

Classroom application   In the classroom, comprehension strategy instruction uses many of the social constructivist principles of scaffolding learning. It may be part of any lesson where reading comprehension is required. Shared or demonstrated reading by the teacher makes these strategies explicit because the teacher 'thinks aloud'. Four steps to the process of teaching comprehension strategies are useful for summarising classroom technique.

1. Teaching the strategy in a real context
2. Shared reading and small group guided practice
3. Pupils practising individually and as part of a group
4. Pupils applying the strategy to a real context

While each technique is suitable for all text, teachers have also to be aware of the different reading demands of fiction and non-fiction. At times, this is a matter of degree. For example, extended fiction reading demands reading stamina or uninterrupted reading skills. Non-fiction reading requires increased skimming and scanning skills plus knowledge of text layout and devices such as subheadings, an index and a glossary.

Sometimes the demands are particular to fiction, non-fiction or to digital text. For example, reading fiction involves understanding story grammar. Story grammar explains how the parts of a story fit together. Even the simplest of stories has characters, a setting, a plot, an opening, a build-up, a resolution and an ending. Most non-fiction reading contains some new and unfamiliar vocabulary. Pupils need to be able to identify and classify it, initially by using clues from the text itself. When using digital text, pupils need to make clear choices about what to read next because the text is not presented in a linear fashion.

Activity

Transferring meta-cognitive reading comprehension skills

Populate the mock weekly primary timetable with opportunities for reading strategy instruction and practice. This class has a learning support assistant for three days a week.

Table 5.3

Time	Monday	Tuesday	Wednesday	Thursday	Friday
8.45	Register and spelling or mental maths practice				
9.00	English	Maths	English	Maths	English

(Continued)

(Continued)

Time	Monday	Tuesday	Wednesday	Thursday	Friday
10.40	Break				
11.00	Maths	English	Maths	English	Maths
12.00	Lunch				
1.00	Register and short physical exercise – outside if weather permits				
1.30	Whole class silent reading and guided reading groups				
2.00	Science	P.E.	Humanities	Swimming	Religious Education
3.00	Story writing and story telling	Music Class story time	Personal interest and topic study time	Swimming	Assembly Class story time
3.45			End of school day		

This activity will have caused you to consider the practicalities of selecting and teaching for the transfer of reading strategies across the primary curriculum. Progression in pupils' reading comprehension can also be monitored through pupils' responses to reading aloud. Comprehension of multimodal sources, such as film, is also possible.

Two established New Zealand researchers suggest five categories of reading comprehension strategy: activating background knowledge, questioning, analysing text structure, creating a graphic organiser and summarising (Dymock and Nicholson, 2010). Although written specifically for non-fiction texts, progression in general comprehension strategies is usefully illustrated using these headings. Dymock and Nicholson have not included pupils' vocabulary development. It has been added to the vignette examples below.

Activating background knowledge

Alerting pupils to the knowledge that they bring to the text increases pupils' ability to predict and anticipate what will be read. These ideas stem from the constructivist idea of schema theory (Rumelhart, 1980), a theory of how knowledge is represented in the mind. Predicting and anticipating reading causes pupils to collate and classify their knowledge in relation to what they already know. The importance of vocabulary development is re-emphasised by schema theory because it is difficult to understand something new without any pre-existing language to express knowledge and understanding.

Activity

Look at the four extracts from an individual reading session, from the pupil vignettes. Record features and suggestions for next steps in progression in activating prior knowledge. The first section has been completed for you.

Table 5.4

Pupil	Extract from an individual reading session	Features of progression	Suggested next steps for progression
Japonica K. Dermott & A. Berk *William Shakespeare –* *His Life and Times*	T: *Why have I chosen this text?* J: *That's easy, it's about William Shakespeare,* *the title tells you that and we have read A* *Midsummer Night's Dream.* T: *Tell me more.* J: *The title says 'times'. I guess this means* *what was happening to everyone else, like* *global warming.*	Relates text to known play, uses title as cue	Use contextual knowledge to improve predictions
John J. Burningham *Edwardo, the* *Horriblest Boy in the* *Whole Wide World*	J: *(Reads title only) This book looks like it's* *going to tell you what to do. I don't think it* *will be very funny or interesting.* T: *How do you know if you are right?* J: *I can flick through the pictures to see if I can* *work out the story.*		

(Continued)

(Continued)

Pupil	Extract from an individual reading session	Features of progression	Suggested next steps for progression
Analyn J. Scieszka The Real Story of the Three Little Pigs (The book is a re-write from the wolf's point of view, one pig survives.)	Analyn has listened to the story read aloud. T: Does this book remind you of anything you have heard before? A: It's like the Three Little Pigs story with the big, bad wolf. T: It is but is there anything different? A: No, the pigs still die.		
Peter C. Mason How Things Work. An Usborne Lift the Flap Book	P: I love this book because it will tell me how things work. T: What sort of things Peter? P: Well it's got flaps so maybe insides of things 'cos you have to lift it to see. My old Spot books had flaps to see inside parcels for Spot.		

〰️ **Reflection questions**

- Does Japonica have an understanding of when Shakespearean times were?
- What other book self-selection strategies will help John to choose books that interest him?
- What evidence is there that Peter may have read fewer science and non-fiction books?

Classroom application   In the classroom, activating background knowledge means preparing pupils to read with purpose. Modelling this orally or using mind-mapping techniques can help pupils to coordinate their previous knowledge. Monitoring progression here is part of speaking and listening observations and assessment. Skimming and scanning skills are required.

Questioning

The progression of questioning skills within reading comprehension is addressed through pupils' understanding of literal, inferential and evaluative questions (Literacy Aotearoa, 2000). Good comprehenders need to be able to formulate and answer each type of question. Pupils need to progress through each type of question with all new material.

🖻 **Activity**

Look at the four extracts from teacher questioning in the pupil vignettes. Record features and suggested next steps for progression and in questioning. The last one has been done for you.

Table 5.5

Pupil and title of book	Extract from teacher questioning with pupil in a guided reading session	Features of progression	Suggested next steps for progression
Japonica K. Dermott and A. Berk	T: *What questions do you have about everyday Shakespearean life before we start reading?*		

(Continued)

(Continued)

Pupil and title of book	Extract from teacher questioning with pupil in a guided reading session	Features of progression	Suggested next steps for progression
William Shakespeare – His Life and Times	J: *The facts of Shakespeare, his life timeline and the main things happening in England then*		
John J. Burningham *Edwardo, the Horriblest Boy in the Whole Wide World*	T: *Who is the main character?* J: *Edwardo* T: *Why?* J: *'cos his picture and name are on every page* T: *How does Edwardo change?* J: *He's naughty then he does jobs for other people*		
Analyn J. Scieszka *The Real Story of the Three Little Pigs*	T: *What happened after the pigs built their houses in this story?* A: *(flicks to page) They were eaten by the wolf* T: *Are there heroes in this story?* A: *Mmmm, it's the last pig because he escaped the wolf* T: *What questions would you ask the wolf?* J: *None because he might eat me*		
Peter C. Mason *How Things Work. An Usborne Lift the Flap Book*	T: *Name four things I can find out about on page 4* P: *Diggers and trucks, cranes and concrete mixers* T: *Who needs the information on this page?* J: *Builders and road menders*	Scans page for literal information, applies facts to real world	Use contents to locate page, formulate pre-reading questions

〰️ **Reflection questions**

- What basic and specific vocabulary would be useful to improve Japonica's comprehension of the text and her ability to locate information?
- How does Analyn show empathy with the characters in the story?
- Which pupils appear to need to practise more prediction, sequence and recall of the text? Why?

Classroom application In the classroom, pupils' progression in answering and asking questions based on text is monitored by observation of carefully structured situations and in free discussion of books and text. Chapter 2 contains practical examples for monitoring the progression of questioning skills. Teachers need to ensure careful use of targeted questions in order not to promote limited or restricted responses from pupils. Pupils' formulation of literal, inferential or evaluative questions before, during and after reading with given and chosen text encourages self-monitoring and structures formative assessment.

Analysing text structure through creating graphic organisers

The bulk of research in this area comes from the functional and critical approaches to literacy outlined in Chapter 1. The use of graphic organisers serves as a bridge between pupils' reading and writing. These charts or diagrams summarise and categorise the meanings within text.

〰️ **Reflection questions**

- John's book has been chosen for its very repetitive structure. How will this help his comprehension?
- How could you extend Peter's science vocabulary using his book?

Classroom application In the classroom, the analysis of text structure is supported through graphic organisers. As well as providing a visual representation of the overall structure of a text, graphic organisers encourage pupils to look for the language features of different genres. Progression is monitored through the complexity of the organiser. For example, a simple linear storyboard can show the beginning, middle and end of a story. More complex activities with text may use established methods like directed activities related to text (Lunzer and Gardner, 1979). These during and post-reading activities include reconstructing modified versions of text or analysing full versions through annotation, labelling or summarising

Activity

Look at four extracts from the class reading logs of the pupil vignettes. Record suggested features and next steps for progression in analysing text structures. The third one has been done for you.

Table 5.6

Pupil and book title	Extract or summary from pupils' class reading log following guided reading session	Features of progression	Suggested next steps for progression
Japonica K. Dermott and A. Berk *William Shakespeare – His Life and Times*	Japonica has drawn a timeline to show Shakespeare's important life dates She has marked the dates of Elizabeth I and the bubonic plague		
John J. Burningham *Edwardo, the Horriblest Boy in the Whole Wide World*	John draws and captions four pictures of Edwardo out of sequence He does not show Edwardo's change of heart		
Analyn J. Scieszka *The Real Story of the Three Little Pigs*	Analyn plays the part of the wolf in a hot seating game She then completes speech bubbles and adds them to a prepared story frieze of the sections of the story	Drama activates and models her vocabulary for related written work	Recall story sequences independently Look for the main idea in a text
Peter C. Mason *How Things Work.* *An Usborne Lift the Flap Book*	Peter asks for the page to read about cars He makes a facts chart of key words and pictures: fuel, tyres, wheels, and engine No contents or index are used		

text. Follow-up activities like this develop pupils' creative and individualised responses to their reading, and comprehension develops.

Summary

An ability to summarise what has been read is a key aspect of progression in reading comprehension. By summarising efficiently, the pupil demonstrates understanding of text beyond individual words and sentences. Good summarisers practise a number of skills. They can pinpoint threads of meaning across a whole text. They can judge the text. Finally, they can précis or re-present the text, sometimes in a different genre. It is of particular use in developing pupils' sense of audience and purpose for the text. The skills of reading and writing are drawn closer together. (Block and Pressley 2003)

Activity

Look at the four extracts from the home-school reading diaries in the pupil vignettes. Record features and suggested next steps for progression in summarising. The second one has been done for you.

Table 5.7

Pupil and book title	Extract from pupils' home/school reading diary	Features of progression	Suggested next steps for progression
Japonica K. Dermott and A. Berk William Shakespeare – His Life and Times	The diary task was to describe a day in the life of Elizabethan England compared to Japonica's day Japonica has written, 'This book is about the life and times of William Shakespeare. It has lots of lift the flap and pull out sections and lots of interesting facts.'		
John J. Burningham Edwardo,	John enjoyed this story. We read a page each then he read it by himself.	Recalls main events and theme of the story, knows	Develop reading stamina to read a whole text alone, find information

(Continued)

(Continued)

Pupil and book title	Extract from pupils' home/school reading diary	Features of progression	Suggested next steps for progression
the Horriblest Boy in the Whole Wide World	*He talked to me about Edwardo's naughty and good deeds after we had chatted through the story again. He said Edwardo was better being good!' Mum's entry in John's home-school log*	main character, beginning to link ideas to his own life	in the text to answer literal questions, predict before reading
Analyn J. Scieszka *The Real Story of the Three Little Pigs* (written from wolf's point of view)	*The diary task was to complete a 4-part storyboard. Analyn has drawn un-sequenced pictures from the story She has written summary sentences: 'The wolf was bad, he ate two pigs. One pig was free. The wolf told the story. He was still bad and had to go away.'*		
Peter C. Mason *How Things Work. An Usborne Lift the Flap Book*	*The diary task was to – draw pictures and write labels in a bubble diagram of trucks and diggers from looking at the relevant page of the book John has completed and added sections to the bubble map provided to show his versions of new types of diggers and trucks*		

〜〜 **Reflection questions**

- Which pupils demonstrate inferential comprehension through their summaries?
- How would you assist Japonica to progress in her ability to summarise the text?
- What advice would you offer to John's mum to develop her son's prediction?

Classroom application Teaching and monitoring summary comprehension skills is an oral and written practice. Firstly, progression includes succinct oral retelling and finding key words and themes in a text. Writing sub-headings for each paragraph is one technique for this process. Secondly, pupils must recognise repetition. Thirdly, pupils must be able to précis.

Reading engagement

Although a pupil may read and understand text well, it does not necessarily follow that they will read for personal reasons or for pleasure. Much of the research in this area has looked at the socio-cultural aspects of reading comprehension. Research suggests that reading engagement is a significant factor in the progression of pupils' reading comprehension (Chapman et al., 2000). Chapter 6 looks at the relationship between reading engagement and reading comprehension in full.

✎ Research focus

Predicting reading comprehension on the Internet

A recent study of 11 to 12 year old pupils compared pupils' online comprehension and reading skills in relation to their offline reading comprehension (Coiro, 2011). Results suggested that on and offline reading comprehension made significant contributions to pupils' online reading skills. Pupils used offline comprehension skills of locating, evaluating, synthesising and presenting knowledge in a similar way online but it suggested that their proficiency with the sequences involved in using the Internet was a mediating factor. For example, in this study *some* pupils with lower levels of subject specific vocabulary performed as well or better than pupils with higher levels of subject specific vocabulary but lower levels of online skills, because they could rapidly search for necessary background vocabulary.

Coiro's research reflects the classroom teacher's responsibility to address reading comprehension progression within and across paper and multimodal sources. Multi-modal sources re-emphasise the essence of reading as communication.

This activity will have caused you to reconsider the elements of reading comprehension in multimodal texts. Like fiction and non-fiction, comprehending multimodal texts means understanding the reading demands of each different type. Understanding their different structures is part of this progression. It involves combing sources of information.

Look at the list of multimodal texts below. Tick the comprehension strategies associated with each activity. What other strategies can you add?

Table 5.8

Multimodal text	Non-verbal communication	Use genre structure and navigation	Literal comprehension	Inference	Evaluation	Audience and purpose
Animated film						
Audio story						
Company website						
Blog						
Online adventure game						
YouTube clip						
Wiki page						
Wordless picture book						
Online newspaper Prezi presentation						

The assessment of reading comprehension

This section examines the assessment of reading comprehension in the light of standardised testing, summative and formative assessment.

Summative assessment
Standardised reading comprehension assessment
All standardised reading assessments contain comprehension questions that assess literal, inferential and evaluative understanding. Some standardised reading assessments measure pupils' reading and **listening comprehension** abilities. The pupil listens to a short piece of text and answers graded questions.

There is a good deal of controversy surrounding the value of standardised reading assessment for measuring progression. Standardised reading results can identify lower, middle and able readers, or at least those who perform this way in reading tests. The same tests make it possible to compare one pupil's results with many others at the same chronological age. They can also reflect the quality of classroom teaching and the range of reading ability. However, most standardised tests only assess certain aspects of reading, such as fluency, accurate decoding or comprehension of ideas in a paragraph or across short pieces of text. This includes computer-based assessment. Other features of pupils' reading progression, such as reading stamina, pupils' established reading interests, the quality of their reading repertoires, their personal responses to text or their motivation to read, are rarely, poorly or never assessed. Nevertheless, effective readers coordinate all of these aspects of reading.

Formative assessment
Formative assessment is truly valid if it provides information to help progression. It should pinpoint current and next steps for achievement with matched teaching suggestions. For these reasons, good formative assessment is always cumulative.

Formative reading comprehension assessment
There are five important data sets for the formative assessments of reading comprehension. Pupils' strategies for word reading also have to be systematically taught and assessed.

1. Knowledge of Standard English
2. Recognition of text type – this includes genre structures and language features
3. Breadth of reading repertoire
4. Quality of pupils' personal reactions to their reading
5. Ability with literal, inferential and evaluative levels of comprehension

Many generic formative assessment procedures can examine these areas such as observation, questioning and mind mapping. Three specific approaches are described here: reciprocal reading, guided reading and reading interviews.

Reciprocal reading approaches seek to address pupils with good decoding but poor comprehension skills (Palincsar and Brown, 1984). In discussion with the teacher, pupils are taught to predict, question, clarify and summarise the text. Formative assessment of reading comprehension during reciprocal reading allows the teacher to measure progression within this subset of meta-cognitive reading comprehension skills.

Guided reading approaches seek to enhance pupils' ability to engage with a full text that is read over one or more guided reading sessions. Typically, these are matched ability group sessions. Guided sessions usually contain sections to teach and assess strategies for word reading, reading aloud and silently, and for personal responses to the text through book discussion. Each session has specific comprehension objectives and assessment points.

Reading interviews are normally one-to-one opportunities for pupil and teacher to discuss reading progress. Typical elements are reading range, interest and an assessment of short passage reading. Useful formative assessment will also involve pupils' self-assessment and realistic goal setting. This is often part of reading interviews.

✍ Research focus

Working together to make meaning from texts: a link between comprehension and classroom talk

Case study research with eight pairs of primary children examined the role of independent group discussion in the development of reading comprehension. Each pair used questions and suggestions to open and structure dialogue (Maine, 2013). Their questions put the text within their own experience. In this way, they discovered deeper meanings and common themes by themselves. Pupils supported and challenged each other using exploratory and cumulative talk as discussed in Chapter 2. Maine argues that if reading comprehension is a creative and active process and not merely measurement of prepared skills, teachers must model and provide pupils with reading discussion groups. It may also be argued that formative, observational assessment of reading comprehension from groups like this has a relevant place in the primary classroom.

Table 5.9 presents the third entry for a matrix of primary English progression. It shows progression in reading comprehension across the primary years. Use this

Table 5.9 Observing progression in reading comprehension

	Activating background knowledge	Questioning	Analysis	Summary	Vocabulary	Examples of links with other four modes of English
Lower primary years	Chooses reading, re-reads and asks for favourites. Recognises familiar and personal experiences and themes in text	Devises and answers literal questions, able to make simple inferences	Recognises simple structures, themes, finds key parts in the text, explains full stops, commas and speech marks	Recalls or identifies main events in a story in sequence	Identifies authors' descriptive words, rhyme and repetition	Links to oral recall and sequencing, familiar with concepts of print: handles book correctly, print direction, difference between word, pictures and sentences
Middle primary years	Predicts with reference to author, similar books and own experience, uses textual features of non-fiction, reads more punctuation	Devises and answers questions at three levels of comprehension, based on prior reading choices, may only find one point as evidence in the text	Predicts and infers using fiction structures, causes, effects, emotions, and plots, uses key words	Recalls and retells most main points in text, explains paragraphs	Begins to judge authors' vocabulary and style for audience and purpose	Reads fiction, non-fiction, uses some forms of multimedia, developing repertoire and interests
Upper primary years	Explains own point using evidence from text, compares and contrasts texts with own ideas	Devises and answers questions at three levels of comprehension, uses quotation, refers to several points of evidence in and related to other texts	Across longer texts, detects fact, opinion and bias, regularly annotates text, judges validity of text	Summary of main points across texts, uses paragraphs and layout, uses genre specific phrases in summary	Judges quality of authors' words and style, including rhetorical devices	Links fiction, non-fiction and multimedia, established reading repertoire and interests

grid as a guide for classroom observation, running records, miscue analysis, monitoring reading logs, reciprocal and guided sessions and in reading interviews.

Summary of chapter

This chapter has summarised the process and progression of reading comprehension under four headings: inferences; using other written information; using genre structures and language features and meta-cognitive reading comprehension processes. Pupil vignettes were used to illustrate the application of comprehension research and theory to classroom practice. The merits of standardised and formative assessment were examined. This chapter has emphasised your role as a classroom teacher in finding efficient and effective ways to develop a relevant context for reading comprehension. Such an approach fosters the stable progression and transfer of reading comprehension across the curriculum and beyond.

? **Self-assessment**

1. List and justify three items that you consider important features or next steps for progression in reading comprehension. Choose items for the oldest, mid-range and youngest pupils in the primary school.
2. Draw Venn diagrams to show the connections between reading acquisition and reading comprehension strategies and the factors that influence their progression.

Annotated further reading

Pressley, M. (2000) What should comprehension instruction be instruction of? In P. Kamil, P.D. Rosentahl, D. Pearson and R. Barr (Eds), *Handbook of Reading Research* (Vol. 3). Mahwah, NJ: Erlbaum. (pp 545–561).
This chapter discusses the research background to reading comprehension instruction.

Further resources

Oczkus, L. D. (2004) *Reciprocal Reading at Work: Strategies for Improving Reading Comprehension.* Newark, DE: International Reading Association Inc.
This practical classroom book details the reciprocal teaching approach.

Dymock, S. and Nicholson, T. (2013) *Teaching Reading Comprehension* [Kindle Edition]. NZCER Press.
This Kindle resource describes practical approaches to reading comprehension in the context of the New Zealand education system.
LDA Thinking Cubes encourage the use of Bloom's Taxonomy type questions. Available at: www.ldalearning.com

References

Barrett, T. C. (1972) *Taxonomy of Reading Comprehension*. Reading 360 Monograph. Lexington, MA: Ginn & Co.

Block, C.C. and Pressley, M. (2003) Best practices in comprehension instruction. In L.M. Morrow, L.B. Gambrell and M. Pressley (Eds) *Best Practices in Literacy Instruction* (2nd edn). New York: Guilford. (pp. 111–126).

Bloom, B. S. (1956) *Taxonomy of Educational Objectives, Handbook I: The Cognitive Domain*. New York: David McKay Co., Inc.

Cain, K. (2003) Text comprehension and its relationship to coherence in children's fictional narratives. *British Journal of Developmental Psychology*, 21, 335–351.

Cain, K., Oakhill, J. and Bryant, P. (2004) Children's reading comprehension ability: Concurrent prediction by working memory, verbal ability and component skills. *Journal of Educational Psychology*, 96, 31–42.

Cain, K. and Oakhill, J. V. (1999) Inference making ability and its relationship to comprehension failure. *Reading and Writing*, 11, 489–503.

Chapman, J. W., Tumner, W. E. and Prochnow, J. E. (2000) Early reading-related skills and performance, reading self concept and the development of academic self concept: A longitudinal study. *Journal of Educational Psychology*, 92, 703–708. doi:10.1037//0022–0663.92.4.703

Child, D. (2011) *Psychology and the Teacher* (8th edn). London: Continuum International Publishing Group.

Clarke, P. J., Snowling, M., J., Truelove, E. and Hulme, C. (2010) Ameloriating children's reading comprehension difficulties: A randomized control trial. *Psychological Science*, 20, 1–11. doi:10.1177/0956797610375499

Clay, M. (1999) *Becoming Literate: The Construction of Inner Control*. Auckland: Heinemann.

Coiro, J. (2011) Predicting reading comprehension on the internet: Contributions of offline reading skills, online reading skills and prior knowledge. *Journal of Literacy Research*, 43, 352–392. doi:10.1177/1086296X11421979

Cunningham, A. E. and Stanovich, E. (1990) Assessing print exposure and orthographic processing skill in children: A quick measure of reading experience. *Journal of Educational Psychology*, 82, 732–740.

DfES (2006) *Primary National Strategy: Primary Framework for Literacy and Mathematics*. London: DfES.

Duke, N. K. and Pearson, P. D. (2002) Effective practices for developing reading comprehension. In A. E. Farstrup and S. J. Samuels (Eds) *What Research has to Say about Reading Instruction* (3rd edn). Newark, DE: International Reading Association. (pp. 205–242)

Duke, N. K. Pearson, P. D., Strachan, S. L. and Billman, A. (2011) Essential elements of fostering and teaching reading comprehension. In S. J. Samuels and A. E. Farstrup (Eds), *What Research has to Say about Reading Instruction*. Newark, DE: International Reading Association. (pp. 51–93)

Dymock, S. and Nicholson, T. (2010) 'High 5' Strategies to enhance comprehension of expository text. *The Reading Teacher*, 64, 166–178. doi:10,1598/RT.64.3.2

Gough, P. B. and Tumner, W. E. (1986) Decoding, reading and reading disability. *Remedial and Special Education*, 7, 6–10.

Kintsch, W. (2004) The construction-integration model of text comprehension and its implications for text instruction. In R. B. Ruddell and N. J. Unrau (Eds), *Theoretical models and processes of reading* (5th edn). Newark, DE: International Reading Association. (pp. 1270–1328)

Krathwohl, D. R. (2002) A revision of Bloom's Taxonomy: An overview. *Theory into Practice*, 41, 212–264.

Literacy Aotearoa (2000) The three level guide. Available at: www.literacy.org.nz/three-level-guide.php

Lunzer, E. and Gardner, K. (1979) *The Effective Use of Reading*. London: Heinemann Educational Books Ltd.

Maine, F. (2013) How children talk together to make meaning from texts: A dialogic perspective on reading comprehension strategies. *Literacy*, 47, 150–155.

National Reading Panel (2000) Teaching children to read: An evidence based assessment of the scientific literature on reading and its implications for reading instruction. Available at: www.nichd.nih.gov/publications/pubs/nrp/documents/report/pdf

Organisation for Economic Cooperation and Development (2000) *Reading for Change: Performance and Engagement across Countries. Results from PISA 2000*. New York: Organisation for Economic Cooperation and Development.

Palincsar, A. and Brown, A. (1984) Reciprocal teaching of comprehension-fostering and comprehension-monitoring activities. *Cognition and Instruction,* 1, 117–175.

Pearson, P.D. (2009) The roots of reading comprehension instruction. In G.Duffy and S. Israel (Eds), *Handbook of Reading Comprehension*. London: Routledge. (pp. 3–31).

Rose, J. (2006) *Independent Review of Early Reading: Final Report*. London: Department for Education and Science.

Roulstone, S., Law, J., Lush, R., Clegg, J. and Peters, T. (2011) *Investigating the Role of Language in Childrens' Early Educational Outcomes*. London: Department for Education.

Rumelhart, D. (1980) Schemata: The building blocks of cognition. In R. Spiro, B. Bruce and W. Brewer (Eds), *Theoretical Issues in Reading Cognition*. Hillsdale, NJ: Lawrence Erlbaum.

Stanovich, K. E. (1986) Matthew effects in reading: Some consequences of individual differences in the acquisition of literacy. *Reading Research Quarterly*, 4 (21), 360–407.

CHAPTER 6

READING ENGAGEMENT

Objectives

1. To identify key features of progression in reading engagement
2. To examine gender, age, ability and motivational based patterns of reading engagement
3. To relate progression in reading engagement to daily classroom practice
4. To evaluate common forms of assessment for reading engagement

Introduction

The joy of reading is the excitement and art of discovery. To love to read is to choose texts for your own purposes and pleasure, to experience immersion in the written word and to understand the power of the printed word. While pupils can experience these features of engagement with film and audio sources, the process of reading itself allows the growth of knowledge and skills that are exclusive to the act of independent reading. Particular types of reading practice also seem to promote wellbeing both at a psychological and at a physiological level (Nell, 1988). As noted in the previous two chapters, learning to read is different from being a reader. While teachers may successfully teach a child to read, becoming a reader requires long-term application and involvement. For this reason, class teachers need to have some familiarity with the common types of reading engagement. They need to know what they look like in the classroom, how they progress and what influences their improvement or deterioration.

The first part of this chapter examines the process of reading engagement. It describes common research findings that underlie our understanding of why pupils choose to read. Many of these findings are applicable to appreciating pupils' motivations for learning.

Activity

What influences your decision to read?

List the influences on your decision to read for academic, work, social and personal purposes. How does the reading's purpose alter your decision to complete it?

This activity will have caused you to consider again your understanding of the nature and purpose of reading from the perspective of a literate adult. A number of factors, such as gender, age and the social capital attached to reading, influence making a personal decision to read. In turn, the effects of each factor can change according to extenuating circumstances such as time, choice, interests, cost and the availability of texts. The reasons for a primary pupil's decision to read are equally complex. For teachers and pupils, reading engagement also encompasses a reflection on what it means to be an effective reader and what part independent reading plays in this process. As well as expanding our understanding of reading strategies, how they are taught and assessed, reflecting on these approaches again now will help you to begin to develop your conception of effective reading. The theme of understanding effective reading reoccurs throughout this chapter.

The process of reading engagement

The processes of reading engagement are part of the body of knowledge that deals with human motivation. Research comes from the fields of psychology and child development. The processes of developing reading engagement can be summarised under three headings. They are part of a social constructivist and constructivist approach to reading engagement.

- Cognition: This area examines the meta-cognitive skills that enable pupils to read independently.
- Emotion: This area examines pupils' beliefs about their reading abilities in relation to their social and cognitive circumstances.
- Social: This area examines the cognitive and emotional effects of pupils' social circumstances upon reading engagement. It includes peer and family relationships as well as those in the broader community.

Table 6.1 presents a categorisation of the reading engagement behaviours of our vignette pupils. The table allows us to track some of the features and suggested next steps for progression that can occur across the primary years of schooling.

In these examples, there are definite patterns in the process of developing reading engagement. Firstly, every vignette pupil reads for personal reasons. Secondly, each vignette pupil is able to name other texts and types of reading that they enjoy. Thirdly, each vignette pupil has experience of a library, guided reading and silent reading times in school. Not all pupils have established reading repertoires or the skills to self-select texts effectively. Not all pupils choose to read regularly or recognise the breadth and potential of different types of text, including the intersection between multimedia, digital text and paper-based texts.

Different types of reading engagement

In essence, there are three broad levels of reading engagement. Pupils may be avid, poor or aliterate. Avid pupils can read and choose to do so for their own purposes. For these pupils the practice of reading is important for building deeper levels of reading comprehension, vocabulary, general knowledge and reading interests. Poor readers cannot read or struggle to read. For these pupils the practice of reading is important for building reading skills, particularly fluency and reading stamina, while developing reading interests. Poor readers who learn to read without reading interests risk aliteracy because they do not have a personal reason to read by themselves. Aliteracy describes pupils who can read but who choose not to read for their own purposes. For these pupils the practice of reading is important for building reading comprehension and reading interest as well as developing confidence with different types of text. Aliterate pupils risk becoming readers who lack understanding of the nature and value of the written word through limited reading practice (Lenters, 2006).

Table 6.1 Summary of reading engagement in the pupil vignettes

	Age	Attainment Level	Key strategies for reading engagement	Features of progression	Suggested next steps for progression
Japonica	10	Within expected levels	Skims and scans text for key ideas, devises questions before reading non-fiction and fiction as part of guided reading, personal reading log shows that she mainly reads Jacqueline Wilson, sustains silent reading during class period, uses school library to find Jacqueline Wilson books, engages in discussion of books chosen and led by the teacher during guided reading.	Seeks meaning from all text, expresses a personal reading preference, demonstrates immersed reading during 30 minutes' silent reading in class, engages in small book discussion, keeps personal log of books and pages read, uses parts of school library, adopts recommendations from fellow Wilson fans and informally discusses Wilson books with these peers	Adopt and comment on recommended books similar to Jacqueline Wilson genre such as Meg Cabot, use reading log to build reading repertoire by setting goals for the next book that she wishes to read, choose texts to read as part of guided reading sessions in class
Analyn	9	EAL pupil at the earlier stages of English language acquisition	Chooses and looks at picture and non-fiction books during silent reading, skims for illustrations, listens to familiar stories read aloud, re-reads familiar fiction often repetitive or rhyming stories, enjoys catalogues, atlases and magazines as well reference books like *The Guinness Book of Records* and selected Internet sites	Seeks meaning from text, established preferences, chooses repetition and rhyming books, this aids comprehension, uses selected text on the Internet when linked to animation, attends to books for up to 15 minutes in silent reading period, only chooses books with covers facing outwards ir the library	Build vocabulary, oral responses during guided reading and class story time, build ability to retell stories, use dual language books, use picture dictionary, widen reading repertoire to include fiction complementary to reading scheme book

	Age	Attainment Level	Key strategies for reading engagement	Features of progression	Suggested next steps for progression
John	7	Below expected levels	Chooses familiar picture books to read with small amounts of text, likes to read and re-read familiar scheme books to adults, skims comics for pleasure, prefers to read aloud, mouths words when reading 'silently'	Seeks meaning from text, established favourite titles such as Dr Seuss, and chooses interactive books with limited texts, including pop-ups, confident to read aloud to an adult	Increase reading stamina during reading silently, reading aloud in a small group, extend reading choices to include fiction complementary to reading scheme book, build basic self-selection skills based on readability of text, build ability to attempt reading challenges based on reading interests
Peter	5	Above expected levels	Reads for interest, always reads non-scheme books, favourite author is Dick King-Smith, reads some non-fiction, reads extended simple early novels, beginning to choose humorous poetry and fairy and folk tale collections	Established personal reading repertoire, mainly chooses fiction, confident digital text reading and navigation through a website for given and devised questions, chooses to read silently for extended periods	Extend self-selection skills based on attempting reading challenges to meet personal reading interest, aim to broaden reading repertoire rather than increase reading level in scheme books immediately because of conceptual level in more difficult texts

---

✎ Research focus

Different types of aliterate pupil

It is easier to understand the reasons for good and poor readers' level of reading engagement but aliterate pupils' reasons for choosing not to read are more complex. Case study research looked at the reasons that pupils chose not to read (Beers, 1996). Over a year, two classes of 12–13 year old pupils were interviewed and observed reading in school. Three distinct groups of aliterate readers emerged: dormant, uncommitted and unmotivated. Dormant readers thought reading was great but were sometimes too busy to read. Uncommitted readers thought reading was a waste of time and did not know if they would become readers in the future. For these pupils the purpose of reading was to provide information for a practical purpose. Unmotivated readers shared the views of uncommitted readers and scorned those who were keen readers as oddities. Neither uncommitted nor unmotivated readers planned to read in the future.

Beers' work highlights the complexity of reading engagement. It forewarns teachers of a decline in reading motivation. A large body of research suggests that this begins in the upper primary school and accelerates during adolescence (for example National Endowment for the Arts, 2007; Office for Standards in Education, 2011). It also encourages teachers to accommodate different levels of reading engagement. In order to do this successfully it is necessary to understand the main elements of reading engagement applicable to its progression.

Cognition and reading engagement

Reading engagement extends particular cognitive skills in addition to those required to decode and comprehend text. Through reading, pupils develop general knowledge, vocabulary, spelling, comprehension, meta-cognitive skills and writing. For example, pupils who read more, generally have wider written vocabularies and a greater control of grammar and structure in their writing. Indeed, good primary classroom practice is to develop pupils' writing using text as a model for shared and independent writing (Wray et al., 2002).

Pupils who consistently read for their own purposes may develop reading stamina and the confidence to adopt reading challenges. Here, reading stamina is defined as the ability to manage increasingly longer pieces of text and to read for extended periods. Most active readers will also read a substantial amount of text and build up a personal repertoire of reading interests and preferences.

✎   **Research focus**

Reading interest and reading challenge

A Canadian study of 56 pupils in upper primary and lower secondary school found that pupils were more likely to tackle challenging text if it was of interest to them (Fulmer and Frijiters, 2011). A reading interest supported their pre-conceived notions about text. It seemed likely that pupils felt in control of the reading task because they knew something of what to expect. This allowed them to persist with the challenging reading ahead of them.

Influential work by leading psychologist Keith Stanovich described good readers becoming 'richer' readers through reading practice and reading amount (Stanovich, 1986). His conceptual analysis of what he called the 'Matthew effect' in reading has a strong practical and experimental basis.

These two pieces of work highlight the importance of personal reading choice for the development of reading skill as well as for reading pleasure. This has implications for many aspects of the assess, plan, teach, practise, apply, and review cycle (DfES, 2006). For example, the use and impact of reading schemes compared to pupils' individual reading choices is of relevance. It is useful to consider how, why and if reading schemes contribute to the development of pupils' reading interests and repertoire while they are learning to read.

Classroom application   In the classroom, planning and teaching for the cognitive aspects of reading engagement chiefly centres on metacognition. Pupils need to be taught key metacognitive skills in order to tackle a wide range of texts. In addition to applying these to comprehend text, explicit teaching of reading self-selection, research and library skills is required. The second section examines the progression of these skills.

Developing confidence to adopt reading challenges is also part of the progression of reading skills and reading interest that lead to sustained reading engagement. Pupils who become very involved in a particular text may experience immersion. This is the feeling of being 'lost in a book'. The text transports the pupil to the world created by the printed word. Significant research has attempted to measure this total immersion or involvement in an activity like personal reading. Four stages summarise its principles. Pupils may favour low skills and challenge. Pupils may have high skills but favour low challenge. Pupils may receive high challenges and possess low skills. Pupils with high skills and corresponding high challenges may experience feelings of total involvement in an activity (Shernoff and Csikszentmihalyi, 2009). Reflecting on these elements can assist primary classroom teachers in understanding the process of experiencing immersed reading and what part this plays in the process of becoming an effective reader. For example, how, and why may immersed reading develop pupils' imagination, concentration and reading stamina?

Activity

Developing reading persistence

Sort the following statements into those with which you agree or disagree from the perspective of a primary classroom teacher. Suitably rephrased, how might a parent and a primary pupil sort them? Does the age of the pupil make a difference?

1. Silent reading is an essential part of every school day for every pupil.
2. Free reading choice is a pupil's right.
3. The only way to develop confidence to tackle challenging texts is through developing confidence with easier ones.
4. Reading for challenge is not a conscious personal choice.
5. Only reading interest guides reading choice.
6. Pupils' free reading choice always needs some adult guidance.
7. Pupils should not have access to library books until they can learn to read fluently.
8. Prescribed reading lists are essential to build pupils' personal reading repertoire.
9. Pupils will naturally extend their reading skills through access to good literature.
10. The only way to enjoy and understand a fiction book is to experience being 'lost' within its pages.

This activity will have caused you to reflect on the nature of reading engagement for different groups of people in relation to pupils' reading progression.

Emotion and reading engagement

Receiving an emotional connection with text is one of the rewards of reading engagement. Reward is part of the study of intrinsic and extrinsic motivation. Responding to extrinsic or intrinsic rewards helps pupils to self-regulate their learning. Extrinsic and intrinsic motivations develop as part of a continuum (Deci and Ryan, 1991). For example, three pupils read a large number of books as part of a sponsored reading event. After the occasion one pupil stopped reading regularly, one pupil began to read regularly and one tried hard to read regularly in the same way that he tried hard at all of his school-work. The extrinsic motivation of the reading event spurned an intrinsic motivation to read in the second pupil. The third pupil was generally moti-vated in school anyway. The first pupil responded to an immediate reward for reading but, at that time, she did not develop an intrinsic motivation to read.

A second aspect of emotion and reading engagement is self-efficacy. Self-efficacy is defined as what you believe you can do with your skills in a variety of different situations (Bandura, 1997). For primary pupils, developing a real-istic and positive reading self-efficacy can lead to an emotional investment in reading. It is part of pupils' academic self-concept. Poor and competent readers show differences in their academic self-concept within the first few weeks of primary school (Chapman et al., 2000).

Social influences on reading engagement

Experiencing a social connection with text is one of the rewards of reading engagement. Social reading rewards may be intrinsic or extrinsic and the effect of them may be felt consciously or unconsciously. Fans of the Harry Potter books by J.K. Rowling, for example, are part of a shared phenomenon that has arguably been responsible for encouraging many children to read for pleasure. For some pupils reading is not part of their social or cultural environment, while for others it has a legitimate position. Sometimes, reading engagement may link to the social capital attached to it more than for the quality of the text itself. The following research contains examples of this idea.

✎ Research focus

Reading self-perception

A survey of over 1,600 9–14 year olds, explored pupils' perceptions of what it means to be a reader (Clarke et al., 2008). A majority were in secondary school. Almost all pupils said that they read some kind of text outside of school. More girls than boys saw themselves as readers. More girls than boys spoke of having friends who read. Readers were perceived positively but also as odd or boring people. When considering that reading was important to do well in life, pupils saw reading as more important than activities such as computer usage. Girls were significantly less likely to know what adults in

(Continued)

(Continued)

school thought about their reading. More girls could state who encouraged them to read at home but it was not significant in relation to boys. Research like this alerts teachers to the significance of pupils' perceptions of being a reader. It suggests a need to revisit these perceptions in secondary school.

Classroom application   In the classroom, developing pupils' emotional and social engagement in reading means fostering an environment where the value of such engagement is explicit. This means modelling, recommending and providing a range of texts to engage pupils' emotions, social and cultural context. Does the classroom contain enough relevant examples of different types of texts? Useful techniques such as reading interest surveys can help the teacher to understand and monitor the progression of pupils' preferred reading interests and reading choices. Monitoring social influences also involves pupils setting reading goals in activities as simple as listing or identifying the texts they want to read next as well as logging what has been read already.

The progression of reading engagement in the primary classroom

This section of the chapter puts reading engagement research into a primary classroom context. Using the pupil vignettes from Chapter 1, it describes and evaluates evidence to support understanding of progression in reading engagement.

> The only motivation for reading that really works is the pleasure of the text or feelings of increasing success and those depend on the reader's own activity… I believe that children say reading bores them when they have to take risks or to make special efforts to understand a text and that their teachers have not made it clear to them what the risks are or what counts as success. (Meek, 1998: 198)

This quotation from the respected British educationalist Margaret Meek highlights the necessity of teaching the skills of reading engagement as part of establishing pupils' reading repertoire. In the classroom, it can be addressed through progression in four areas, which illustrate opportunities for pupils to practise and apply reading in a relevant context.

1. Book or text discussion
2. Reading aloud, reading silently and listening to literature

3. Library and reading self-selection skills
4. Reading research skills

Book or text discussion

Research suggests that book or text discussion improves reading comprehension, fluency and word recognition (Fountas and Pinnell, 1996). All are important for developing reading engagement. In particular, book or text discussion provides a vehicle for pupils to practise their metacognitive reading strategies and relate them to their own reading choices.

 Activity

Look at the four samples of reading from the pupil vignettes. Record features and suggested next steps for progression in cognitive, social or emotional aspects of reading engagement through book discussion. The second section has been completed for you.

Table 6.2

Pupil	Extract from guided reading notes or individual pupil and teacher interviews	Features of progression	Suggested next steps for progression
Japonica	Japonica's reading attitude survey shows that she feels anxious about starting a new book		
	During an individual discussion with her class teacher she explains that thick and unfamiliar books are especially daunting, even more so if she is told to read them by an adult		
John J. Burningham The Magic Bed	J: I love this book. I've got a racing car bed cover and at night I dream that I am Coultard driving T: Where did the magic bed go in this story?	John relates the story to his own experience, creates mental images from reading the text, questions text, and recalls part of the text	Sequence the events of the text in order, summarise the story for someone else, tell someone else why it is good to read

(Continued)

(Continued)

Pupil	Extract from guided reading notes or individual pupil and teacher interviews	Features of progression	Suggested next steps for progression
	J: *It went to the jungle, out to sea with pirates and into the dark. How come the magic word began with M?* T: *What do you think would be a good magic word?* J: *Monkey to go to the jungle, motorcar to go to Brands Hatch!*		
Analyn J. Scieszka *The Stinky Cheese Man and other Fairly Stupid Tales*	*Analyn has been pair reading the Frog Prince tale with her teacher.* A: *I like this story, it's like Disney* T: *How?* A: *It's got a princess* T: *Which part is your favourite?* A: *I like the princess who wiped her mouth, the frog kissed her! Yuck!*		
Peter	*Peter's reading attitude survey shows that he feels largely positive about his reading except for reading worksheets in school. He does not like answering questions about what he has read*		

〰 Reflection questions

- How and why would you encourage Japonica to read thick and unfamiliar texts?
- Analyn cannot read Scieszka's book completely by herself. How is she encouraged to believe that she enjoys and understands it?
- How would you encourage John to choose books?

Classroom application   In the classroom, progression in reading engagement through book discussion is largely measured through pupils' personal response to texts. This may include an emotional response. Pupils' responses have progressively more evidence to support their views.

Reading aloud, reading silently and listening to literature

Reading aloud, silently and listening to literature are reading skills and experiences that develop pupils' reading stamina and comprehension. They can also serve to recommend and highlight digital and paper-based reading material as a way of widening pupils' reading repertoire. Literature here refers to non-fiction and fiction texts as well as poetry and current affairs.

 Activity

Look at the four observations from the pupil vignettes. Record the features and suggested next steps for progression in cognition, emotional or social aspects of reading engagement through reading aloud, silently or by listening to literature. The last section is completed for you.

Table 6.3

Pupil	Extract from classroom observations	Features of progression	Suggested next steps for progression
Japonica	Japonica is observed listening to her class teacher read the First World War poem, 'In Flanders Fields' by John McCrae, to the class as part of their national Remembrance Day observance She is moved to tears by the reading. In the following days, Japonica borrows more war poetry from the school library, having searched online for the most famous poems with guidance from her father.		

(Continued)

(Continued)

Pupil	Extract from classroom observations	Features of progression	Suggested next steps for progression
John	*John is observed over a series of regular silent reading sessions. He regularly chooses books for browsing such as 'Where's Wally' by Martin Handford or the 3D Magic Eye, visual illusion books, by N.E. Thing Enterprises. He occasionally browses comics. John changes his book or comic up to four times during a 30-minute session.*		
Analyn	*Analyn is observed using an audio taped non-fiction book about the supermarket. She 'reads' along with the tape while listening with a friend. The book is new to her. She has a short discussion about the book with her friend when it is finished. They go back together and find the funny pages they have enjoyed.*		
Peter	*Peter is observed reading a simplified play script, 'Fantastic Mr Fox' by Roald Dahl, as part of a drama lesson. He reads with intonation and expression. When his audience laugh at his excellent characterisation, Peter improvises more lines and actions and adds dramatic pauses to engage his audience.*	Stamina, fluency and intonation in reading aloud, detects effect of author's humour and develops own ideas from it	Try simple novels or poems by Roald Dahl in order to broaden repertoire, refer to the text for evidence of how author engages the reader

﹏﹏ Reflection questions

- Describe the social influence of adults or peers on some of the pupils.
- How does Peter's knowledge of the audience and purpose of *Fantastic Mr Fox* engage his audience?
- For John, what are the benefits and drawbacks of browsing books?

Classroom application In the classroom, teachers need to ensure daily opportunities for pupils to choose and read text independently. Teachers need to be aware of the quality of pupils' silent reading, adapting and scaffolding it with the aim of increasing reading stamina and facilitating immersed reading. A regular class novel or continuous text read aloud increases pupils' listening comprehension skills, provides opportunities to listen to complete stories, highlights popular texts for recommendation and builds a positive classroom atmosphere. It should not be a practice reserved for younger primary school children.

Library and reading self-selection skills

Library and reading self-selection skills are reading skills and experiences that develop pupils' reading choices. They include pupils' ability to use technological sources to find 'just right' reading material. Recent research suggests that effective reading self-selection skills are not automatic. Some boys, for example, can be especially prone to selecting less challenging books, a behaviour that can accelerate amongst both genders in early adolescence where a return to popular primary school titles has been observed (Topping, 2010, 2011).

Activity

Look at the four observations from the pupil vignettes. Record the features and suggested next steps for progression in cognitive, social or emotional aspects of reading engagement through library and reading self-selection skills. The first section has been completed for you.

Table 6.4

Pupil	Extract from observation in the school library, book fair or class book corner	Features of progression	Suggested next steps for progression
Japonica	Japonica is observed during the weekly school library visit. She goes to the Jacqueline Wilson shelf but finds it empty. The librarian offers an alternative author, Jean Ure, but Japonica is unsure, saying that it looks too hard. She says that none of her friends read Jean Ure.	Established favourite author, discusses reading with peers, reading stamina for interesting reading	Attempt recommended texts, use evidence to express reading preferences, find other authors and sections of the library

(Continued)

(Continued)

Pupil	Extract from observation in the school library, book fair or class book corner	Features of progression	Suggested next steps for progression
John	John is observed in the book corner during wet play time. He is flicking through the pages of a pile of comics. When asked which is his favourite comic John says that he likes the comics that have free gifts like catapults or itching powder.		
Analyn	Analyn is observed during silent reading time. She has selected three favourite picture books that she has read before, plus her new reading book. Her mum and her class teacher have carefully kept her reading log. It shows that she receives a house point every time she finishes a book and chooses to read it again on her own.		
Peter	Peter is observed trying to read 'George's Marvellous Medicine' by Roald Dahl at the book fair sale. When asked he says that his class teacher has challenged him to read it to see if he thinks it is a great book too. He explains that he normally reads books by Dick King-Smith but this book cover did look very 'cool'.		

〰 Reflection questions

- How and why would you encourage Japonica to try similar authors?
- Which pupils are responding to extrinsic reading rewards?
- How could you use paired reading to support John to select and read his favourite comics?

Classroom application In the classroom, monitoring progression in self-selection and research skills means providing sufficient time and choice for pupils to choose what they wish to read. Constructive browsing is a key skill to be modelled or explicitly taught. The most avid readers will employ a range of selection skills, often based on what they already know about the text or their reading interest. The least able readers have far fewer skills, risking the danger of eventually giving up the task of looking for something to read.

Reading research skills

Research skills illustrate pupils' ability to apply their reading skills. Chapter 5 discussed the progression of reading comprehension skills for academic work. Research skills can also provide a context for pupils' reading practice and reading choices.

Research focus

Concept Orientated Reading Instruction

The Concept Orientated Reading Instruction approach uses specific 'hands on' practical activities in the classroom (Guthrie et al., 2006). The practical activities promote collaborative reading, autonomy, practical application for reading and pupils who subsequently set personal reading goals. Focused play and exploration are part of a meaningful context that stimulates reading engagement.

Activity

Look at the four observations or samples of written work from the pupil vignettes. Record the features and suggested next steps for progression in social, emotional and cognitive aspects of reading engagement in reading research skills. The third section has been completed for you.

(Continued)

(Continued)

Table 6.5

Pupil	Extract from classroom observation and written work	Features of progression	Suggested next steps for progression
Japonica	*Japonica has summarised the processes of respiration and digestion for the class science competition. She submits two poems, 'The Journey of a Jam Sandwich' and an acrostic poem using the word respiration. She includes a flow chart of her notes and a list of books she has used.*		
John	*John is completing a grid: 'What I know and want to know' before he begins a class topic on plants. He lists names of plants but no questions.*		
Analyn	*Analyn is observed during silent reading time. She has selected a shopping catalogue and is busy making a picture dictionary by cutting out pictures and copying out the English words for objects she has chosen to write beside them.*	Motivated to develop vocabulary, matches words to pictures, finds catalogues alone	Dictionary usage and application
Peter	*Peter shows the class a diary he has made over the summer holidays. As well as a written account it also contains photos, leaflets and souvenirs, he has added a related imaginary story or a labelled picture to most pages.*		

~~~ **Reflection questions**

- What are Peter and Japonica's extrinsic motivations for their work?
- What are Analyn and John's intrinsic motivations for their work?

Classroom application   In the classroom, monitoring progression in reading engagement through research skills means providing structured, cross-curricular opportunities for pupils to practise and develop them, including systematic planning of access to genre as well as research skills. Pupil choice is part of this process.

The assessment of reading engagement

This section evaluates formative examples of classroom reading assessment in reading engagement. Currently, summative assessments of reading engagement are not common but some well-researched reading attitude surveys are available. References appear at the end of this chapter.

Activity

Reading repertoire

1. Name the last six books that you have read for pleasure.
2. Name the last six children's books that you have read.
3. Name your three most influential books or texts as an adult or child.
4. Name the three books or texts that you would recommend to the youngest and oldest children in the primary school.

This activity will have caused you to consider the breadth and depth of your own reading repertoire. Unfortunately, research suggests that some primary school teachers are not keen readers. This has the effect of limiting their use and understanding of children's literature. It also means that they are less able to model the practices of an enthused reader and build a reading community within their classroom without structured training (Cremin et al., 2008; Cremin et al., 2009).

There are three main aspects to assessment in reading engagement: reading attitudes, reading repertoire and reading self-selection. An understanding of the purpose and audience for reading enriches them all.

Reading attitudes

Reading attitude surveys measure what pupils believe about their own attitudes towards reading. The surveys generally examine a spectrum of influences including pupils' attitudes towards reading challenge, reading self-concept, social and emotional reading attitudes. Reading interviews can also focus on these aspects but in a less formalised way. Reading attitude surveys link to classroom practice and improve pupils' English attainment by providing teachers with details of what pupils think about independent reading outside of school, as well as reading for academic purposes. Used cumulatively, they may measure changes in reading attitudes but teachers also need to be aware of the reliability of pupils' self-reporting. It is beneficial to use attitude surveys as part of a range of evidence for reading engagement.

Reading repertoire

Formative assessments of pupils' reading repertoire incorporate a written record of what and how pupils have responded to what they have read. This assessment links to classroom practice and improves pupils' English attainment by providing teachers with information about the quantity, quality and range of materials that pupils choose to read. Traditional approaches include reading logs or reading diaries. These require pupils or an adult listening in detail to the pupils' comprehension and emotional response to what has been read. Some logs require pupils to choose and read a set range of genres, sometimes called reading 'passports'. Home/school reading logs involve parents and carers. Guided reading logs link to regular teaching sessions. Year-group reading logs link to criterion-referenced assessment for pupils of a particular age.

More summative assessments attempt to measure the frequency of pupils' general access to print. For example, the Title Recognition Test (Cunningham and Stanovich, 1990) was developed as a quick measure of pupils' awareness of current and established titles for a particular age group.

Reading self-selection

Formative assessment of pupils' reading self-selection skills entails observation, monitoring and training, and it complements pupils' pre-determined choices and purposes for selecting a text to read. The essence of reading self-selection can be summarised as pupils' quest for readability. How then does an effective reader self-select text? Is it a pupil looking for optimal comprehension and decode-ability? Is it a pupil with pre-determined reasons for choosing, such as an author known to give pleasure and interest? Your answers to these questions will cause you again to consider the effective reader and what part self-selection plays in its progression.

Although all pupils may benefit from the modelling of self-selection skills, only some will require specific training. Nevertheless a regular screening assessment of pupils' self-selection skills can provide teachers with diagnostic information. For example, pupils with limited reading repertoires may lack the skills and confidence to select books other than those they can decode or only select other books to browse. Keen readers may only read one particular author because similar but alternative authors have not been recommended. Aliterate readers may possess limited self-selection skills because they do not know what to read or how to describe and find what does interest them.

Table 6.6 Observing progression in reading engagement

	Reading attitude survey	Reading self-selection skills	Reading repertoire and reading interests	Reading stamina and reading fluency	Vocabulary, comprehension and research skills	Examples of links with other 4 modes of English
Lower primary years	Speaks and shows personal feelings toward reading	Browses and selects books, mostly based on front covers for new books	Knows favourite reads, may ask for adults to re-read them as well as by themselves, beginning to choose particular genres, authors or multimedia	Developing fluency, may mouth words when reading alone, listens to stories, imitates and retells familiar stories	Joins in with repetitive stories and rhymes, browses books using illustrations and captions, uses index and contents, finds key words, has some simple questions	Uses library to find named and own books in some sections, discusses favourite characters and plots
Middle primary years	Completes and reflects on reading attitude survey from personal perspective	Uses a full range of reading self-selection skills but inconsistently	Beginning to establish reading interests plus authors and genres, uses some recommendations	Fluently reads aloud, sometimes becomes 'lost in a book', tries some reading challenge, developing reading of extended texts	More emotional responses to text with increasing use of evidence to support views, summary skills developing, devises some questions about the text	Chooses increasing range of texts for own interests and for relaxation inside and outside school, not just in library, recalls and may list texts read and to be read
Upper primary years	Completes, evaluates, devises reading attitude survey from their own and another perspective	Uses a full range of reading self-selection skills consistently	Established reading interests, genres and authors, may be very influenced by peers' choices, uses some recommendations	Attempts most reading challenges, reads extended texts, fluent reader who can easily become immersed	Summary skills established, emotional and response to text with evidence, adapts to other points of view, devises own questions	As for middle primary years, may begin to set reading goals to address other interests

Pupils may select a book or text based on:

- Titles
- Front covers
- Interactivity of the book (for example pop-up books or Internet linked books)
- Back of the book or text summaries
- Previous knowledge of genre, topic or author
- Scanning and skimming the text
- Reading part of the text
- Illustrations
- Recommendations
- Media influences
- Available time to read
- Cost or availability
- Usefulness for pre-determined issue
- Thickness of book or length of text
- Prescribed reading level

While some of these strategies are positive for self-selection, others may not be effective in developing pupils' reading repertoire. Teachers need to be alert to pupils' strategy use, particularly for poor and aliterate readers. Pupils' ability to use a library naturally partners reading self-selection skills. Table 6.6 presents the next entry for a matrix of primary English progression. It shows progression in reading engagement across the primary years. Use this grid as a guide for classroom and library observation, interpreting reading attitude assessments, monitoring reading logs, reciprocal and guided reading sessions and in reading interviews. These assessments are designed to gauge the breadth of pupils' reading repertoire, reading interests and reading attitudes and to give examples of how pupils apply reading to their personal needs.

Summary of chapter

This chapter has summarised the process and progression of reading engagement from three perspectives: cognition, emotion and social influences on reading engagement. Research and theory, largely from a constructivist and social constructivist perspective, were examined and linked to classroom practice. Pupil vignettes illustrated individual examples of progression. The nature of effective readers has been a key feature of this chapter. Sharing a clear and reasoned understanding of effective reading is central to enabling teachers and pupils to becoming engaged readers as part of a classroom reading community. In this way, the skills, benefits, rewards and challenges of being a reader are made explicit and progression can be monitored.

? **Self-assessment**

1. List and justify three items that you consider important features or tipping points of progression in reading engagement. Choose items for the oldest, mid-range and youngest pupils in the primary school.
2. Draw Venn diagrams to show the connections between reading acquisition, reading comprehension strategies and reading engagement and factors that influence their progression.
3. Write a definition of an effective reader for the oldest, mid-range and youngest pupil in the primary school. Note the similarities and differences between them.

Annotated further reading

Elkin, S. (2010) *Unlocking the Reader in Every Child*. Winchester: Ransom Press.
A resource book of excellent ideas for developing the reluctant reader.

Layne, S. L. (2009) *Igniting a Passion for Reading: Successful Strategies for Building Life-long Readers*. Portland, ME: Stenhouse.
This practical book provides excellent ideas to support upper primary and lower secondary readers.

Lockwood, M. (2008) *Promoting Reading for Pleasure in the Primary School*. London: Sage.
This practical book contains details of the practice and theory of reading engagement.

Further resources

Details of the Concept Orientated Reading Instruction approach and reading attitude surveys are available at: www.cori.umd.edu/

The Elementary Reading Attitude Survey from American researchers M. C. McKenna and D. J. Kear is available at: www.professorgarfield.org/parents_teachers/printables/pdfs/reading/readingsurvey.pdf

The Power of Reading Project, based at the Centre for Literacy in Primary Education in London, aims to develop use of children's literature in the primary school. It is available at http://por.clpe.org.uk/

References

Bandura, A. (1997) *Self Efficacy: The Exercise of Control.* New York: Freeman and Company.

Beers, K. (1996) No time, no interest, no way. The three voices of aliteracy: Part 1 & 2. *School Library Journal*, 2 & 3, 30–33; 110–113.

Chapman, J. W., Tumner, W. E. and Prochnow, J. E. (2000) Early reading-related skills and performance, reading self concept and the development of academic self concept: A longitudinal study. *Journal of Educational Psychology*, 92, 703–708. doi:10.1037//0022–0663.92.4.703

Clarke, C., Osborne, S. and Akerman, R. (2008). Young people's self-perceptions as readers: An investigation including family, peer and social influences. London: National Literacy Trust.

Cremin, T., Mottram, M., Bearne, E. and Goodwin, P. (2008) Exploring teachers' knowledge of children's literature. *Cambridge Journal of Education*, 38, 449–464. doi:10.1080/03057640802482363

Cremin, T., Mottram, M., Powell, F. and Safford, K. (2009) Teachers as readers: Building communities of readers. *Literacy*, 43, 11–19.

Cunningham, A., E. and Stanovich, E. (1990) Assessing print exposure and orthographic processing skill in children: A quick measure of reading experience. *Journal of Educational Psychology*, 82, 732–740.

Deci, E. L. and Ryan, R. M. (1991) Motivation and education: The self-determination perspective. *Educational Psychologist*, 26, 325–346.

DfES (2006) *Primary National Strategy: Primary Framework for Literacy and Mathematics.* London: DfES.

Fountas, I. C. and Pinnell, S. (1996) *Guided Reading.* Portsmouth, NH: Heinemann.

Fulmer, S. M. and Frijiters, J. C. (2011) Motivation during an excessively challenging reading task: The buffering role of relative topic interest. *Journal of Experimental Psychology*, 79 (1), 185–208.

Guthrie, J. T., Wigfield, A., Humeick, N., Perencevich, K., Taboada, A. and Barbosa, P. (2006). Influences of stimulating tasks on reading motivation and comprehension. *The Journal of Educational Research*, 99, 232–245.

Lenters, K. (2006) Resistence, struggle and the adolescent reader. *Journal of Adolescent and Adult Literacy*, 50, 136–146.

Meek, M. (1998) *On Being Literate* (4th edn). London: Random House.

National Endowment for the Arts (2007) *To Read or Not to Read: A Question of National Consequence: Research Report #47.* Washington, DC: National Endowment for the Arts.

National Primary Strategy (2006) *Excellence and Enjoyment: Learning and Teaching in the Primary Years.* (Ref: 0521–2004). London: Department for Education.

Nell, V. (1988) The psychology of reading for pleasure. *Reading Research Quarterly*, 23, 6–50.

Office for Standards in Education (2011) *Removing the Barriers to Literacy*. London: Office for Standards in Education.

Shernoff, D. and Csikszentmihalyi, M. (2009) Flow in schools: Cultivating engaged learners and optimal learning. In R. H. Gilman, E. Scott-Huebner and M. J. Furlong (Eds.), *Handbook of Positive Psychology in Schools*. London: Routledge. (pp. 131–145).

Stanovich, K. E. (1986) Matthew effects in reading: Some consequences of individual differences in the acquisition of literacy. *Reading Research Quarterly*, 4 (21), 360–407.

Topping, K. (2010) *What are Kids Reading? The Book Reading Habits of Pupils in British Schools 2010*. London: Renaissance Learning.

Topping, K. (2011) *What are Kids Reading? The Book Reading Habits of Pupils in British Schools 2011*. London: Renaissance Learning.

Wray, D., Medwell, J., Poulson, L. and Fox, R. (2002) *Teaching Literacy Effectively in the Primary School*. London: Routledge Falmer.

CHAPTER 7

WRITING COMPOSITION

Objectives

1. To identify key features of progression in writing composition
2. To examine key models of the process of writing composition
3. To relate progression in writing composition to daily classroom practice
4. To evaluate common forms of assessment for writing composition

---

Introduction

This is the first of three chapters that look at the progression of writing in primary pupils.

In school there are two aspects to writing: learning to write and writing to learn (Britton, 1972). Learning to write is different from writing to learn. Writing to learn is about writing fluency; it requires motivation and a reason to write as well as an environment that prizes the production of independent and unique pieces of text in a range of genres. Writing can lead to different forms of thinking as well as providing a vehicle for emotional development and personal creativity. Like reading, speaking and listening, the act of writing is affected by cognitive, emotional, motivational, social and physical factors.

Writing is a difficult task for primary school pupils. Unlike reading, independent writing requires pupils to create and be skilled at transcribing their thoughts on to the page. When pupils begin to write they move from the physical act of representing their ideas through play and drawing, to using words, letters and sentences. Language supports this transition. Even when the pupil is an accomplished writer, play and drawing continue to support the writing process. For example, a pupil may use symbols or sketches on a comic strip to plan a narrative story developed through role play.

Although writing is closely linked to pupils' progression in language it is more than speech written down. Speech relies on a visible or audible context and social interaction. The participants understand the tone of the speech and may interpret non-verbal cues because speech occurs in an immediate context. In contrast, writing requires the pupil to anticipate and predict the reader's response to their composition. Although it can be solitary, multimodal forms have increased collaborative writing opportunities. A text may also be written for the author. In each instance the process of creating a piece of text has a number of different purposes, all of which can have a number of different effects on the author and the reader.

This chapter looks at how pupils compose text. Pupils' progression through the physical processes of writing composition links to their language capability (Clay, 1998; Wells, 1985), which is in turn enriched by an active reading repertoire. Like speaking, listening and reading, writing composition progresses within a language-rich environment that celebrates the diversity of text and within one that provides the necessary scaffolding to establish independent writing of a wide range of genres and for different purposes.

Activity

Distinguishing speech and writing

Text types contain different levels of spoken and written language according to the context, audience and purpose of the writing. Complete the following table to illustrate some of these differences.

Table 7.1

Text type	Context	Purpose	Audience	Language features
Love letter	Written for private consumption	To declare love	A loved person	May contain fragments of speech-like phrases such as pet names and personal terms of endearment

(Continued)

(Continued)

Text type	Context	Purpose	Audience	Language features
Adventure story				
Shopping list				
Recipe				
A text message for a friend				
An email request for tutorial support from an academic				

This activity may have caused you to reconsider the role of language in the progression of reading, writing, speaking and listening. Understanding levels of written and spoken language in written text requires pupils to identify when, why and how standard and non-standard, formal and informal language forms are used. For example, sending a text message to a friend is an immediate and potentially transient form of writing. It may read like abbreviated speech. It may use colloquial phrases and non-standard grammar. In contrast, a written letter to a friend on paper and posted is a delayed and potentially lasting form of writing. It requires planned description. Being able to transmit your own thoughts to paper or to the screen like this involves two skills: composition and transcription. These relate to pupils' pragmatic use of language. They understand what and why written language is used in particular contexts.

Transcription is the skill of recording what you wish to write, and concerns the secretarial aspects of writing. Elements of transcription include handwriting, layout, presentation and spelling. Composition is about authorship. Composing a text is also about the physical processes of planning, drafting, editing and revising the text in order to match the author's interpretation of the finished product. It includes the creation of ideas, developing pupils' own writing voice, writing in different forms for a range of purposes and audiences, gathering ideas, selecting words and the use of grammar in sentences, across and within paragraphs and whole pieces of text. Different types of writers compose in different ways. For example, some writers use a prepared plan. Others may commit all of their thoughts to paper in a stream of consciousnesses, followed by editing and drafting. A third type of writer may use a plan that is adapted as the writing evolves.

Activity

Classifying writing attainment

Classify the following examples of writing from across the primary age range. The first one has been done for you.

Table 7.2

Writing example	Transcription	Composition	Lower primary	Middle primary	Upper primary
Use apostrophes	✓			✓	
Hold a pencil correctly					
Circular scribble					
Write simple captions					
Write own name					
Write paragraphs with **Point Evidence Analysis and Refer** structures					
Write a punctuated **complex sentence**					
Spell 50 high-frequency words					

It is important to understand the difference between composition and transcription because of the nature of writing progression in primary pupils and its link to spoken language development. Four stages can summarise the process (Kroll, 1981):

1. Preparation: At this stage pupils learn to use a pencil and begin to explore spelling. Oral composition happens.
2. Consolidation: At this stage writing is similar to speech written down. Long compound sentences joined by 'and' are often evident.
3. Differentiation: At this stage, writing for different audiences and purposes becomes apparent.
4. Integration: The pupils' own writing voice begins to mature. The pupil can easily select particular language to engage the reader.

As pupils' writing develops, handwriting, spelling and the presentation of written text becomes more automatic; short-term memory is freed up for pupils to address the content of the writing (Flower and Hayes, 1980). However, learning to write is not a linear process, confined to teaching the technical aspects of grammar and punctuation. It is recursive. It is driven by the need to write for a relevant context (Dombey, 2013). As pupils' writing matures they are increasingly able to write for specific audiences and purposes because they have precise writing goals.

The processes of writing composition

The processes of writing composition can be viewed from three main angles: cognitive, socio-cultural or linguistic. Multimodal texts, digital literacy and meta-cognitive emphases are included.

Cognitive psychological approaches to writing composition suggest that writing is a problem-solving approach that involves the retrieval and storage of ideas in the memory. The process has been summarised in three stages: reflection, production and interpretation. Each is affected by writing motivation, context and pupils' working memory (Hayes, 1996). An analogy with the simple view of reading (Gough and Tumner, 1986) shows pupils' memory underlying their writing ideas, supported by transcription and editing skills in a simple view of writing (Berninger et al., 2002).

Critics of purely cognitive approaches to writing composition suggest that they have omitted the social context for writing. Socio-cultural perspectives on the writing process emphasise the development of socially constructed tools for writing. These are language, genres, technology and the development, history and values attached to writing in different cultures and communities. Pupils' writing identities are debated. Some aspects of social-cultural writing research are relevant to understanding writing progression. These include gender and pupils with English as an additional language. For example, evidence surrounding boys' poor literacy progress in comparison to girls, is part of this area (Mullis et al., 2007).

✍ Research focus

Expert and beginning writers

Beginning writers have been described as 'knowledge-telling' and expert writers as 'knowledge-transformers' (Bereiter and Scardamalia, 1987). Knowledge-telling pupils compose writing as a record of information and skills, retrieved from the long-term memory. These pupils pour out their ideas until no more ideas occur. Language and social experience are the source of the writing. These pupils are contrasted with expert knowledge-transforming writers who compose writing with added depth that sets out to address pre-prepared writing goals. It may also be problem-solving and it will be written specifically for the reader. Expert writers like this tend to have a greater understanding of what they have composed than that drawn from social interaction alone. In their later work the authors liken pupils with knowledge-transforming skills to members of a knowledge-building community, facilitated by the critical use of the Internet (Scardamalia and Bereiter, 2006).

Bereiter and Scardamalia's ideas may link to the other modes of English. For example, a comparison between casual or critical readers is possible. They also highlight the importance of the link between comprehension and composition and the roles of general knowledge, vocabulary and wider reading in the progression of writing composition. It is hard to write with your own authentic voice unless you have a true understanding of the content and the contexts from which different types of text can be written.

Linguistic approaches to writing progression examine the grammatical context for writing. These approaches include the study of pupils' ability to write using established and blended genre structures for particular audiences and purposes.

Multimodal forms of writing have spawned the development of collaborative, problem-solving approaches to writing. These approaches examine pupils' ability to interpret and integrate images and text on screen and on paper. Multimodal sources of writing blur the traditional boundaries between producers and composers of text (Myhill and Watson, 2011). For example, without careful monitoring and education, pupils may only cut and paste written work directly from the Internet and plagiarism may develop. In contrast, multimodal sources of writing, such as online feedback, shared Google documents or Twitter, can allow for collaborative composition that enhances pupils' editing skills.

The progression of writing composition can be summarised under four headings. In the classroom these aspects of writing are often categorised as structural and language features.

1. Audience, purpose and context: this area includes development of the writers' own voice and their ability to adopt appropriate formal or informal writing styles.
2. Cohesion: this area includes sentence structures and vocabulary choices that organise and unify the meaning of the text as a whole.
3. Structure: this area includes knowledge of text forms, genres, narrative and non-narrative constructions and paragraph writing techniques.
4. Language choices: this area includes vocabulary and sentence structures chosen for effect.

Table 7.3 presents a categorisation of the writing composition skills of our vignette pupils. The table allows us to track some of the features and next steps for progression that can occur across the primary years of schooling. In these examples, there are definite patterns in the process of developing writing progression. Spelling errors have not been included. Further examples are required to monitor consistency. Each pupil writes logical English independently, except for using spelling aids. Every pupil can read their work aloud. Note the influence of pupils' prior knowledge or experience of the writing content. How does it affect their work?

Progression in writing composition

In the classroom, the progression of writing composition relies upon a process approach to teaching. The process approach to teaching writing is typified by the seminal work of Donald Graves. His work emphasised the importance of using pupils' prior knowledge for an audience and purpose that they had decided. Gradually pupils' writing voice is established. 'Voice is the imprint of ourselves in our writing ... the dynamo of the writing process ... take the voice away and the writing collapses of its own weight. There is no writing, just words following words' (Graves, 1983, p. 227).

The process method requires teachers to know the mechanisms and progression of the writing process and how they are applied within and across a range of genres. The alternative, product approach to writing, emphasises the final result. Composition skills sit within both of these approaches but the former is more characteristic of a constructivist approach to learning because of its development of meta-cognitive skills and the meta-language associated with composition.

Early writing progression

Writing grows from language and literacy experiences in a social setting. Like reading, speaking and listening, writing grows alongside language development, phonological awareness and an understanding of narrative, rhymes and songs. In very young pupils, literacy experiences also include drawing and play '... make believe play, drawing and writing can be viewed as different moments in an essentially unified process of the development of written language' (Vygotsky 1978 p. 116). This means learning the technical rules of writing and what writing can do.

Learning the rules of writing

Case study research in the 1980s documented the progression of young children's literacy development in relationship to early language progression. Evidence ranges from single case study analysis (Bissex, 1980) to longitudinal

Table 7.3 Summary of writing composition in the pupil vignettes

	Age	Attainment level	Writing sample	Key strategies for writing composition	Selected features of progression	Suggested next steps for progression
Japonica	10	Within expected levels	**Story opening** _One very hot summer's day there was a very excited dog called Scamp was due to emigrate to Canada. He was to be adopted by a gorgeous new family called the Smythes. He was due to arrive at Heathrow airport by rail because it was too far away to travel by car. Canada was a long way away so they had to be at the airport early. When they arrived at the airport Scamp was put in a small crate. He howled like a wolf._	A sensible number of characters are clearly described. She has used story phrases such as, 'one hot summer's day' to fit the ideas together. Beginnings of sentences help to put events in order.	The opening has a sensible chronological order. The setting and tone of the story is consistent, seeks to engage the reader, mixture of sentence types creates pace.	Add further detail to descriptions, add dialogue, paragraphs, start sentences in different ways.
Analyn	9	EAL pupil at the earlier stages of English language acquisition	**First page of mini autobiography – accompanies self-portrait** _My name is Analyn. I am nine years old. I come from the Philippines. I like to dance. I like to sing. I like to run. I like to read books. I like school._	Uses personal experience, chooses suitable information, ideas are in order, repeats a familiar sentence structure, first person used.	The writing makes sense, content is appropriate.	Expand vocabulary choices, add description for added interest, expand sentence structures.

(Continued)

Table 7.3 (Continued)

	Age	Attainment level	Writing sample	Key strategies for writing composition	Selected features of progression	Suggested next steps for progression
John	7	Below expected levels	**John describes a Victorian child chimney sweep** *The boy is called Ben and he can't write or read and he is five yrs old, he can work good and he is small. He can dress on his own. He can tie shoes on his own. He can wash on his own.*	Uses ideas that relate to self, contains introductory sentence, lists of ideas, and includes some added description.	The writing makes sense, contains some detail.	Punctuation, add relevant description, expand sentence structures.
Peter	5	Above expected levels	**Thank you letter after school trip** *Dear Sir* *I enjoyed my visit to your museum. I liked your spiders they had lots of different kinds and it told you about them. I wrote a poem about it this is it. Spiders are scary spiders are small spiders run and creep all over the floor. I enjoyed your museum. From* *Peter*	Applies own interests to new situation, engages reader, uses conventions of letter writing, adds detail, some repetition of phrases, clear opening and ending.	Uses written letter format, seeks to engage the reader, mixes genres by adding own poem, well described, adds personal voice.	Layout of poem, vary sentence openings, develop description and significant detail.

studies of patterns of development in young children (Clay, 1989). In essence these studies suggest that early writers show similar characteristics in mark making on paper through to the formation of letters and words. Clay summarised a series of six principles of emergent writing progression with which to classify pupils' patterns of early mark making. Such early mark making is part of young pupils' invented symbol 'writing', often seen in their exploratory play writing and drawing which the pupil may 'read' back, showing an awareness that marks on a page can translate into spoken language. Clay's stages of emergent mark making are summarised below.

1. The recurring principle – these marks and symbols repeat.
2. The directional principle – these marks and symbols occur in a specific direction.
3. The generating principle – these marks and symbols are combined to make patterns.
4. The inventory principle – these marks and symbols are listed.
5. The contrastive principle – these marks and symbols are compared and contrasted.
6. The abbreviation principle – these marks are deliberate abbreviations to imply a familiar word.

Other research has emphasised the role of young pupils' drawings as an expression of identity. Pupils convey meaning using similar themes through their drawing, imaginary and symbolic play (Kress, 1997; Ring, 2010). These ideas illustrate how pupils begin to learn what writing may be for.

Audience, purpose and context

Like effective readers, effective writers understand the importance of an audience, purpose and context for text. They understand the structure and language features of different genres and how particular types of writing are laid out on the page. Like effective readers, knowing this helps effective writers to comprehend texts with layers of meaning to entice or inform their readers.

After a period of experimenting and playing with symbols and mark making, pupils begin to compose written text. Typically pupils write lists, labels and captions to illustrations. Early simple recounts may sound like speech but also contain simple phrases from favourite stories such as 'once upon a time'. As pupils' transcription and language skills progress the pupil learns to manipulate written language for given and personal purposes and for audiences other than the class teacher. The oldest pupils consistently use their own writer's voice. This enables critical writing to develop.

Classroom application In the classroom, planning and teaching for progression in audience and purpose combines the four modes of English to integrate real contexts for writing. For example, children's literature may be a hook to stimulate pupils' key questions, leading to personal research, written and oral presentations. The work is preceded by activating pupils' relevant prior knowledge. Previous knowledge encourages the pupil to make informed writing choices and seeks to align pupils' literacy practices from home and school.

Research focus

The impact of writing and writing instruction on reading progression

A report from the USA examined the impact of writing and writing instruction on reading development in adolescents across 93 comparative classroom strategies. Overall writing achievement was improved by three key teaching strategies (Graham and Hebert, 2010).

1. Pupils must write about what they have read.
2. Pupils must know and apply the processes of writing.
3. Pupils must write often and write increased amounts of text.

These findings echo the principles of the 'Matthew effect' in reading, discussed in Chapter 6 (Stanovich, 1986). Good readers become better readers by reading larger amounts of text than poorer readers, who read less. They also show the importance of reading as a basis for composition and the need for writing stamina. Lastly, this research with adolescents offers points for writing progression in upper primary classes as pupils prepare for transition to secondary school.

Cohesion

The overall sense of a whole piece of text is supported by pupils' progression in their understanding of how texts fit together. Texts can be coherent such as when the setting, characters and sequences of events are consistent. Paragraphs can be coherent such as when introductory sentences are expanded sequentially and the last sentence in the paragraph signals a connection with the next. Sentences can be cohesive such as when pronouns and tenses are used consistently.

Structure

The overall structure of a whole piece of text is supported by pupils' progression in their understanding of different types of text. A key point for progression in understanding the structure of composition is pupils' ability to write both chronological and non-chronological texts (Perera, 1984). Multi-modal texts present different challenges since they may be a mixture of both with the addition of visual and auditory content.

Genres define types of text. They include fiction, non-fiction, multi-modal texts and poetry. Standardised genres have common structural and language features. For example, imperatives are a feature of instruction. Understanding genres also means knowing that they are not fixed entities because they evolve according to the audience and purpose for which they are written.

Research focus

Comprehension and coherence in telling stories

This study investigated the relationship between pupils' understanding and their ability to tell stories. It found that pupils with poor comprehension skills told stories with weaker structures. More coherent stories contained a better use of connectives. Pupils' story telling improved with the use of simple prompts to aid the sequence of the story. For example *'How the pirates lost the treasure'* (Cain, 2003). Developing narrative structure like this depends upon using simple plot structures, often based on familiar stories. Telling the story beforehand and reading their work out loud helps pupils to listen to their writing, to hear the effect it has on the reader and to alter it accordingly.

Classroom application   In the classroom, planning and teaching for progression in cohesion and structure relies on three factors:

1. Knowledge of whole text structures
2. Knowledge of paragraph construction
3. Effective and accurate use of cohesive ties such as connectives, pronouns and tenses

Teaching cohesion involves pupils recognising weak examples of poorly constructed text and systematically improving them. This can take place via shared, guided and collaborative group writing. A useful preamble to looking at cohesion in whole written texts is to use film. This introduces pupils to the analogy of looking at and tracking themes, broadly as in the use of music, light or colour to indicate mood, or closely, as in the use of costume for characterisation.

> ### Activity
>
> **Engaging with text and film**
>
> Choose your favourite book to film adaptation. How do the film trailer and the back of the book summary compare as effective summaries of the plot? Which of the following are present in each: authorial intent, stylistic expectations, generic expectations, emotional responses, identification with character, personal investment in the text and modality? (Bearne and Bazalgette, 2010)

Meta-cognition and writing composition

Structure and cohesion are also supported through the use of meta-cognitive support materials, which scaffold the process of composition. Examples are sentence stems, writing frames, writing skeletons, graphic organisers and vocabulary building tools such as topic specific dictionaries or word walls in the classroom. These tools can help pupils to organise, categorise and sum marise ideas. Additional marking ladders and recipes for genres specify the required elements for each composition. In order for pupils to understand, apply and transfer these elements of composition, pupils benefit from devising their own support materials through investigation and collaboration. Once mastered, pupils develop conscious usage of each technique in the planning, editing and re-drafting stages of composition across the curriculum. Properly taught, they can become an instinctive part of pupils' independent writing.

Scaffolding writing composition like this incorporates a distinction between immediate, extended and sustained writing practice. Immediate writing is completed in one short session. Extended writing is completed over a number of sessions. It incorporates planning, editing, drafting and revising. Sustained writing requires the pupil to produce longer pieces of completed text in set periods of time. This develops writing stamina. It is useful preparation for formal written examinations in the upper primary classes.

Language choices

The impact of a piece of text is supported by effective language choices. This includes technical vocabulary and the diversity of vocabulary necessary to convey subtleties of meaning. The importance of vocabulary development is re-emphasised by the constructivist ideas of schema theory (Rumelhart, 1980). Pupils need a language for composition and thought.

✎ **Research focus**

Vocabulary and composition

A study of upper primary school pupils found that they appeared to select writing vocabulary according to genre (Olinghouse and Wilson, 2013). Different types of words added to the quality of different types of genre. The quality of persuasive writing was predicted by wider and varied vocabularies. The quality of informative writing was predicted by the level of subject specific vocabulary and the maturity of the pupil. Story writing was predicted by wider and varied vocabulary. The authors note the need to support pupils' awareness of key vocabulary for each genre. It also highlights the importance of applying writing genres across the curriculum.

Classroom application   In the classroom, planning and teaching for vocabulary links to comprehension. As with reading comprehension, if a word is not part of a pupil's spoken or mental dictionary it will not be immediately used in print.

The progression of writing composition in the primary classroom

This section of the chapter puts writing composition research into a primary classroom context. Using research and the pupil vignettes from Chapter 1, it describes and evaluates evidence to support understanding of progression in writing composition.

Overall there is less research devoted to writing composition than for grammar and spelling. In the classroom, two strands are useful as a basis for understanding progression at the primary level: cognitive strategies and social practices. Cognitive strategies include the systematic development of structure and vocabulary. Social practices include the systematic development of writing context, including out-of-school writing and the choice of formal or informal language. Linguists call the latter register. Register can also refer to the language of subject areas such as science. Each area progresses from simple to increasingly abstract ideas for composition. In this section we discuss influential approaches to teaching writing composition: talk for writing and the genre writing approach. It is useful to reflect on the interlinking of cognitive and social ideas of composition within them.

Talk for writing

Talk for writing maximises the links between pupils' spoken and written language. The benefits of using pupils' talk as part of the process of composition have been shown by recent studies which show the positive effects of oral language work for boys (Myhill and Fisher, 2005) and for novice writers (DCSF, 2008). Group discussion, predictions, questions and improvised drama can all help to assist pupils in capturing their ideas for composition across the primary age range. This is particularly so when these activities are linked to written, symbolic and pictorial planning frames. The relationship between storytelling and story writing has been popularised in English schools by the practical resources produced by Pie Corbett (Corbett and Strong, 2011). Their work encourages pupils to remember and reuse familiar and cultural story structures and ideas.

Activity

Look at the four independent writing samples, from the pupil vignettes. Record the features and suggested next steps for progression in the use of talk to support writing composition. Think about how the pupils construct an audience, purpose and a context for their composition. How does this affect their choice of language? The second section has been completed for you.

Table 7.4

Pupil and preceding talk	Writing sample	Features of progression	Suggested next steps for progression
Japonica Japonica has written an advert after seeing a film about a flying car and designing one.	*Whizzing wild wacky car! Its big, its fast, yes it's the wild, wacky, flying car. This is the car to help you, when you're in a car like this no traffic jams! But the best thing is- it's fast, so fast it will blow your hair style off. This car is new, it's modern. This is the car for you! It also needs only water.*		

Pupil and preceding talk	Writing sample	Features of progression	Suggested next steps for progression
John H. Oram *Angry Arthur* John has seen and heard an online version of this story.	*Arthur's anger was shouting. He wanted sweets. Arthur's anger was stamping feet. Arthur's anger was kicking the chair.* He was scared and stopped and went to bed with no sweets. John can retell most of the original correctly.	Keeps plot and sequence of the original story, adapts to a familiar context, recalls original, draws own pictures to match captions	Develop descriptive vocabulary
Analyn Analyn is writing instructions after making her sandwich.	*Making a sandwich* 1. *Put fat on bread.* 2. *Put cheese on it* 3. *Put bread on plate* 4. *Cut bread* 5. *Eat bread and cheese*		
Peter Peter has read, heard and recited the poem 'Down behind the Dustbin', by M. Rosen.	Peter is writing speech bubbles for a comic strip of the poem. *Hello Sid the dog. Hello Peter. Do you know me? Yes I do. You are my friend. Come to my house Sid. I like the bin!*		

〰️ **Reflection questions**

- How and why could role play help Japonica to restructure her advertisement?
- Identify alternative forms of recording for Analyn's instructions that will broaden her vocabulary.

Genre writing

The genre approach to writing originates in the work of Australian academics in the 1980s, among them the linguist M.A.K. Halliday (Halliday, 2009). This work researches the structure of language and its usefulness. For young children, Halliday separated two purposes for language: its content and how it is used by different people in different circumstances, such as when formal or informal language is used. This has links with the pragmatic or communicative aspects of spoken language. Other academics applied these ideas to pupils' writing development (Martin et al., 1987). It was suggested that taught writing genres were too narrow in school; wider experience was necessary in order to acknowledge pupils' out-of-school literacy practices.

The following sequence for genre teaching and monitoring composition is adapted from the former English National Literacy Strategy materials (National Strategy, 1999).

1. Familiarise the pupil with the genre and its context.
2. Focus on the structure and language features through looking for patterns across different examples of text.
3. Define the genre. This involves pupils defining genres for themselves and recognising exceptions to definitions.
4. Scaffold the writing. This involves the use of structural devices such as writing frames.
5. Increase independence in writing. This stage may include adaptations and extensions such as 'genre exchanges' where one type of writing is rewritten in another form.

Critics of genre approaches note the dangers of formulaic writing. Written genres do not necessarily always have the same structure and language features because they are affected by different social and cultural circumstances. Language and written language is constantly evolving. For example, a blog is a multi-dimensional written form moulded by its author. Website construction is a further example. Websites are not necessarily constructed in a uniform and linear fashion. Out-of-school literacy practices are part of this socio-cultural perspective of how literacy is shaped and acquired. However, using a flexible genre approach in the classroom can provide a basis for pupils' writing composition, given sufficient context and pupil choice to encourage motivation through creativity and relevance.

✐ Activity

Look at the four independent writing samples, from the pupil vignettes. Record the features and suggested next steps for progression in the use of genre to support writing composition. Think about how the pupils manage cohesion and structure in their composition. How does this affect their vocabulary choices? The first section has been completed for you.

Table 7.5

Pupil	Writing sample and preceding scaffolding	Features of progression	Suggested next steps for progression
Japonica Extract from a script written for a short film using stick figure animation software	*Imaginary Elizabethan groundlings are discussing 'A Midsummer Night's Dream'* G1: *The play was great! I like Puck, he's wicked, an imp do you think?* G2: *Yes, stealing magic potions like that was bad news for Titania* G1: *Do you think Oberon should've put him in the stocks?* G2: *No, imps are dangerous, all that magic and stuff no way!*	Script layout used, adds humour, uses colloquial phrases, and interprets themes from play and period	Add stage direction, add names to characters
John Advice for new pupils using sentence starters	*New pupils need to do this.* **Find**... *their coat peg and their drawer.* **Always**... *listen to the teacher.* **Never** ....*shout out in class.* **Sometimes**... *stay for after school clubs.* **Our school** *is fun.*		
Analyn A recount of the school day using a list of connectives and photographs	*Firstly we have assembly. Next we have maths, then we have playtime and snack. Then we have literacy and reading. I have packed lunch. After lunch we have music and painting. Then we go home.*		

(Continued)

(Continued)

Pupil	Writing sample and preceding scaffolding	Features of progression	Suggested next steps for progression
Peter A story using a three part frame: beginning, middle and end	*One night I saw a bright light outside. It was dark and wet. A yappy dog helped me we went off and he pulled me more but I jumped away from him because he barked he ran back barking for me. I could see the light and it was a man with a torch he was looking for his dog but it was gone so he was sad. I went home sad too.*		

Reflection questions

- How would you extend the length of John's sentences?
- What elements of Peter's writing show coherence at a sentence level?
- Other than using photographs, how else would you support Analyn's understanding of chronology in her recount?

The assessment of writing composition

This section examines the assessment of written composition. Both multimodal and traditional forms of text composition need assessment across the curriculum. The assessment of writing composition examines pupils' ability to select appropriate writing structures and language features in order to match the audience, purpose and context for a piece of writing.

Summative assessment

Summative writing assessments are snapshots of pupils' written performance. Summative assessment of composition is normally part of a larger measure which contains grammar, spelling and handwriting. Summative writing assessments do not usually assess the processes of composition. They tend to assess the finished product.

Like reading, standardised writing assessment makes it possible to compare one pupil's results with many others of the same chronological age and therefore the range of writing ability in a classroom. Standardised writing assessments are often administered for statutory purposes, with specified levels of curricular achievement such as the use of particular sentence structures. While these grammatical elements are relatively straightforward, identifying their contribution to the composition of the text involves a complex judgement of the overall success of the piece of writing for its reader. This requires some interpretation by the marker because readers respond to text in different ways.

Formative assessment

Formative assessment is truly valid if it provides information to help progression. It should pinpoint current and next steps for achievement with matched teaching suggestions. For these reasons, good formative assessment is always cumulative. In the context of writing composition, formative assessment examines pupils' ability to plan, draft and edit work as well as an assessment of the finished product. Writing drafts, particularly those with visible alterations, can assist teachers to see the process of composition. It also assesses pupils' ability to make connections with their reading. For example, reading back the work out loud will cause editing. Links to pupils' own reading repertoire are also possible as different writing styles are absorbed.

There are two main areas to consider in the formative assessment of writing composition. These can be seen in the product and process of composition.

1. An appropriate match for audience, purpose and context
2. Evidence of authorial intent, leading to the inclusion of the authors' personal writing voice

Many generic formative assessment procedures can examine these areas, such as observation, guided group work and dramatic improvisations that summarise ideas for writing, such as through '**hot seating**'. Three specific approaches are described here: focused marking, rubric self-assessments and guided writing. The three approaches address social and cognitive perspectives of writing composition.

Focused marking

Focused marking is a formative assessment of pupils' writing composition using specified assessment criteria. Areas to assess for composition are evidence of planning and alteration, evidence of writing for a deliberate purpose and reader, such as through structure layout and deliberate vocabulary choices, word play and sentence constructions. These may provide evidence of pupils' own writing voice. Integrating summative and formative assessment data is possible with cumulative examples of focused marking for individuals and specific groups of pupils. This latter type of 'teacher assessment' has been a feature of statutory criterion referenced writing assessment in English primary schools. Here it can provide teachers with a shared language, raise expectations and improve consistency as part of a thorough understanding of formative assessment (Ofsted, 2011).

Assessment rubrics

Assessment rubrics are pre-prepared criteria for writing tasks. Pupils are encouraged to self-assess their work in tandem with the class teacher. The rubrics are sometimes called marking ladders. They can be usefully used in conjunction with the success criteria for individual lessons. Other versions add to pupils' overall English curriculum targets for progression. Pupils' ownership and understanding of the content of assessment rubrics is important. Some of this understanding comes from pupils devising the rubrics for themselves and collaboratively. Rubrics for pupils' self-assessment can contain different levels of writing challenge.

Research focus

Using writing rubrics for self-assessment

A study from the USA examined the relationship between pupils' writing composition and their use of self-assessment rubrics (Andrade et al., 2010). Pupils in the upper primary and lower secondary school were asked to analyse a good writing example to create their own rubric for assessment of the same type of writing. Results from the 162 pupils suggested that this process of using criteria devised from good writing examples benefited their first drafts of the same type of writing.

Guided writing

Guided writing is part of a trilogy of teaching approaches: modelled, shared and guided writing. Modelled and shared writing allow the class teacher to observe pupils' contributions to the joint construction of shared pieces of text. Guided writing extends these whole class activities to small group work. The format of guided writing varies. It may be used to observe or measure pupils'

Table 7.6 Observing progression in writing composition

	Audience, purpose and context	Cohesion	Structure	Language choices	Examples of links with other four modes of English
Lower primary years	Writing personal recounts, speech-like constructions	Links to simple narrative structure, may use 'and' to link strings of ideas	Simple recount structures, lists and captions May imitate simple genre constructions and stories	Labelling vocabulary, early descriptive words	Link to play, drawing, mark making, familiar stories, songs and rhymes, and favourite stories
Middle primary years	Some evidence of writing for specific audience and purpose contains ideas that connect and build Beginning to use evidence to support ideas Mostly appropriate language register in context	Meanings are clear; clauses are linked with a range of words Some use of paragraphs	Openings established but structure may be irregular Writes ending Uses common genre structures and specific texts with some variations Writes own versions	Sentences vary but some resemble speech, sentences may often start in the same way Some vocabulary and language devices like simile, chosen for purpose and effect	Differences between writing and speech: character, plot development and choice of language register through role play
Upper primary years	Identifies goals prior to writing Pace of writing mostly consistent Uses evidence to support opinion Appropriate language register in context	Uses paragraphs and layout appropriate to genre	Confident adaptations of common genre structures, and specific texts, most sections developed Writes a range of texts independently	Deliberate vocabulary and sentence choices, technical vocabulary used, plus description for effect	Write notes and plans for writing using graphic organisers that link to organising and presenting research topics

progress in specific writing areas. It can also be an opportunity to model, extend and discuss the process of composition and to set joint writing goals.

Table 7.6 presents the next entry for a matrix of primary English progression. It shows broad areas of progression in written composition across the primary years. Use this grid as a guide for classroom observations, initial marking, guided writing and pupil interviews.

Summary of chapter

This chapter has summarised the processes of writing composition and progression in writing from cognitive, linguistic and socio-cultural perspectives. Research and theory were examined and linked to classroom practice. Pupil vignettes illustrated individual examples of progression. Two important themes have featured in this chapter. Firstly, the importance of using pupils' out of school practices and secondly linking writing composition to pupils' reading and speaking and listening skills. Understanding these links reinforces the essence of primary English, to make meaning. Sharing a clear understanding enables teachers and pupils to compose writing for real and relevant contexts.

? **Self-assessment**

1. List and justify three items that you consider important features of or suggested next steps for progression in writing composition. Choose items for the oldest, mid-range and youngest pupils in the primary school.
2. List linguistic, socio-cultural and cognitive perspectives of writing composition.
3. List linguistic, socio-cultural and cognitive aspects of writing composition.

Annotated further reading

Bearne, E. and Bazalgette, C. (Eds) (2010) *Beyond Words: Developing Children's Response to Multimodal Text*. Leicester: UKLA. This resource suggests progression frameworks for multimodal texts in the primary school. Useful case studies are included.

Clay, M. (1999) *Becoming Literate: The Construction of Inner Control*. Auckland: Heineman. Chapter 5 in this seminal text examines pupils' early introduction to print.

Corbett, P. and Strong, J. (2011) *Talk for Writing Across the Curriculum*. Maidenhead: Open University Press/McGraw Hill Education. This text contains details and resources for the talk for writing approach.

Further resources

Pivot: free stick figure animation software, available at www.snapfiles.com/get/stickfigure.html

Audacity: free downloadable audio editing software, available at http://audacity.sourceforge.net

Steps Professional Development from Australia provides interlinked assessment and resources across the four modes of English. Materials are based on maps of development in literacy progression. Available at: www.det.wa.edu.au/stepsresources/detcms/portal

Scholastic writing guides provide a range of printed writing scaffolds for composition. Available at: www.scholastic.co.uk

References

Andrade, H. L., Du, Y. and Mycek, K. (2010) Rubric-referenced self-assessment and middle school students' writing. *Assessment in Education: Principles, Policy and Practice*, 17, 199–214.

Bearne, E. and Bazalgette, C. (Eds) (2010) *Beyond Words: Developing Children's Response to Multimodal Text*. Leicester: UKLA.

Bereiter, C. and Scardamalia, M. (1987) *The Psychology of Written Composition*. Hillsdale, NJ: Lawrence Erlbaum.

Berninger, V., Vaughan, K., Abbott, R., Begay, K., Byrd, K., Curtin, G., et al. (2002) Teaching spelling and composition alone: Implications for the simple view of writing. *Journal of Educational Psychology*, 94, 291–304.

Bissex, G. L. (1980) *GNYS At WRK: A Child Learns to Read and Write*. Cambridge, MA: Harvard University Press.

Britton, J.N. (1972) *Writing to Learn and Learning to Write. The Humanity of English*. Urbana, IL: NCTE.

Cain, K. (2003) Text comprehension and its relationship to coherence in children's fictional narratives. *British Journal of Developmental Psychology*, 21, 335–351.

Clay, M. (1989) *What Did I Write?* Oxford: Heinemann.

Clay, M. (1998) *By Different Paths to Common Outcomes*. York, ME: Stenhouse.

Corbett, P. and Strong, J. (2011) *Talk for Writing Across the Curriculum*. Maidenhead: Open University Press/ McGraw Hill Education.

DCSF (2008) *Talk for Writing: Primary National Strategies*. London: HMSO.

Dombey, H. (2013) *Teaching Writing: What the Evidence Says*. Leicester: UKLA.

Flower, L. and Hayes, J. (1980) The dynamics of composing: Making plans and juggling constraints. In L. Gregg and E. Steinberg (Eds), *Cognitive Processes in Writing*. Hillsdale, NJ: Lawrence Erlbaum Associates. pp. 31–50.

Gough, P. B. and Tumner, W. E. (1986) Decoding, reading and reading disability. *Remedial and Special Education*, 7, 6–10.

Graham, S. and Hebert, M. (2010) *Writing to Read: Evidence of how Writing can Improve Reading*. Washington, DC: Carnegie Corporation of New York

Graves, D. H. (1983) *Writing: Teachers and Children at Work*. Portsmouth, NH: Heinemann.

Halliday, M. A. K. (2009) *The Essential Halliday*. London: Continuum.

Hayes, J. R. (1996) A new framework for understanding cognition and affect in writing. In C. M. Levy and S. Ransdell (Eds), *The Science of Writing: Theories, Methods, Individual Differences and Applications*. Mahwah, NJ: Erlbaum. pp. 1–27

Kress, G. (1997) *Before Writing: Rethinking the Road to Literacy*. New York: Routledge.

Kroll, B. (1981) Developmental relationships between speaking and writing. In B. Kroll and R. J. Ivan (Eds), *Exploring Speaking and Listening Relationships: Connections and Contrasts*. Urbana, IL: NCTE. pp. 32–54.

Martin, J. R., Rotheray, J. and Christie, F. (1987) Social processes in education: A reply to Sawyer and Watson (and others). In I. Reid (Ed.), *The Place of Genre in Learning: Current Debates*. Deakin: Deakin University.

Mullis, I. V. S., Martin, M., O., Gonzalez, E. J. and Kennedy, A. M. (2007) *Progress in international literacy study [PIRLS]*. Boston, MA: International Association for the Evaluation of Education.

Myhill, D. and Fisher, R. (2005) *Informing Practice in English: A Review of Recent Research in Literacy and the Teaching of English*. London: Ofsted.

Myhill, D. and Watson, A. (2011) Teaching writing. In A. Green (Ed.), *Becoming a Reflective English Teacher*. Maidenhead: Open University Press. pp. 58–73

National Strategy (1999) *Training Modules*. London: DfEE.

Ofsted (2011) *The Impact of the 'Assessing Pupils' Progress' Initiative*. London: Ofsted.

Olinghouse, N. G. and Wilson, J. (2013) The relationship between vocabulary and writing quality in three genres. *Reading and Writing*, 26, 45–65.

Perera, K. (1984) *Children's Writing and Reading: Analysing Classroom Language*. Oxford: Blackwell.

Ring, K. (2010) Supporting a playful approach to drawing. In P. Broadhead, J. Howard and E. Wood (Eds), *Play and Learning in the Early Years*. London: Sage. pp. 113–126.

Rumelhart, D. (1980) Schemata: The building blocks of cognition. In R. Spiro, B. Bruce and W. Brewer (Eds), *Theoretical Issues in Reading Cognition*. Hillsdale, NJ: Lawrence Erlbaum.

Scardamalia, M. and Bereiter, C. (2006) Knowledge building: Theory, pedagogy and technology. In K. Sawyer (Ed.), *Cambridge Handbook of Learning Sciences*. New York: Cambridge University Press. pp. 97–118.

Stanovich, K. E. (1986) Matthew effects in reading: Some consequences of individual differences in the acquisition of literacy. *Reading Research Quarterly*, 4 (21), 360–407.

Vygotsky, L.S. (1978) *Mind in Society: The Development of Higher Psychological Processes*. Cambridge, MA: Harvard University Press.

Wells, G. (1985) *Language Learning and Education*. Windsor: NFER Nelson.

CHAPTER 8

GRAMMAR

Objectives

1. To identify key features of progression in written grammar
2. To examine key models of the process of sentence construction
3. To relate progression in written grammar to daily classroom practice
4. To evaluate common forms of assessment for written grammar

Introduction

This is the second of three chapters that look at the progression of writing in primary-aged children.

Grammar is the organisation of language. It includes words (morphology), sentence structure (syntax), meaning (semantics) and sounds (phonology). In the primary classroom, the written grammar curriculum addresses the knowledge and structure of words, sentences and whole texts. Progression in written grammar is underpinned by pupils' speaking and oral comprehension.

It is also linked to reading. The use of syntactic reading cues such as reading on and back in a sentence to determine meaning illustrate this link.

Activity

Match the following written or spoken language as examples or definitions of dialect, **Received Pronunciation**, Standard English, slang or informal language.

- *'He's a boffin!'*
- *'When using English abroad, I choose to pronounce words in this way because they are probably more easily understood.'*
- *'It's the English heard on the school playground.'*
- *'She ain't my BFF!'(best friend forever)*
- *'When I was a nipper, me mam always pulled the clinkers from the fire.'*
- *'I write my primary English assignments in this type of English because it is the required standard for formal written composition.'*

This activity will have caused you to clarify your understanding of key terms in defining written and spoken grammar and to consider the differences between them. The glossary at the end of this book is one reference point for the grammatical terminology used in this chapter. Understanding the distinctions between written and spoken grammar contributes to pupils' grammatical progression. Your judgement of 'correct' or 'incorrect' use of grammar in the examples above relates to the context in which they were used. Typically, these choices of Standard English, accent, dialect or Received Pronunciation are affected by social class, the social group, working group and formal or informal situation in which they occur.

The purpose of grammar in the primary school curriculum had been the subject of some debate. Some of this discussion concerns the value of discrete or traditional grammar instruction versus functional or context-embedded language instruction. Traditional grammar teaching is often prescriptive, characterised by separate grammar lessons that teach grammatical knowledge and skills, mainly from a written perspective. Functional grammar teaching links to genre based pedagogy (for example, Halliday, 2009). It places grammar teaching in the context of pupils' language and literacy across the curriculum and beyond. Intrinsic to a functional approach to grammar is an understanding of audience and purpose.

Understanding pupils' implicit and explicit knowledge of grammar can affect the way it is taught (Myhill and Watson, 2014). Pupils usually come to school with a good grasp of spoken grammar. Exceptions are pupils for whom English is a second language. Early writers can also write grammatically, without specific instruction. Pupils can do this because they have an implicit knowledge of grammar. These ideas link to the work of Noam Chomsky and the theory of innate language acquisition, as discussed in Chapter 2.

Explicit grammar knowledge is taught. It builds on an implicit foundation. Critics, however, suggest that an overemphasis on explicit grammar teaching stunts native speakers' natural language experience, creativity and motivation to write for a genuine purpose, resulting in formulaic writing (Pullman, 2005). Progression in implicit and explicit grammar acquisition in primary school depends upon a classroom environment that is rich with relevant opportunities for language and literacy, linked to pupils' social and cultural awareness of English and language in society.

The distinguished linguist David Crystal provides a useful summary of the importance of grammar. 'Without grammar we are left with a jumble of words and word parts and nothing makes sense' (Crystal, 2000: 6). He lists five main reasons for learning grammar. These are summarised below.

1. Grammar underpins languages.
2. Knowledge of grammar is necessary in order to detect where, when and how language has been used for particular purposes. Critical readers and writers recognise and use grammar in this way.
3. Knowledge and understanding of the power of the English language grows through understanding how language works.
4. Knowledge of grammar is necessary in order to enhance effective writing and speech.
5. Knowledge of English grammar can assist in learning a second language.

Activity

Classifying grammatical writing attainment

Classify the following examples of grammatical skills from across the primary age range. The first one has been done for you.

(Continued)

(Continued)

Table 8.1

Writing example	Transcription	Composition	Reading cue	Speaking and listening	Lower primary	Middle primary	Upper primary
Use full stops	✓	✓	✓		✓		
Write a simple sentence							
Use modal verbs							
Use adjectives							
Identify types of subordinating conjunctions							
Expand noun phrases							
Write a mix of sentence structures to persuade							
Re-read and read on from a sentence in order to decipher meaning							
Use a sentence which contains a fronted adverbial							

This activity will have caused you to revise grammatical terminology and to appreciate the breadth of grammatical knowledge required by primary pupils. The application of grammatical skills incorporates different aspects of the four modes of English.

The elements of grammar

Grammar is the study of words and sentences. The study of words includes word classes (parts of speech), such as adverbs, and word structures, such as suffixes and compound words. The study of sentences includes sentence types, such as statements or questions, and three main sentence structures: **simple, compound** and **complex**. Sentences are examined as parts of paragraphs and whole texts. Punctuation marks help the reader to demarcate and interpret the meanings of written sentences in more detail.

✎ Research focus

Sentence construction and writing improvement

A systematic review of 64 papers across a range of English-speaking countries looked at the effects of direct grammar instruction on pupils' writing attainment in a range of English-speaking countries (Andrews et al., 2006). It compared teaching correct word order and the technique of combining sections of sentences to build sentence types. Sentence combining appeared to have a greater effect on the quality of pupils' writing. However, as noted by the authors, this review did not address social or cultural influences on grammatical development. They note that the improvement may also have been due to pupils applying grammatical knowledge with the process of sentence combining itself. The small sample of studies for review was also recorded. This review underlies the importance of context in the process of learning grammar for writing.

Elements of written grammar can be summarised under four headings: words, sentences, punctuation and paragraphs. In the classroom these aspects of writing are often divided into grammatical form and function. Grammatical forms are the characteristics of word classes, morphemes and parts of a sentence. Grammatical function deals with meaning such as knowing what verbs can do within a sentence.

Within a context and process-driven approach to teaching for progression in written grammar, the form and function of grammar is frequently taught

Table 8.2 Summary of written grammar in the pupil vignettes

Pupil	Age	Attainment level	Writing sample	Key strategies of written grammar	Features of progression	Suggested next steps for progression
Japonica	10	Within expected levels	**Story ending** *Outside the castle, snow was falling. Inside, the castle, a man cried with sadness. What was he to do? His heart was broken but suddenly, without warning, he lifted his head. His puffy, red eyes opened widely after an amazing idea flashed across his mind. 'That's it, I know,' he shouted then ran into the snow.*	Writes with clear idea of audience and purpose Consistently uses commas to separate clauses Confident with basic genres Paragraphs group ideas and use opening sentences Uses question marks, apostrophes, speech marks	Uses a mix of sentence constructions. Includes questions, statements and exclamations Uses a mix of subordinating and coordinating conjunctions Uses fronted adverbials	Use greater range of subordinating conjunctions consistently Begin to use a range of different lengths of sentences Consolidate use of commands Edit paragraphs to show change of emphasis
Analyn	9	EAL pupil at the earlier stages of English language acquisition	**Retell traditional tale** *Once upon a time there livd a mum and Jack. One day Jack went to sell a cow but he has beans. The beans grow then Jack climbd the stalks and sawed the giant in the castle but the giant chasd Jack down the stalks so Jack chopd the stalk down and the giant was dead. He livd happily ever after.*	Retells basic events Uses full stops Compound sentences joined by 'and', 'so and 'but' Sentences are opened in different ways Uses capital letters for names and to begin sentences Ideas presented in order	Written in past tense with some errors Uses story introduction and ending Uses verbs in different ways	Use a greater range of description Vary sentence types Expand noun phrases Consolidate tenses and plurals Add paragraphs

Pupil	Age	Attainment level	Writing sample	Key strategies of written grammar	Features of progression	Suggested next steps for progression
John	7	Below expected levels	**Recount of weekend family trip** *We went to mcdonlads and had chips and burger and filly of fish. Mum had coke and I had ice creme. We went becos it wos my birthday.*	Writes speech-like sentences; writes familiar recounts; writes three-part stories using three box planning grid Uses some capital letters for sentences and proper nouns	Compound sentences joined by 'and' or 'because'; uses word banks to add vocabulary, often adjectives or synonyms for action verbs	Consistent use of capital letters Develop description Develop non-fiction writing, instructions
Peter	5	Above expected levels	**Leaflet** *This leaflet of new pupil in St Marys school and to find there class.* *What is in school?* *Its fun. You will do PE, maths, reading and swim.* *Dinner* *You will eat lunch in the hall where diner peple help you and you eat the hot diners or the cold packd lunch.* *When is playtime?* *You go outside to find the balls and do the run to be it game.*	Logical sequence of ideas Uses plurals Clauses joined with 'and' Full stops Commas in a list Repeats sentence openings Some sections more like instructions than written as an information leaflet	Separates ideas with sub-headings Expands some noun phrases Writes for audience and purpose Uses a word bank	Investigate apostrophe for omission Look at 'there', 'their', 'they're' Consolidate 'ed' endings Consolidate use of adverbs Develop question and exclamation marks Develop conjunctions 'when', 'if', 'so', 'but'

through reading and writing for particular text types, or genres. Writing simple recounts are one example. Here pupils learn to identify both language features, such as time connectives, and the organisational features, such as writing settings, events and endings. Although many real life examples of genres are hybrids, in the primary classroom, teaching basic forms allows pupils to imitate them, leading to an ability to compare and contrast basic and hybrid texts through writing for an authentic context.

Table 8.2 presents a categorisation of the grammatical features of writing in the vignette pupils. Combined with pupils' writing composition, the table allows us to track some of the features and next steps for progression that can occur across the primary years of schooling. In these examples, there are definite patterns in the process of developing sentences, paragraphs, punctuation and word classes. Morphemic spelling mistakes have been included. Note how grammar progression builds on sets of basic skills. They are not learnt in isolation. Further written examples are required to monitor consistency.

Progression in written grammar

In the classroom, the progression of writing composition involves a process approach to teaching grammar. Both the form and function of grammatical terms are taught at an appropriate level of difficulty for primary school pupils. This provides pupils with an accessible meta-language to talk about language. This meta-language allows pupils to choose the most effective grammar for each writing task. Meta-language is more than defining grammatical terminology. It involves pupils and teachers confidently knowing how different word classes function in different sentences and types of writing (Myhill et al., 2013). It also asks pupils to write with an intention to be understood in varying degrees of sophistication, to write like a reader. These processes are reinforced as pupils learn to read between the lines and search for degrees of meaning in written text. Meta-language is supported by numerous classroom strategies including mnemonics, colour coding sentence sections, table top aide memoires, cumulative audits of grammar knowledge and self-assessment using rubrics that contain relevant grammatical terms.

✍ Research focus

Grammar teaching and writing quality

A randomised controlled study of young adolescents suggests that teaching grammar enhances writing attainment (Myhill et al., 2011). It emphasised the importance of pupils making specific grammatical choices in order to write effective sentences and construct text. Over the course of one academic year, pupils were exposed to the same teaching foci in planned teaching units. One group received additional detailed grammar lesson plans based on the premise that grammatical knowledge was a tool for making effective writing choices. Qualitative observation and interview data was included. The main finding was that embedded grammar teaching could improve writing attainment. A further analysis suggested that able writers in the additional grammar teaching group made significant progress. The able writers in the non-additional grammar group made less progress than the less able writers. Teachers' own grammatical subject knowledge also played an important role.

Words

Progression in pupils' use of words links to the development of spoken and written vocabulary and to spelling. Knowledge of words or vocabulary growth is a measure of pupils' understanding of the meaning of language but it does not necessarily indicate pupils' ability to apply new vocabulary to a range of contexts. Growth in pupils' grammatical knowledge of words is also like this. Listing and categorising a word class is useful but pupils' ability to transfer it to written work requires the words to be part of pupils' language to report, inform, describe, instruct, explain, persuade and discuss.

Progression in the grammatical use of written words can be divided into the use of word structures and word classes. Grammatical word structures address morphemes, the smallest units of meaning in a word. Written progression in the use of morphemes is part of pupils' spelling development. Structured spelling programmes normally contain a mix of phonic and morphemic word structures plus high frequency words and topic related vocabulary. Word classes are divided into structural or lexical word classes. Structural words form the framework for a sentence such as pronouns and **determiners** and **conjunctions**. **Lexical terms** are nouns, adjectives, verbs and adverbs (Reedy and Bearne, 2013).

Most pupils begin school with a good vocabulary for naming and describing. In school, pupils' early writing generally resembles aspects of the grammar of early speech (for example, Perera, 1984). For example, early experimentation with inflectional endings such as –s and –ed also happens in early speech. Similarly, once beyond the emergent writing phase, young writers write labels. Later, simple sentences and similar compound sentences emerge with popular **coordinating conjunctions** such as 'and'. Many of these early written sentences have speech-like patterns. As pupils' writing matures it begins to reflect more complex sentence constructions that require a sophisticated choice of words and punctuation. Part of this is an understanding of how the same word can perform different functions and therefore be a different word class, depending on where it is placed in a sentence.

Activity

Identifying the form and function of words

Make a list of words that can be part of more than one word class. Construct sentences to show their different functions. For example: The sum is right (adjective). The man came right on time (adverb). Fresh water is a right (noun). I must right this wrong (verb).

Classroom application In the classroom, developing knowledge of words is a cross-curricular practice that links to vocabulary and genre development. This approach enables the pupil to see links and to gather specific vocabulary from different subjects. Such connections place words in a real context. Additional practice at playing with words as part of a structured spelling programme also enables pupils to develop the confidence to investigate word structures and word classes for themselves. Daily challenges that build word-based skills such as dictionary usage, spelling exceptions, anagrams or mnemonics, exemplify this approach. A simple investigation of etymology, or the origins of words, can be included. Consistent defining and word building practice like this also reduces opportunities for pupils to use words incorrectly. Misuse of **subordinating conjunctions** is one such example. For instance, a younger child writing 'I went to the shops however I ran there' should use the coordinating conjunction 'and'. Pupils often misuse conjunctions when they cannot group them according to their function in a sentence or associate them with different text types. Once pupils progress beyond using simple coordinating conjunctions, choosing these correctly relies on investigating their purpose through model examples in real contexts.

Sentence structure

Progression in sentence structure can be divided into learning to write a sentence and to adapting it. Learning the concept of a sentence begins when young pupils are able to separate their thoughts into discrete chunks of meaning. It is hard for young writers. They may be able to speak using many joined clauses but use simple sentences when writing. This again highlights the distinction between written and spoken language. Young pupils learn that a sentence makes sense on its own and to distinguish it from whole words and individual phonemes. Teaching sentences in a shared reading and writing context is essential classroom practice at this early stage (DfEE, 2001).

As pupils mature, sentences grow more complex. Clauses are added to expand phrases and to add layers of meaning to produce compound and complex sentences. Functional grammar and genre-based approaches attribute this progression to the contexts for which pupils use language. Pupils move from writing about concrete ideas to more abstract thinking and use known grammatical structures to express these ideas. For example, sentences may contain logically related clauses using conjunctions to add information, to compare and contrast, to give examples or to reinforce an idea, to show cause and effect and to show time and place.

Classroom application   In the classroom, planning and teaching for progression in sentence construction means teaching in a real context as an integral part of the composition process. Within the 'familiarise, focus, define, scaffold and independent teaching' framework outlined in Chapter 7 (National Strategy, 1999), teachers may use shared and guided writing practices to address common areas of misconception or to extend sentence structures with targeted groups or individual pupils. Guided writing techniques include segmenting, blending and expanding parts of a sentence, adding and subtracting punctuation and exchanging parts of a sentence for specific writing effects. Young pupils often need guidance to write continuous prose rather than writing each sentence on a new line. It is also useful to imitate and critique sentence constructions in real and invented examples of text written for different purposes.

Research focus

Using exploratory talk to develop sentence structures in able writers

A short-term practitioner research study looked at the impact of exploratory talk on the sentence structures of able writers (Robins, 2011). This small-scale research looked at upper primary school pupils over one term. Based on the constructivist principles of using a common language to develop knowledge, the pupils were trained in the techniques of exploratory talk (Mercer and Hodgkinson, 2008). Exploratory talk involves pupils using talk to elaborate thinking and challenging others to do the same. Able writers then used exploratory talk to manipulate clauses and prepositional phrases in independent group work. This group showed greater stamina, embraced challenge and demonstrated higher levels of writing skill. Robins' practitioner-based study reaffirms the underlying significance of speaking and listening to grammar and writing progression.

Punctuation

Progression in pupils' use of punctuation is linked to the development of writing grammatical sentences. It marks sentences, clauses, some phrases and adds tone to aid the reader. There is currently less direct research into the effect of punctuation on writing progression, compared to grammar (French, 2012). There are particular stages in pupils' use of punctuation. They are not necessarily linear. Initially, after the emergent writing phase, pupils learn to demarcate sentences with full stops, use commas within lists and to separate clauses. Other end-of-sentence punctuation, such as question and exclamation marks, emerge as pupils begin to write written questions and add emphasis. More advanced punctuation develops as pupils' range of writing expands alongside their confident use of complex sentences.

✎ Research focus

The development of punctuation knowledge

A qualitative research project looked at the development of written punctuation in 7–11 year olds. Amongst the pupils, the development of punctuation was not a linear process. The study found that in these middle and lower ability pupils, punctuation was linked to its symbolic appearance more than to its use (Hall, 2002). As pupils matured, accuracy with speech marks and apostrophes grew. The purposeful use of punctuation to separate grammatical parts of sentences was less well-developed. Pupils rarely used a meta-language. Hall was critical of de-contextualised grammar teaching.

More recent case study research with 6 year old children (French, 2012) showed that teaching children about the punctuation of quoted speech through writing and reading aloud helped pupils to develop an active awareness and increased use of the correct punctuation. Although both studies illustrate the benefits of contextualised grammar, a greater range of punctuation research was requested by both authors.

Classroom application   In the classroom, progression in the use of punctuation links to pupils' development in sentence construction. Pupils learn to expand and contract different sentence types and to add the necessary punctuation. Alone, punctuation marks are abstract symbols. As with phonics, pupils often initially benefit from interactive, multisensory approaches that allow them to investigate, see, hear and feel where punctuation is required as well as numerous opportunities for over-learning and revision. Attaching physical mimes to punctuation marks is one type of multisensory method. Using punctuation as sentences are constructed is the goal.

Paragraph construction

Paragraphs are part of what linguists call discourse. Discourse describes how larger pieces of spoken language and writing are structured. Unlike speaking and listening, asking pupils to write independently requires them to write without a shared experience. Paragraphs contribute to this process by helping pupils to order ideas and clarify threads of meaning across whole pieces of text.

Coherent texts are written for particular contexts. Progression in structuring coherent paragraphs begins when young children reproduce simple beginning, middle and end narratives. Setting, characters, problem, build-up and resolution structures typically follow this order. Older fiction paragraph structures include other generic formats such as flashbacks or dual narratives. Specific fiction genre structures such as myths and science fiction are added.

Early non-fiction paragraphing structures are generally recounts. Pupils also learn paragraphing in standard non-fiction structures: non-chronological reports, instruction, persuasion, discussion and explanation. Specific non-fiction genre structures such as newspapers are added. Paragraph progression here is supported by using discourse markers. These are sentences that signpost the reader. They may introduce a paragraph, link it to the next or conclude. It is sometimes useful to encourage pupils to use mini subheadings for paragraphs as part of the planning process.

Cohesive texts also contain a choice of language to knit it together across and within sentences and across whole texts. Examples include substituting alternative words or clauses to avoid repetition and using synonyms, conjunctions, and pronouns. Poor use of conjunctions can alter the meaning of a sentence.

Classroom application In the classroom the development of paragraph constructions links to pupils' understanding of the differences between written and spoken text. Pupils learn to use a graded set of sentences within each paragraph that logically build and connect ideas within them and across whole pieces of text. Exposure to, and investigation of, a wide variety of text is necessary. In particular, digital texts such as Twitter posts, Facebook, email or text messaging may require abbreviated or précised ideas that do not use traditional paragraphing structures but which still require cohesive elements, for instance pronouns and conjunctions.

The progression of written grammar in the primary classroom

This section of the chapter puts research into written grammar into a primary classroom context. Using research and the pupil vignettes from Chapter 1 it describes and evaluates evidence to support understanding of progression in written grammar. As with the composition of writing, two strands are useful as a basis for understanding progression at the primary level: cognitive strategies and social practices. Cognitive strategies include the systematic development of words, sentences and paragraphs and whole texts. Linguistic knowledge is included. Social practices include the systematic development of different types of writing, including hybrid genre, multimodal texts, out-of-school writing, popular culture and the choice of formal or informal language. A multisensory and meta-cognitive approach to grammar teaching is emphasised in this section. This reflects a constructivist approach to learning.

Word choice and word play

Word choice and word play address pupils' knowledge of word classes and the structure or morphology of words. Two areas are important because they provide a starting point for expanding pupils' current vocabulary. Firstly, knowing how the same word can function as different word classes in a single sentence. Secondly, recognising root words and knowing how suffixes and prefixes build on them.

Activity

Look at the four independent writing samples, from the pupil vignettes. Record the next steps and features of progression in the use of word classes to support writing composition. Think about the choice of word classes for effect and how they may address an intended audience and purpose for writing. The first section has been completed for you.

Table 8.3

Pupil talk and preceding scaffolding	Writing sample	Features of progression in word class use and morphology	Suggested next steps for progression in word class use and morphology
Japonica Investigating root words, suffixes and prefixes using a combined thesaurus and dictionary	*Medicine medic medicinal medicate medical medicinally*	Japonica is able to categorise new vocabulary into word classes with examples to show where single words function as different word classes.	Use these words in editing own writing as part of sentence combining exercises to add, subtract or change meaning or change the emphasis in a sentence. Retain these words as part of a personal topic based dictionary or vocabulary book.

Pupil talk and preceding scaffolding	Writing sample	Features of progression in word class use and morphology	Suggested next steps for progression in word class use and morphology
John John takes part in drama improvisation prior to writing.	Linking action verbs and adverbs. *The pig runs pretty fast.*		
He is describing movement in a character from *The Sheep Pig* by Dick King-Smith.	*It likes to run quickly on the fields and see the sheep eating grass slowly.*		
Analyn Analyn listens to a short story. With the rest of the class, she stands up when she hears a pronoun and sits down when she hears a proper noun.	*Analyn has difficulty keeping up with the speed of the rest of the class. She confuses 'you' and 'your'.*		
Peter Using *The Very Hungry Caterpillar* (Eric Carle) to expand a noun phrase. Peter uses prepared adjective and adverb cards to add to a selection of cut up sentences extracted from the story.	*Peter forms the following sentence:* In the light of a bright moon **a tiny, little**, white egg lay on a leaf. *He spontaneously invents another sentence.* **A very green and stripy caterpillar looked for food.**		

〰️ Reflection questions

- What sort of sentence combining games will help John?
- Other than listing new words, how can Peter practise new vocabulary?
- Which paired speaking and listening games are appropriate for Analyn to consolidate her knowledge of pronouns?

Sentence construction and punctuation

Sentence construction and punctuation address pupils' knowledge of phrases and clauses. Knowledge of punctuation is part of this. Progression in sentence construction is characterised by pupils' ability to manipulate the parts of a sentence. Pupils understand how and why this affects the meaning of the sentence itself and the context in which it is written. Learning to manipulate sentences in this way should have a clear routine, value and purpose to enable pupils to transfer the skill to their own writing.

Activity

Look at the four independent writing samples, from the pupil vignettes. Record the features and suggested next steps of progression in the use of sentence construction and punctuation to support writing composition. Think about how the pupils use sentence constructions to address an intended audience, and their purpose for writing. Identify the elements of multisensory teaching and learning. The second section has been completed for you.

Table 8.4

Pupil talk and preceding scaffolding	Writing sample	Features of progression in sentence construction and punctuation	Suggested next steps for progression in sentence construction and punctuation
Japonica Using silent film to create dialogue plus **relative clauses**. The film shows meerkats in the wild.	It is a hot day in the desert. 'I can see the meerkats which live near the sand dunes,' says the man. The man disturbs the meerkats that he sees sunbathing which upsets the two lookouts. The other meerkats, who have not seen him yet, dig holes.		

Pupil talk and preceding scaffolding	Writing sample	Features of progression in sentence construction and punctuation	Suggested next steps for progression in sentence construction and punctuation
John Joining sentences beyond using 'and' and 'then' – using conjunctions. Examples using one given sentence stem. *Given list: if, because, so, when.*	*I can see the man because he is happy.* *I can see the man so then I went home.* *I can see the man when he jumps up.* *I can see the man if he jumps up high.*	Uses given conjunctions	Experiment with moving the conjunctions to alter meaning. Check tense. Experiment with pairs of phrases and clauses and longer conjunctions lists.
Analyn Analyn takes part in a paired speaking and listening game, turning her partner's question or statements into the other.	P: *Is it Christmas Day?* A: *It is Christmas Day.* A: *Are we dancers?* P: *We are dancers.* P: *Is it a good book?* A: *The book is good.* A: *Will you come for a sleepover?* P: *I did sleepover.*		
Peter Use prepositions in writing. Peter writes instructions for hiding clues before a class scavenger hunt.	*Put the clues in a bag before you go so no one sees.* *Put the first clue under the seat, not in playtime because class 2 will see before the hunt.*		

〰️ **Reflection questions**

- How would you help Analyn to extend her spoken sentences?
- How has Peter applied his understanding of prepositions?
- How would a restructuring of this task have allowed Japonica to use paragraphs?

Paragraph construction

Paragraph construction addresses pupils' ability to sort and order ideas. Progression in paragraph construction is characterised by pupils' ability to both plan and structure key themes across and within paragraphs and whole texts. This has links to pupils' inferential and evaluative reading comprehension and their ability to replicate similar layers of meaning in their own writing. For example, in fiction writing pupils may write hooks to entice the reader to anticipate plot lines.

Activity

Look at the four independent writing samples, from the pupil vignettes. Record the features and suggested next steps for progression in the use of paragraph construction to support writing composition. Think about how the pupils structure the text for an intended audience and purpose for writing. Identify the elements of multisensory teaching and learning. The fourth section has been completed for you.

Table 8.5

Pupil talk and preceding scaffolding	Writing sample	Features of progression in the use of paragraphs	Suggested next steps for progression in the use of paragraphs
Japonica Developing links within a paragraph *Japonica writes a review.*	*Review of* The Wolves in the Walls *(Neil Gaiman).* *This book is top class. It is funny and scary but not very frightening. Suddenly you laugh at the wolves' actions then you think about the Lucy's battle with them. After that it's the family who are the fools really because they don't listen.*		
John Use consistent tense forms	*My team is Chelsea I go to football games with Jack my granddad.*		

Pupil talk and preceding scaffolding	Writing sample	Features of progression in the use of paragraphs	Suggested next steps for progression in the use of paragraphs
John writes about his love of football.	*I am at the game we shouted for Chelsea to win and granddad is singing and I was happy I singed too.*		
Analyn Use headings and subheadings to group material *Analyn has described her family.*	*My mum My mum is kind and nice and we have a dog. My dad My dad is tall and big and he is a postman. He likes dogs but some bit him. I am Analyn and mum and dad and me are family.*		
Peter Use headings and subheadings to group material *Peter has written a chronological report of his trip to the London Science Museum.*	*We went on the bus acros London to see the space ships and the astronauts. The bus ride was long. I had sandwichs and joos s. In the museum we saw the astronauts food, bed and space knickers! It was like a nappy. We got home late and it was dark.*	Three distinct sections Events are in order	Use subheadings to signal further ideas in planning for each paragraph Increase description Include paired and group discussion

---

〰 Reflection questions

- Japonica struggles to finish this book review after her opening paragraph. What discourse markers can you suggest that will use subordinating conjunctions or **fronted adverbials**?
- Do subheadings help Analyn? What do you notice about her sentence constructions?

The assessment of written grammar

This section examines the assessment of written grammar in the light of standardised testing and formative assessment. Like many aspects of primary English, the complexity of grammar for writing is assessed and revised regularly. Grammar concepts are usefully taught by carefully increasing the level of difficulty. Both the form and function of grammar is assessed.

Summative assessment

Summative assessment is a snapshot of pupils' performance. Summative assessment of grammar for writing can be part of a longer writing assessment that contains composition, spelling and handwriting. Summative assessments of grammar can also be discrete measurements of pupils' explicit knowledge. The latest governmental draft frameworks in England for 7 and 11 year olds, due for testing in 2016, are recent examples (Standards and Testing Agency, 2014).

Data from statutory grammar assessments such as these are used to judge national trends and to 'ascertain what children have achieved in relation to the areas of the national curriculum (2014) describing grammar, punctuation and spelling' (Standards and Testing Agency, 2014, p. 4). Classroom teachers may also judge pupils' attainment in comparison to their own written grammar assessments.

Formative assessment: What sets of data are most valuable for daily classroom practice?

As noted in previous chapters, formative assessment is truly valid if it provides information to help progression. It should pinpoint current and next steps for achievement with matched teaching suggestions. For these reasons, good formative assessment is always cumulative. The formative assessment of grammar is not an exception. There are five main areas to consider. These can be considered from functional language and traditional approaches to teaching grammar.

1. Sentence constructions and punctuation
2. Sentence types
3. Word classes
4. Morphology
5. Standard and non-Standard English

Many generic formative assessment procedures are suitable for these areas. Observation, shared writing, structured questioning and guided group work are suggested. Three particular formative assessments are described here, regular class grammar tests, mental starters and sentence combining.

Grammar tests

Regular grammar tests, like weekly spelling tests, are most usefully adopted as part of a cumulative, contextual and multisensory approach to teaching and learning. This involves building grammatical knowledge through identifying and improving text examples for a named purpose. Pupils are allocated differentiated grammatical knowledge which is assessed on a regular, often weekly basis, depending on ability. Like spelling tests, assessing grammar in this way builds knowledge and skill simultaneously. As with spelling tests, peer and pupil self-testing and marking leads to an ability to identify personal grammatical writing errors and to add these areas to future tests. This links to pupils' ability to edit and proof read. As with spelling tests, there are dangers in pupils only learning for a weekly test and not receiving opportunities to revise, practise or apply their knowledge to their own writing.

✍ Research focus

Using immediate feedback to develop knowledge of grammar

An investigation into the effects of immediate formative feedback increased pupils' knowledge of grammatical terminology (Sheard and Chambers, in press). Pupils used electronic handsets to answer individual questions generated from an electronic database. The class teacher used immediate access to pupils' speed and accuracy in order to give instant electronic feedback. Immediate formative feedback was especially beneficial to low and middle ability pupils and in classes that used the handsets more frequently. The effects did not generalise into a separate writing task. The authors note the need to develop more knowledge of how pupils transfer this discrete grammatical knowledge into their own writing.

Mental starters

Grammar mental starters are short whole class or guided group work activities designed to practise and apply grammatical concepts in a fun and amusing way. It is useful to build pupils' confidence with a stock of familiar techniques such as anagrams, moving clauses and phrases, generating a family of words based on the root word, expanding and contracting phrases and generating synonyms and features of a sentence, such as tense. Teachers may use these techniques for formative assessment.

Table 8.6 Observing progression in written grammar

	Words	Sentences and punctuation	Paragraphs and whole texts	Examples of links with other four modes of English
Lower primary years	Use plurals Distinguish words and sentences Describe and name actions, objects, people, and places	Full stop, capital letter, exclamation mark and question mark Use capital letters for names Use coordinating conjunctions, 'and', 'so', 'but', 'or', and simple subordinating conjunctions, e.g. 'because' Commas in a list	Join sentences in simple recounts, regular tenses Simple three-part story structures Simple instructions Recounts	Recounts are possible across the curriculum Mark for grammatical consistency across the curriculum Consider grammatical elements of speaking and listening such as Standard English
Middle primary years	Investigate suffixes and prefixes, wider use of word classes such as adverbs and prepositions, root words	Apostrophe for omission More advanced use of conjunctions Add detail to expand sections of a sentence such as noun phrases Speech marks and some commas to separate clauses	Begin to separate ideas into paragraphs There are overall ideas across paragraphs Wider range of generic non-fiction and fiction genres used with scaffolding	A range of written genres are possible across the curriculum Mark for grammatical consistency across the curriculum Consider grammatical elements of speaking and listening such as Standard English
Upper primary years	Use suffixes and prefixes confidently Deliberate choice of words for audience and purpose Use different types of verbs with confidence	Use a fuller range of punctuation Consistent use of commas to show meaning in a sentence Full range of conjunctions	Wide use of connectives and conjunctions as discourse markers within and across paragraphs Link ideas in different ways such as to give examples and to show a time sequence	A range of written genres are possible across the curriculum Mark for grammatical consistency across the curriculum Consider grammatical elements of speaking and listening such as Standard English

Sentence combining

Sentence combining is a formative assessment technique and a teaching process (Saddler, 2005). Pupils add and subtract features of a sentence. The purpose is to assess skills in manipulating grammatical sentence features. These can be word classes, clauses, phrases and related punctuation. Sentence combining can be a physical process which expands or contracts sentences. Sets of pre-made sentences on card, cut up and ready to manipulate are a useful resource. The essence of sentence combining is to judge the impact of the new sentence (Myhill, 2010).

Table 8.6 presents the sixth entry for a matrix of primary English progression. It shows broad areas of progression in written grammar across the primary years. Use this grid as a guide for classroom observations, initial marking, shared and guided writing.

Summary of chapter

This chapter has summarised four aspects of progression in written grammar. Functional language and traditional approaches to grammar have been discussed and linked to classroom practice. Pupil vignettes illustrated individual examples of progression in written grammar with words, sentences and punctuation, paragraphs and whole texts. The chapter has emphasised the importance of a progressive, functional and multisensory approach to teaching and learning grammar underpinned by speaking and listening. In this way pupils' written grammar has a firm foundation as part of written composition across a range of digital, traditional and multimodal texts.

> **? Self-assessment**
>
> 1. List and justify three items that you consider important features or next steps for progression in written grammar. Choose items for the oldest, mid-range and youngest pupils in the primary school.
> 2. List linguistic, socio-cultural and cognitive influences on written grammar.
> 3. Describe contrasting and comparable elements of written grammar in examples of digital and multimodal texts.

Annotated further reading

Reedy, D. and Bearne, E. (2013) *Teaching Grammar Effectively in the Primary School.* Leicester: United Kingdom Literacy Association.
This practical resource covers all aspects of grammar in the new English national curriculum across the primary age range. It provides a useful mix of case studies, practical

classroom examples and terminology revision. The book contains many examples of links to children's literature and the four modes of English.

Saddler B. and Asaro-Saddler, K. (2010) Writing better sentences: Sentence-combining instruction in the classroom. *Preventing School Failure*, 159–163. DOI: 10.1080/10459880903495851.
This article demonstrates practical classroom strategies for sentence combining.

Wilson, A. and Scanlon, J. (2011) *Language Knowledge for Primary Teachers* (4th edn). Abingdon: Routledge.
This is a well-written and accessible book for developing grammatical subject knowledge.

Further resources

Corbett, P. (2010) *Jumpstart Literacy: Games and Activities for Ages 7–14.* Abingdon: Routledge.

Corbett, P. and Strong, J. (2014) *Jumpstart Grammar: Games and Activities for Ages 6–14.* Abingdon: Routledge.

The British Library *Sounds Familiar* website provides details of accent and dialect in the United Kingdom. It is available at: www.bl.uk/learning/langlit/sounds/regional-voices/lexical-variation/

References

Andrews, R., Torgerson, C., Beverton, S., Freeman, A., Locke, T., Low, G., et al. (2006) The effect of grammar teaching on writing development. *British Educational Research Journal*, 32, 39–55.
Crystal, D. (2000) *Discover Grammar*. London: Longman.
DfEE (2001) *Developing Early Writing* (DfEE 0055/2001). London: DfEE.
French, R. (2012) Learning the grammatics of quoted speech: Benefits for punctuation and expressive reading. *Australian Journal of Language & Literacy*, 35, 206–222.
Hall, N. (2002) *The Development of Punctuation Knowledge in Children Aged Seven to Eleven Years*. Project report number: ROOO2383348: ESRC
Halliday, M. A. K. (2009) *The Essential Halliday*. London: Continuum.
Mercer, N. and Hodgkinson, S. (Eds) (2008) *Exploring Talk in Schools*. London: Sage.
Myhill, D. (2010) Making textual music with grammar and punctuation. In D. Wyse, R. Andrews and J. Hoffman (Eds), *The Routledge International Handbook of English Language and Literacy Teaching* (pp. 170–181). Abingdon: Routledge.
Myhill, D. and Watson, A. (2014) The role of grammar in the writing curriculum: A review of the literature. *Child Language Teaching and Therapy*, 30, 41–62.

Myhill, D. A., Jones, S. and Bailey, T. C. (2011) Grammar for writing? An investigation of the effects of contextualised grammar teaching on pupils' writing and pupils' metalinguistic understanding. Swindon: ESRC End of Award Report. pp.1241–1263.

Myhill, D., Jones, S., Watson, A. and Lines, H. (2013) Playful explicitness with grammar: A pedagogy for writing. *Literacy*, 47, 103–111.

National Strategy (1999) *Training Modules*. London: DfEE.

Perera, K. (1984) *Children's Writing and Reading: Analysing Classroom Language*. Oxford: Blackwell.

Pullman, P. (2005) Common sense has much to learn from moonshine., *The Guardian*. Available at: www.theguardian.com/education/2005/jan/22/schools. wordsandlanguage

Reedy, D. and Bearne, E. (2013) *Teaching Grammar Effectively in the Primary School*. Leicester: United Kingdom Literacy Association.

Robins, G. (2011) The effect of exploratory talk on the development of sentence structures in able writers. *Literacy*, 45, 78–83.

Saddler, B. (2005) Sentence combining: A sentence-level writing intervention. *Reading Teacher*, 58, 468–471.

Sheard, M. K. and Chambers, B. (in press) A case of technology-enhanced formative assessment and achievement in primary grammar: How is quality assurance of formative assessment assured? *Studies in Educational Evaluation*. doi:http://dx.doi.org/10.1016/j. stueduc.2014.02.001

Standards and Testing Agency (2014) English grammar, punctuation and spelling test framework KS1 & KS2 (draft).

Ref: ISBN 978–1–78315–341–1, STA/14/7099/e

Ref: ISBN 978–1–78315–340–4, STA/14/7098/e Available at: www.gov.uk/government/ collections/national-curriculum (accessed 30 March 2014).

CHAPTER 9

SPELLING AND HANDWRITING

Objectives

1. To identify key features of progression in spelling and handwriting
2. To examine key models of the process of spelling and handwriting
3. To relate progression in spelling and handwriting to daily classroom practice
4. To evaluate common forms of assessment for spelling and handwriting

Introduction

The penultimate chapter of this book concludes the three writing chapters by looking at two transcriptional skills, spelling and handwriting. Spelling can present particular difficulties for a number of pupils, some of whom will require specialist diagnostic assessment and teaching. For this reason, understanding progression in spelling means that class teachers must have a thorough knowledge of the processes of spelling development and be able to recognise what irregular spelling development looks like. With this knowledge teachers are able to tailor the spelling curriculum for maximum impact.

Like spelling, handwriting can also present difficulties and challenges for primary pupils. These can have significant effects on pupils' writing composition and motivation to write. Handwriting fluency is also an aspect of spelling development (Medwell and Wray, 2010). In addition to this, the relationship between keyboarding skills and handwriting needs consideration. Research suggests that handwriting uses knowledge of letter patterns or common strings of letters, while spelling also uses knowledge of phonics (Berninger and Amtmann, 2004).

Despite the convenience of word processing tools such as spellcheckers, auto-correct, predictive text and typed text, both spelling and handwriting are important features of writing progression. Traditionally both of these skills were taught separately from the compositional aspects of writing. Weekly spelling lists and daily handwriting practice exercises typify this approach. However, attention to spelling and handwriting are part of pupils' awareness of writing for an audience and a purpose, integrated into the writing process. In addition, learning to spell successfully is about teaching pupils to use consistent self-correction strategies that build on their personal spelling strengths and preferred methods of learning to spell. Learning to handwrite is about developing a fluent, legible and personal style that enables the pupil to write at speed. Older pupils develop handwriting stamina in preparation for secondary school and beyond.

There is an interconnection between spelling and reading. At its most basic level this is the link between encoding and decoding. Spelling is the ability to encode. Encoding print is the opposite of decoding print, which is part of the reading process. While decoding print, pupils may decipher phonemes, letter strings and whole words to read each word. Reading print also provides contextual clues which independent spelling does not use (Dombey, 2013). Independent spelling asks pupils to read, recall and write each word from memory. This is why spellings are best tested by placing the words in context. A number of different skills may be used to spell such as using mnemonics, rehearsing syllables, onsets and rimes, recalling whole words, blending phonemes and building up parts of words as in compound words or the use of suffixes and prefixes. As well as reading, spelling is also linked to writing fluency (O'Sullivan and Thomas, 2007). The glossary at the end of this book is one reference point for the spelling terminology used here and in the remainder of this chapter.

Activity

Spelling test

Take a spelling test using the following list of words. Use the table to analyse your answers. Use the final column to note the difficult aspects of spelling in each word.

(Continued)

(Continued)

Table 9.1

Words for dictation	Spelling attempt	Order of letters confused/ missing/ reversed/added	Phonemically plausible/ implausible	Random spelling	Other	Analysis
Anaesthetic						
Diarrhoea						
Definitely						
Grammar						
Independent						
Jewellery						
Unnecessary						
Occurrence						
Receipt						
Underrate						

This activity will have caused you to consider your own spelling strategies. You may have used favoured spelling techniques and aspects of the spelling process such as using spelling 'rules', recalling a mnemonic, recognising familiar letter patterns, sounding out phonemes and syllables and writing out different versions to see if it 'looks right'. These strategies are amongst a range of approaches underpinned by visual, auditory and kinaesthetic skills. Learning to spell using a range of approaches like this is called multisensory learning. This approach lies at the heart of learning to spell. Multisensory approaches underlie the importance of equipping pupils with personalised spelling strategies. In the classroom this means that spelling is taught as part of writing composition, rather than always separately from it. In this way it becomes part of a natural editing and proof reading process.

Spelling processes

The processes of learning to spell in an alphabetic system are part of the body of knowledge that deals with phonological, phonemic, orthographic and morphemic knowledge. Each of these can be further subdivided into six areas, which are listed below, adapted from a resource document produced by the Irish National Council for Curriculum and Assessment (Kennedy et al., 2012).

1. Alphabetic knowledge: this is knowledge of letter names and the sequence of the alphabet. In addition to phonemic awareness, it is also essential for later skills such as indexing and dictionary use.

2. Phonemic awareness: this is the ability to discriminate phonemes, aurally and visually, and to be able to pronounce them. It includes the reversible processes of segmenting and blending phonemes.
3. Common English letter patterns or strings of letters in English: this includes being able to discount phoneme sequences not found in English. It is called orthographic knowledge.
4. Phonological awareness: this is the ability to discriminate sounds. It includes knowledge of rhyme, rhythm, onset, rime and syllables.
5. Modifying root words: this is the ability to use morphemic knowledge as a basis for building words. It includes inflections. It may include etymology.
6. **High frequency sight words** are used most often in written text and can include common phonically irregular words. They are often divided into progressive lists for whole word memorisation.

Like writing composition, spelling processes can be viewed from three main angles: cognitive, socio-cultural or linguistic. Like composition, learning to spell also takes place in the context of multimodal texts and digital literacy. Similarly, an investigative approach to learning to spell is a meta-cognitive process.

Cognitive approaches to spellings include the concept of developmental spelling. In general these cognitive approaches suggested that pupils progress from phonological to orthographic and morphological spelling.

Research focus

Staged models of reading and spelling development

Building on earlier staged theories of reading development, the psychologist Uta Frith proposed three stages of spelling and reading (Frith, 1985). In the logographic stage pupils may recognise a small number of whole words by sight. To do this the young child may use the word's shape, colour, font and its context. In the alphabetic stage pupils may use onsets and rimes to find patterns within words and match graphemes to phoneme correspondences (GPCs). In the orthographic stage pupils may use spelling patterns and units of words that are common to written English. There is researched evidence for aspects of Frith's model. For example, exposure to print appears to be related to knowledge of orthographic letter patterns in young primary children (Cunningham and Stanovich, 1991).

Frith's model compares to the well-cited sequence of spelling acquisition developed by J. Richard Gentry (Gentry, 1982). He classifies five stages of spelling development, summarised below.

(Continued)

(Continued)

1. The pre-communicative stage: pupils record random single letters and strings of letters that do not relate to GPCs. Some random numbers may appear.
2. The semi-phonetic stage: pupils record some examples of correct GPCs plus random letters.
3. The phonetic stage: pupils spell phonetically.
4. The transitional stage: pupils use a mix of phonetic spelling and common English orthography.
5. The correct stage: pupils spell correctly.

Critics of staged approaches to spelling express similar arguments to those of staged theories of reading acquisition, discussed in Chapter 4. Not all pupils necessarily pass through each stage because children learn in different ways, have different social and cultural circumstances and have different levels of language acquisition. Instead of learning to spell in a sequential manner it is suggested that pupils use a series of skills that overlap according to circumstance. Older pupils, for example, may revert to phonetic spelling with unfamiliar or foreign words. Research suggests that certain young children use orthographic patterns before their phonemic knowledge is fully formed (summarised in Bourassa and Treiman, 2010). For others, a solid language base combined with frequent reading and writing does not automatically result in good spelling. Some good readers who are poor spellers, for example, fail to use their orthographic reading skills and appear to rely on inconsistent visual cues and phonetic strategies (O'Sullivan and Thomas, 2007). The teachers' role is therefore to distinguish between persistent or fleeting misspellings and early 'invented' or exploratory spelling and to identify potential barriers to spelling development.

Research focus

Socio-cultural and constructivist approaches to spelling

In the 1980s the work of educationalists such as Donald Graves emphasised the importance of creative written composition as part of pupils' socio-cultural development (Graves, 1983). His whole language approach to writing composition has already been discussed in Chapter 7. Graves outlined the importance of pupils' invented spelling as part of other writing processes. Using pupils' written work as evidence, he noted five stages of invention, showing pupils' progressive use of consonants and vowels. For Graves, the content of pupils' work was of paramount importance. Spelling was part of pupils' editing and proof reading process, best addressed with the class teacher's individual help. More recently the work of Gunther Kress describes spelling as a cultural act, as a code learnt and taught as part of the writing process (Kress, 2000). He argues for the place of meaning in the process of learning to spell as part of writing composition, alongside linguistic and cognitive routes. As a consequence teachers need to credit pupils' spelling attempts as well as their accuracy. The work of Graves and Kress reflects socio-cultural and constructivist approaches to learning. Pupils play an active and investigative role in their own learning, enhanced by their use of the meaning and context of words. Developing a progressive and systematic approach to proof reading skills is part of this approach.

Linguistic approaches to spelling incorporate pupils' development in relation to language. In order to spell, pupils must obviously have an oral vocabulary. It is hard to spell if you do not know the words or their meaning. In addition, spelling requires auditory, visual and kinaesthetic skills. These include an ability to pronounce phonemes, syllables, onsets and rimes and to detect analogy (Goswami and Bryant, 1990). Some of this work has particular significance in understanding phonological deficits in dyslexic pupils.

Activity

Associated spelling skills

Decide whether you agree or disagree with the following statements. Rank them in order of importance for lower, middle and upper primary school aged pupils.

1. Pupils who read well will automatically be able to spell correctly by default.
2. Cursive handwriting contributes to orthographic spelling skills.
3. Both printing and cursive handwriting assist phonemic development.
4. Frequent independent writing practise develops writing stamina, writing fluency and independent spelling.
5. Spelling should be taught as a cumulative set of rules alongside proof-reading skills.
6. Pupils should be encouraged to 'have a go' at spelling the words they need.
7. All pupils need to know how to use a dictionary.
8. Spelling must be correct in all final writing drafts.
9. All spelling errors should be corrected by the teacher and re-learnt by the pupil.
10. An interest in words will assist spelling development.

This activity will have caused you to consider the relationships between spelling and the four modes of English, including handwriting. You may have begun to plot the progression of spelling skills across the primary years. You may have looked at the statutory requirements of prescribed curricula and begun to match each of the six aspects of spelling progression noted above. For example, the primary national curriculum in England provides statutory spelling requirements for each year group. Using similar documents it is useful to isolate spelling skills that bridge year groups and those which characterise them individually.

The elements of handwriting

Although there is a good deal of research into the nature of handwriting it has not recently received as much attention in primary schools. Part of the reason for this may be due to a persistent separation between composition and transcription. While the process and emergent models of writing have encouraged the development of pupils' writing composition and owner-ship, the place of handwriting has received less emphasis (Medwell and Wray, 2010).

In order to control the formation of print pupils need to be stable in their upper bodies. They need to have a stable pencil grip to facilitate a fluent writ-ing style. In order to write, pupils must coordinate their eyes, arms and hands. In order to write, pupils must know their grapheme-phoneme correspond-ences and the conventions of writing in English, such as the flow of print from left to right and the sequence of letter formations.

Children come to school at different stages of readiness for handwriting. Early stages of mark making and letter formation have been discussed in Chapter 7. A key point of progression is when pupils know the difference between draw-ing and writing and that print has meaning (Clay, 1999).

The early work of Rosemary Sassoon is of relevance here. She recommends six areas for attention: direction, movement, letter height, capital and lower case letters, spacing and letters with mirror images, reversals or inversions (Sassoon, 2003: 70). Each is significant in developing a fluent and individual writing style from the early years of schooling. Sassoon notes the primary importance of developing correct letter formation alongside pupils' early attempts at writing. 'Once children can write as much as the letters of their own names, they need to be taught the correct movement of each letter. If this is not done, incor-rect movements become habits that are progressively more difficult to alter' (Sassoon, 2003: 2). As handwriting develops, Sassoon observes the balance between correct letter formation and neatness. Correct letter formation comes before letters are joined. Sometimes neatness, as in the production of an ele-gant, copperplate handwriting style, is not conducive to the legible and speedy handwriting skills required at secondary-level schooling. More recently the need for automaticity in handwriting has been linked to orthographic spelling patterns and to composition at the lower and upper ends of primary schooling (Medwell et al., 2007, 2009; Wray and Medwell, 2013).

✎ **Research focus**

Handwriting and keyboard skills

Findings from a study of three hundred primary school children suggested that there were links between handwriting and keyboarding skills (Connelly et al., 2007). None of the sample had been referred for handwriting difficulties. The children did not receive specific touch-typing instruction but children who were fast handwriters were generally fast keyboarders. Some older pupils had better keyboarding than handwriting skills. In the second part of the study the quality of handwritten and typed compositions were compared. Pupils who received higher composition scores were generally those who had the most fluent handwriting. The authors argue for the need for touch-typing instruction in order to maximise word processing skills for written composition.

Table 9.2 presents summaries of the spelling and handwriting skills of our vignette pupils. The table allows us to track some of the features and next steps for progression that can occur across the primary years of schooling. The summaries show different patterns of spelling and handwriting skills.

The progression of spelling and handwriting in the primary classroom

Progression in spelling content incorporates alphabetic knowledge, phonemic awareness, common English letter patterns or strings of letters in English, phonological awareness, modifying root word and high frequency words. An analysis of pupils' spelling errors can reveal pupils' spelling strategies as well as providing insights into the six aspects of spelling progression noted above. Such strategies include visual approaches that focus on recognising common letter patterns. One of the most common visual spelling strategies is summarised in the look-cover-write-check routine (Peters and Smith, 1993). Variations of this routine, such as look-say-cover-write-check or look-say-cover-picture-it-in-your-head-write-check have added visualisation and speaking and listening cues. Other strategies include segmentation and blending, use of syllables, phonemic selection, use of suffixes and prefixes, analogy, and selecting words based on their meaning. The latter can be practised by building words from root words or looking for smaller words within larger ones.

Table 9.2 Summary of spelling and handwriting in the pupil vignettes

Pupil	Age	Attainment level	Key strategies for spelling	Key points in handwriting	Features of progression	Suggested next steps for progression
Japonica	10	Within expected levels	Uses dictionary after writing Uses spell check during word processing Uses mix of root words and morphemes to spell, resorts to phonemes for unfamiliar words	Uses nylon tipped handwriting pen Uses cursive style with some letters abutted rather than joined Letters correctly formed and sized Writes at speed, notes and from dictation Can write for up to 45 minutes independently	Corrects spelling at point of composition and in editing process Evidence of Gentry's transitional and correct stages of spelling	Use thesaurus, and etymology cues Further investigate root words Use own reading interests as part of investigative approach to building orthographic knowledge
Analyn	9	EAL pupil at the earlier stages of English language acquisition	Uses high frequency words from the first 200 word lists Uses suffixes, ed, s, ing, es, ly Some tense confusions	Uses nylon tipped handwriting pen Copperplate handwriting style Slow handwriting speed	Evidence of Gentry's transitional stage of spelling Polysyllabic spelling attempts	Link spelling skills to vocabulary development Dictation to link spelling to word meaning, underlining own errors

Pupil	Age	Attainment level	Key strategies for spelling	Key points in handwriting	Features of progression	Suggested next steps for progression
John	7	Below expected levels	Requests unknown words for personal dictionary before writing Some transfer from taught phonic sessions into own writing High frequency words Weak self-correction	Uses triangular pencil to promote tripod grip, prints, heights inconsistent tailed letters, others correctly formed, and sizes vary Some b/d p/q reversals and inversions Does not form capitals Q, R, H, G Slow handwriting and keyboarding	Spells at point of composition Segments and blends, marks phonemes manually on 'have a go' notepad Evidence of Gentry's phonetic stage of spelling Mainly CVCC, CCVC and CVC patterns	Assess spelling through written sentences to develop word meaning Handwriting patterns to develop fluency plus letter formation through regular phonics teaching
Peter	5	Above expected levels	During some composition, uses 'have a go' notepad Uses word banks found in the classroom, during composition	Uses pencil, tripod grip Print script with entry and exit joins attached but letters are not joined Letter size inconsistent, not on line, formation is mostly correct	Evidence of Gentry's phonetic and transitional stage of spelling	Develop word processing skills alongside handwritten work Monitor letter formation

As with all forms of primary English it is useful to look at a number of different examples from different contexts in order to build a picture of pupils' knowledge and skills. Contexts for spelling and handwriting include independent writing samples, observations of handwriting, sentence dictation, testing spelling in a context, single word spelling tests and the monitoring of pupils' use of spelling aids. These include dictionaries, rough spelling practice notepads to try out unknown spellings, and the use of classroom aids, for example word walls and word banks. Electronic aids such as handheld spellcheckers can assist pupils who have sufficient phonemic skills to input approximations and sufficient vocabulary and visual spelling skills to select from the similar examples that spellcheckers produce.

Analysing spelling errors

Analysing pupils' spelling enables you to detect patterns of error and provides insights into pupils' favoured spelling strategies. These may be phonological, phonemic, orthographic, morphemic, a weak set of high frequency words or visual errors such as where pupils confuse the order and number of letters in a word (Ott, 2007).

ᗌᗺ **Reflection questions**

- What evidence is there for Analyn's ability to experiment with her spelling? How would you rate her spelling confidence?
- How would you address Japonica's difficulty with **homophones**?
- How and why would you encourage polysyllabic spelling?
- Which pupils have confused the morpheme *ed*?

Classroom application   A classroom where pupils are afraid to make spelling errors can upset pupils' confidence to tackle new written vocabulary and reduce their fluent writing (Bearne, 2002). However, this does not mean that pupils should ignore correct spelling in the process of writing composition. In the classroom, pupils learn to be independent spellers gradually, by making spelling mistakes, recognising them and developing strategies to address spelling correction that work for them. These strategies are pupils' spelling strengths. They may use a combination of kinaesthetic, aural, oral and visual strategies and cues. These are part of a multi-sensory approach. Word meaning is part of this. For some pupils a single route dominates, which teachers may exploit. For example, pupils with weaker visual memories may benefit from more opportunities to segment and blend aurally. As reading develops pupils are exposed to a wider written vocabulary.

Activity

Look at the examples of independent writing from the pupil vignettes. Record the evidence of spelling content and suggested next steps and add to the evidence of possible spelling strategies for each pupil. The second section has been completed for you.

Table 9.3

Pupil	Sample of independent writing	Evidence of spelling content	Evidence of spelling strategies	Suggested next steps in spelling progression
Japonica	*My street is full of rubbish. It is not nice because it smells in the summer and it is blon all over the place in the winter. Their are people who drop litter, there not thinking of others. But we also need less packging to throw away in the first place. Another nasty thing is dog muck on the pavement. Wreckless owners do not clean up after there dogs. It's distgusting! They're should be a program to show them that dog muck is dangrous.*		She learns weekly spellings using look, say, cover, write and check She corrects spelling after composition	
John	*I tok the tost for my brekfst and got into my tente on the campsit in the forist.*	43 words, 14 spelled incorrectly	Relies mainly on phonic strategies with some visual strategies	Develop polysyllabic words, introduce long vowels,

(Continued)

Pupil	Sample of independent writing	Evidence of spelling content	Evidence of spelling strategies	Suggested next steps in spelling progression
	It rand and there saw thunder. Mum brot me a picnic with litle sanwchs. I slep in the tent and wockd up in the moning	His vocabulary choice is not restricted to familiar spelling. Some short vowel errors. Does not use ai, ea, oa, oo. Order of letters is sometimes mixed (was/saw). Inconsistent use of 'magic e' (split vowel digraph). High frequency words mostly correct	Uses blends and consonant digraphs correctly. Sounds out phonemes, matching to his fingers as he counts, writes and says them together	consolidate consonant vowel digraphs
Analyn	*It was a windi day. The lade has a red hat on. She is a prette lady but she is sad and cring She has lost a dog. The dog is gon. She walked home sadly.*		Learns spellings orally by rote, reciting phonemes	
Peter	*One day there was a hen who wanted to plant some seed in the midel of a feld. Who will help me. Not i said the dog. not i sed the cat, not i sed the mouse. I will do it mysef sed the hen. Who will help me cut the whet sed the hen. The dog, the mouse and cat sed no. The hen made new bred. The dog, cat and mouse wantd to eat it but the hen sed no. I will do it mysef.*		Visual and auditory memory for whole words, confident to have a go at spelling the words he wishes to use. Uses peer marking to circle incorrect words	

Spelling aids

This section is designed to present a range of practical spelling aids and resources for pupils' day-to-day classroom use. Some of these resources are designed to exploit particular spelling strategies; others employ a multi-sensory approach. The range includes materials to develop phonological, phonemic, orthographic and morphemic spelling, plus high frequency words. More generic activities to promote an interest in words have not been included. These are part of a regular spelling curriculum.

ᔑᔑ Reflection questions

- Why does Peter appear to use the fewest physical examples of spelling aids?
- What are the benefits and drawbacks of using dictionaries for each pupil?
- In terms of a multi-sensory approach to spelling, how would you describe Japonica's and Analyn's preferred spelling strategies?
- Which pupils also use word meanings to aid their spelling?

Classroom application In the classroom, exploiting pupils' use of spelling aids begins by building an interest in words and by encouraging pupils' spelling attempts. Self-regulation is central. This may be developed by individual usage but also through peer marking and partnered spelling testing. For older pupils, some selection for their own list of misspellings for testing can contribute to pupils' awareness of patterns of spelling errors, as well as patterns of spelling strength. Spelling aids include:

- personal, alphabetised word books for collecting unknown spellings;
- customised spelling dictionaries, including those for phonics or subject terminology;
- various commercial dictionaries and thesauruses;
- 'have a go' practice notepads;
- computer spelling packages for reinforcement, speech recognition software and talking word processors;
- handheld spellcheckers;
- classroom word walls or word banks;
- misspelling reminder posters;
- generic spelling strategy tips;
- key word displays such as days of the week, months and numbers;
- topic specific word displays;
- interactive word displays;

Activity

Look at the examples of the use of spelling aids from the pupil vignettes. Record suggested next steps for progression and add to the evidence for spelling strategies possible for each pupil. The fourth section has been completed for you.

Table 9.4

Pupil	Examples of the use of spelling aids	Evidence of spelling strategies	Suggested next steps in spelling progression
Japonica	Uses standard dictionary, Spellchecker, edits work after completion but not always thoroughly. Collects examples of derivations from root words in rough book planning. Rough book drafts show crossings out and multiple spelling attempts during composition. Enjoys crosswords and word searches.	She learns weekly spellings using look, say, cover, write and check Refers to common misspellings wall chart	
John	Personal phonic dictionary, classroom word walls, 'have a go' notepads, blends and segments using magnetic letters. Some written words have marked phonemes. Order of letters can be mixed up when he copies out given spellings.	Sounds out phonemes, matching to his fingers as he counts, and then writes and says the phonemes before blending to say the whole word	
Analyn	Dual language picture dictionary. Classroom dual language signage. Copies correct spelling from captioned visual prompt cards for individual lessons.	Learns spellings orally by rote, reciting phonemes	
Peter	Uses and contributes to the word walls in the classroom. Draws a blank 'magic' line if attempting adventurous words with some unknown phonemes. Words are clearly spaced. Uses rhyme to write words that sound the same: make, take, cake, ball, small, tall etc. Enjoys age appropriate word searches.	Visual and auditory memory for words, confident to have a go at spelling the words he wishes to use	Confident use of simple dictionaries

- classroom labels;
- alphabet and phoneme charts.

Observing and analysing handwriting

The purpose of observing and analysing pupils' handwriting is to measure the progress of letter formation and handwriting fluency. Examining a range of handwriting samples in context can also alert teachers to specific issues that may require additional intervention. These include physical coordination and visual problems. Areas for observation and analysis include letter formation, posture, pencil grip, letter size and proportion and letters on the line, spacing, consistent joins in cursive script and the consistency of hooks on letters in pre-cursive script.

Activity

Look at the observations and descriptions of handwriting from the pupil vignettes. Record suggested next steps for handwriting progression and their links to spelling for each pupil. The first section has been completed for you.

Table 9.5

Pupil	Observation of handwriting behaviour	Description of independent handwriting	Suggested next steps in handwriting progression	Links to spelling progression
Japonica	Japonica can take legible notes from speech and film. She can write legibly for up to 45 minutes, without strain, using nylon tipped handwriting pens. She is right handed with a tripod grip. She tilts the page to the left to suit her slightly slanted cursive script. She lifts her pen in the middle of words to form un-joined letters.	Japonica uses cursive script with some letters partially joined. Her words are evenly spaced and of equal sizing. There is evidence of developing personal style; she draws small circles above the letter i, shorter joins help her to write faster.	Use different handwriting implements. Monitor written work for consistent presentation across the curriculum.	Observe the speed and fluency of written spelling test dictations.

(Continued)

(Continued)

Pupil	Observation of handwriting behaviour	Description of independent handwriting	Suggested next steps in handwriting progression	Links to spelling progression
John	*John is right handed. He can copy and trace print. He uses a tripod grip but it is not stable. He uses a triangular pencil to develop his tripod grip. He does not write fluently and avoids handwriting if the keyboard is available. He tends to rest his head on his non-writing arm. He does not enjoy drawing or colouring.*	John writes an uneven print. K is inconsistently formed. Round letters are mostly correct but irregular in size. John has most difficulty writing fluent zigzag strokes as part of handwriting stroke practice. His words are not evenly spaced.		
Analyn	*Analyn is right handed. She uses a nylon tipped handwriting pen but is capable of using a cartridge pen. She takes extreme care to produce very neat work. She writes slowly and carefully.*	Analyn uses an upright copperplate style.		
Peter	*Peter is left handed. He uses a pencil. He enjoys drawing, colouring and manipulative tasks. Although he tilts his book to write, Peter finds it difficult to write on lines. He writes fluently but slowly in his work books but more freely elsewhere.*	The sample shows print with attached entry and exit hooks on round letters as part of pre-cursive handwriting preparation.		

〰️ **Reflection questions**

- How can John's writing fluency be developed through his phonics programme?
- What playful handwriting and drawing exercises would increase Peter's writing speed?
- What are the benefits and possible drawbacks of Analyn's copperplate writing as part of a multisensory approach to spelling?

Classroom application In the classroom, handwriting can be taught as part of the spelling process. Handwriting is a kinaesthetic route as part of a multisensory spelling approach. The second aspect for classroom teaching is handwriting fluency, leading to the ability to handwrite automatically. Short, sustained and extended writing provides daily writing opportunities. Pupils also benefit from discrete teaching of letter strokes and oval letter formations. A number of commercial schemes are available for this or individual schools may develop their own teaching package. Teachers need to consider the benefits and drawbacks of whole class handwriting teaching as opposed to small guided writing groups.

The assessment of spelling and handwriting

Summative assessment of spelling includes standardised spelling tests that give a spelling age for comparison with pupils' reading and chronological ages. Typically, summative spelling assessments ask pupils to insert missing words into sentences or to write words read aloud by the tester. The meaning of the word is made specific.

Diagnostic spelling assessment aims to uncover areas of weakness and strength across phonological, phonemic, orthographic and morphological areas of spelling. They identify pupils' visual and auditory spelling processes. Sensory impairment such as intermittent hearing loss can affect the progression of spelling in the primary years. Particular physical impairment such as dyspraxia or cerebral palsy can affect the progression of handwriting. Teachers need to be alert to the implications of physical and sensory impairment and to be proactive in addressing potential barriers to progression.

The activity may have caused you to summarise spelling errors into broad phonemic and visual categories. You may have noted missing and additional letters. Generally, errors are considered by looking at spelling across a number of pieces of pupils' written text in order to see patterns of spelling strategies

Activity

Analysing spelling errors

Complete the table to indicate possible spelling strategies. One entry has been added.

Table 9.6

Example	Actual word	Possible phonemic strategy	Possible orthographic strategy	Possible morphological strategy	High frequency word or homophone error	Notes
they're	there					
wet	went	✓			✓	Possible incomplete visual recall of high frequency word and/or confusion with sounding nt
playn	plane					
Yor	your					
begining	beginning					
Spshll	special					

as well as errors. Some pupils use random spellings that do not approximate to English spelling (Peters and Smith, 1993). If pupils in receipt of structured spelling and phonics programmes continue to use a majority of random spellings in independent writing, further specialist teaching advice may be necessary.

Spelling tests

Spelling tests are both summative and formative methods of assessment. Although they have a traditional place in primary classrooms, both the quality and purpose of spelling tests needs consideration. The purposes of spelling tests are to assess understanding of the taught spelling curriculum and see the transference of knowledge and skills into pupils' everyday writing. Summative test results may also be required by external bodies to judge pupils' ability against national or chronological benchmarks. Summative assessments are also a measure of the effectiveness of teaching and the rigour of the spelling curriculum itself.

 Activity

Look at the examples of spelling tests from the pupil vignettes. Record suggested next steps and spelling content for each pupil. The third section three has been completed for you.

Table 9.7

Pupil	Examples of single word spelling tests	Evidence of spelling content	Suggested next steps in spelling progression
Japonica	Act, react, activity, actor, action, sign, signature, signal, significant		
John	staem (steam), red (read) grass, spot, ship, shed, tent, tree		
Analyn	Things (think), going, agian (again), everyone (everywhere), hoped (hopped), Plaid (played), said, pip(pipe)	Uses high frequency words. Some evidence of whole word and phoneme substitutions. Phonetic spelling with transitional elements	Develop common word endings. Consolidate split vowel digraph and range of alternative spellings for phonemes

(Continued)

(Continued)

Pupil	Examples of single word spelling tests	Evidence of spelling content	Suggested next steps in spelling progression
Peter	Playground, football, playtime, handbag, farmhouse, hairgrip, eggcup		

∿ Reflection questions

- Characteristically, Japonica achieves 100 per cent for most of her spelling tests but continues to misspell some tested words. She does not use them in her regular writing. How would you address this issue?
- Analyn spells 'think' as 'things', why?
- What aspects of spelling are assessed in the lists for Japonica and Peter?

Formative assessment of spelling concerns the development of pupils' spelling strategies and their ability to apply these strategies to their own writing. For the class teacher this will also include careful records of taught spelling and its assessment through pupils' reading and writing. Useful approaches include short, cumulative spelling lessons that culminate in weekly spelling tests, pupil self- and peer testing, differentiated spelling groups, activities to promote an interest in words and allocated proof reading and editing time. Establishing routines for monitoring spelling is a key part of formative spelling assessment. A consistent, relevant and manageable marking policy, for instance, allows pupils to address their spelling errors and to be praised for their spelling attempts.

The assessment of handwriting has tended to focus on two descriptors: style and speed. Style is assessed through general descriptors of letter formation and the legibility of the script. These are often part of commercial handwriting schemes. Handwriting speed is often assessed when pupils have particular difficulties. Sometimes a separate commercial assessment of handwriting speed is required to fulfil criteria for additional support in formal examinations. It is important to remember the kinaesthetic aspects of handwriting assessment since these will affect written outcomes and writing speed.

Table 9.8 Observing progression in spelling and handwriting

	Alphabetic knowledge	Phonological awareness and spelling strategies	Phonemic awareness	Orthography and high frequency words	Morphology and mnemonics	Handwriting letter formation and fluency
Lower primary years	Recites alphabet Distinguishes upper and lower case letters, reorders letters of the alphabet Simple dictionary and word bank use	Confidence to attempt exploratory spelling Generates, recognises, discriminates rhyme and rhythm patterns, onset and rime, use of analogy	Know common GPCs Segments and blends phonemes orally, visually and aurally, phonemically feasible spelling attempts	High frequency words Uses single, double and polysyllabic words Find difficult spelling elements in given words	Beginning to use prefixing and suffixing in spelling Beginning to use compound words, and to recognise simple homophones	Secure handwriting grip Uses pencil Developing letter formation of print script or early cursive, spaced words Early keyboard and word processing skills
Middle primary years	Dictionary, word bank and indexing skills	Continue use of analogy plus syllables, developing own spelling strategies	Segments and blends phonemes orally, visually and aurally, confident use of polysyllabic words	High frequency words Find difficult spelling elements in words Reading repertoire builds written vocabulary	Suffix and prefix rules become established May use mnemonics, and simple spelling rules, extends homophones	Secure handwriting grip Fluent handwriting with developing stamina Developing cursive script, correct formation
Upper primary years	Confident use of a range of dictionaries, thesaurus and indexing skills	Established use of syllables, phonemes and analogy, describes own spelling strategies	Segments and blends phonemes orally, visually and aurally May use phonemes as primary strategy with unknown words out of context	Recognises irregular spelling patterns for the English language, visual strategies Wider reading repertoire builds written vocabulary	Established strategies for own proof reading routines e.g. spelling rules, mnemonics and building words from root words, secure homophones	Fluent, speedy and sustained cursive script contains elements of personal style Uses pen Established keyboard and word processing

Table 9.8 presents a matrix of primary English progression observing broad areas of progression in spelling and handwriting. Use this grid as a guide for classroom observations, initial marking, shared and guided writing.

Summary of chapter

This chapter has summarised the elements of handwriting and the processes of spelling. Multisensory approaches to spelling have been emphasised along with the development of a fluent handwriting style. Spelling and handwriting have been considered as an essential part of the process of writing composition in order that the pupil may transfer discrete spelling and handwriting skills to their independent writing. Pupil vignettes illustrated individual examples of progression in the use of spelling aids, the spelling curriculum and individual spelling strategies. Observations and descriptions of handwriting were included.

? **Self-assessment**

1. List and justify three items that you consider important features or next steps for progression in spelling or handwriting. Choose items for the oldest, mid-range and youngest pupils in the primary school.
2. Relate linguistic, socio-cultural or cognitive research perspectives to common examples of classroom practice in the teaching of handwriting or spelling.
3. List evidence for the importance of monitoring handwriting and spelling as part of writing composition; include digital and multimodal texts.

Annotated further reading

Wyse, D. Andrews, R. and Hoffman, J. (Eds) (2010) *The Routledge International Handbook of English Language and Literacy Teaching*. Abingdon: Routledge.
Read Chapter 16, Bourassa, D. and Treiman, R., Linguistic foundations of spelling development. Also useful is Chapter 17, Medwell, J. and Wray, D., Handwriting and writing. Both chapters provide succinct overviews of key issues in spelling and handwriting.

Sassoon, R. (2003) *Handwriting* (2nd edn). London: Paul Chapman Publishing.
This classic handwriting textbook provides classroom materials and guidance.

Further resources

Bearne, E. (2002) *Making Progress in Writing*. London: Routledge.

Ott, P. (2007) *How to Manage Spelling Successfully*. London: Routledge.
Both texts present a wealth of practical classroom resources and guidance for monitoring progression.

Allcock, J. (2009) *The English Spelling Dictionary*. New Zealand: MJA Publishing (ISBN 9780958293099).
This notebook dictionary is useful for developing pupils' familiarity with spelling classifications. It contains space for pupils to record their own spelling. Available at: www.papakuraeducation.co.nz/index.php/teachers/english-spelling-dictionary-by-joy-allcock.html

References

Bearne, E. (2002) *Making Progress in Writing*. London: Routledge.

Berninger, V. and Amtmann, D. (2004) Preventing written expression disabilities through early and continuing assessment of handwriting and/or spelling problems: Research into practice. In L. Swanson, K. Harris and S. Graham (Eds), *Handbook of Research on Learning Disabilities*. New York: Guilford. pp. 345–363.

Bourassa, D. and Treiman, R. (2010) Linguistic foundations of spelling development. In D. Wyse, R. Andrews and J. Hoffman (Eds), *The Routledge International Handbook of English Language and Literacy Teaching*. Abingdon: Routledge.

Clay, M. (1999) *Becoming Literate: The Construction of Inner Control*. Auckland: Heinemann.

Connelly, V., Gee, D. and Walsh, E. (2007) A comparison of keyboarded and handwritten compositions and the relationship with transcription speed. *British Journal of Educational Psychology*, 77, 479–492.

Cunningham, A. E. and Stanovich, K. E. (1991) Tracking the unique effects of print exposure in children: Associations with vocabulary, general knowledge and spelling. *Journal of Educational Psychology*, 83, 264–274.

Dombey, H. (2013) *Teaching Writing: What the Evidence Says*. Leicester: UKLA.

Frith, U. (1985) Beneath the surface of developmental dyslexia. In J. Patterson, J. C. Marshal and M. Coltheart (Eds), *Surface Dyslexia*. Mahwah, NJ: Lawrence Erlbaum Associates. (pp. 301–330).

Gentry, J. R. (1982) An analysis of developmental spelling in 'GNYS at WRK'. *The Reading Teacher*, 36, 192–200.

Goswami, U. and Bryant, P. (1990) *Phonological Skills and Learning to Read*. Hillsdale, NJ: Lawrence Erlbaum.

Graves, D. H. (1983) *Writing: Teachers and Children at Work*. Portsmouth, NH: Heinemann.

Kennedy, E., Dunphy, E., Dwyer, B., Hayes, G., McPhillips, T., Marsh, J., et al. (2012) *Literacy in Early Childhood and Primary Education (3–8 years)*. Dublin: National Council for Curriculum and Assessment.

Kress, G. (2000). *Early Spelling: Between Convention and Creativity*. London: Routledge.

Medwell, J., Strand, S. and Wray, D. (2007) The role of handwriting in composing for Y2 children. *Journal of Reading, Writing and Literacy*, 2, 18–36.

Medwell, J., Strand, S. and Wray, D. (2009) The links between handwriting and composing in Y6 children. *Cambridge Journal of Education*, 39, 329–344.

Medwell, J. and Wray, D. (2010) Handwriting and writing. In D. Wyse, R. Andrews and J. Hoffman (Eds), *The Routledge International Handbook of English Language and Literacy Teaching*. Abingdon: Routledge.

O'Sullivan, O. and Thomas, A. (2007) *Understanding Spelling*. Abingdon: Routledge.

Ott, P. (2007) *How to Manage Spelling Successfully*. London: Routledge.

Peters, M. L. and Smith, B. (1993) *Spelling in Context*. Windsor: NFER Nelson.

Sassoon, R. (2003) *Handwriting* (2nd edn). London: Paul Chapman Publishing.

Wray, D. and Medwell, J. (2013) Handwriting automaticity: the search for performance thresholds. *Language and Education*, 28, 34–51.

CHAPTER 10

LOOKING FORWARD

Objectives

1. To summarise current issues in primary English across examples of pedagogical and cross-disciplined research
2. To relate these themes to daily classroom practice

Introduction

The final chapter of this book is designed to introduce examples of current issues related to primary English progression and to link them to classroom practice. The chapter is divided into two sections. The first section looks at examples of current pedagogical issues in primary English progression. Examples of research from education, cognitive neuroscience, ethnography and psychology appear. This cross-disciplined approach is designed to strengthen understanding of broader factors in primary English progression. The second section revisits the themes of progression in learning found in Chapter 1.

One of the roles of the practising class teacher and student teacher is to be informed by current curriculum and pedagogical innovations. Increasing your professional knowledge enhances your judgement of the relevance of the myriad of teaching approaches, resources and official directives that are part of the process of education in school.

After initial teacher training and a statutory period of probationary classroom teaching, teachers build their professional knowledge through five main routes:

1. Classroom practice and dialogue with colleagues
2. Regular in-service training
3. Membership of subject associations and teaching unions
4. Additional specialist teaching qualifications and further academic study
5. Published literature, including 'classroom ready' resources, the educational press, peer reviewed academic journals and regulatory reports such as those produced by the Office for Standards in Education in England (Ofsted)

It is hard for busy classroom and student teachers to devote enough time to exploit these resources. In-service training may be initially directed to immediate training priorities in the current school. Teachers' preparation time is prioritised for planning, marking, preparation of resources and assessment as well as seasonal demands such as annual report writing.

Activity

Barometers of English and literacy issues

Since 1997, the International Reading Association in the USA has produced a regular survey to determine the significance of a range of issues related to reading, literacy and English education (Cassidy et al., 2010). These 'What's Hot and What's Not' surveys are completed mostly by university professors. Each collates popular themes and those which are receiving less publicised attention. Neither are necessarily the same areas popular in English and literacy research at the time. Similar surveys were conducted by the National Literacy Trust in England in 2008 and 2009 (National Literacy Trust, 2009).

Look at the examples of recurring themes taken from both surveys below. Rate them in order of importance for lower, middle and upper primary school children. Add examples of evidence to support your ratings. Make links between the four modes of English and to linguistic, socio-cultural or cognitive frameworks. Multimodal texts and meta-cognitive references may be included. One example has been completed for you.

Table 10.1

Key literacy issues	Rating	Examples of evidence	Possible theoretical framework	Suggested links to four modes of English
Phonics	Key element of early reading acquisition and primary spelling	Rose, J. (2006) *Independent review of early reading: Final report.* London: DfES. Statutory non-word reading test for youngest primary pupils in England Dombey, H. (2010) *Teaching reading: what the evidence says.* Leicester: UKLA Use of multimodal resources as part of multisensory phonic teaching	Mix of socio-cultural, cognitive and linguistic frameworks	Decoding print and spelling
Comprehension				
Vocabulary				
Reading for pleasure				
Literacy in the early years				
Parental involvement				
Reading intervention				

This activity will have caused you to evaluate the importance of some key areas of primary English and to review again the links between the four modes of English in the context of school and pupils' homes and communities. You also may have identified an imbalance in your knowledge of a range of evidence to support your ratings. Perhaps you have mainly used Ofsted reports or the popular press with less reference to research or professional literature. Not all classroom practice is based on peer reviewed research and not all peer reviewed research is based on classroom practice, but both may inform the other to some degree. Many issues in primary English and literacy also adopt a mixed theoretical framework, embedded in a pragmatic approach to meeting the diversity of pupils' needs found in the classroom.

Pedagogical issues in primary English progression

Research is a very important element of learning to teach but classrooms are complex places to observe and understand the processes of learning. While surveys and summative assessments can measure attainment, collate opinion and gather pupil data, details of the context for such evidence can provide much more information about effective teaching and learning. Research from other disciplines also can contribute. It is this combination that allows classroom teachers to identify patterns of effective teaching and learning for their own school contexts.

This section looks at some of the recurring pedagogical issues in primary English progression. It has used three main sources: the international Progress in Reading Literacy Survey (PIRLS) (Mullis et al., 2012), North American and English versions of the 'What's Hot and What's Not' surveys of reading and literacy cited above, and recent Ofsted reports. The selections are not exclusive sources for all primary English issues but are intended to give a flavour of international and national issues while comparing and contrasting different types of evidence to support them.

International reading achievement data surveys

The international Progress in Reading Literacy Study has been noted in Chapter 1. It measures reading ability in the 9–10 year old age range. In 2011 the summary report noted that girls continue to outperform boys. In particular, girls were better readers of literary fiction. Non-fiction presented fewer difficulties for either gender. The highest performing countries had more pupils capable of using higher order reading skills. Taking part in early literacy activities such as reading books, playing with alphabet toys and word play games, a supportive home environment and positive reading attitudes, contributed to higher reading attainment. The quality of physical school resources were linked to attainment as were pupils' basic nutrition and amounts of sleep.

The Office for Standards in Education

In England, the Office for Standards in Education (Ofsted) is a national regulatory body, responsible for monitoring standards of education in state schools. Similar bodies exist in other countries such as the Educational Review Office in New Zealand and the School Excellence Model in Singapore (Teen, 2003). The actual process of school inspection has a different emphasis and structure in each country.

As well as being responsible for inspecting schools, Ofsted produces a number of annual and specialist reports. Each report offers recommendations and directives to improve attainment, teaching and learning. In English, girls continue to achieve more than boys. A tail of underachievement is also recorded (Ofsted, 2008, 2011a, 2011b, 2012).

School inspections reveal that effective English teaching is characterised by engaging pupils through challenge, rigour and excellent differentiation for all aspects of English, including those pupils who require additional intervention. In schools identified as centres of excellence for English teaching and learning, boys do as well as girls. Pupils' English knowledge and skills from outside of school are incorporated into daily classroom practice.

The 'What's Hot and What's Not' surveys in the US and in England

It is possible to classify the themes from the English and North American 'What's Hot and What's Not' surveys into four categories: philosophies and approaches, curriculum content, classroom resources, assessment and age of schooling (Cassidy et al., 2010; Cassidy & Ortlieb, 2011). Under these broad headings themes recur in the US and in England. The US authors note decreasing emphasis on reading fluency, phonics and phonemic awareness, noting that they have become embedded in a range of established classroom practices such as guided reading and discrete phonics teaching. However, comprehension and vocabulary development are now a focus for concern (Cassidy et al., 2010). The 2009 survey in England prioritised reading for pleasure, literacy in the early years and parental involvement (National Literacy Trust, 2009).

Common strands

An analysis of the three sources of evidence shows common areas of concern. Table 10.2 shows overarching issues to affect English progression: gender, parental involvement, independent learning, marking and curricular targets and transition. Overarching curriculum issues are also represented: cross-curricular literacy, high stakes testing and **balanced approaches** to teaching literacy and English. Lastly, specific literacy issues are shown: phonics and early reading, reading motivation and comprehension, developing writing and interventions. The appearance of adolescent literacy points to the importance of laying strong English foundations in the primary school. It also links to cross-curricular and transition issues.

Table 10.2   Issues in English progression

Issue	What's Hot and What's Not data	Ofsted	PIRLS
Gender	X	X	X
Reading comprehension	X	X	X
Reading motivation	X	X	X
Non-fiction	X	X	X
Parental involvement and home environment	X	X	X
Early reading and phonics, early intervention	X	X	
Adolescent literacy	X	X	
Cross-curricular literacy, balanced approaches to teaching English	X	X	
Developing writing	X	X	
High-stakes testing and test preparation	X	X	
Transitions between early years and secondary		X	
Independent learning		X	
Marking and curricular targets		X	

Teaching to address these common issues incorporates a balanced approach to English teaching. This integrates the four modes of English, critical thinking skills and the use of digital and multimedia texts (Cassidy and Ortlieb, 2013). Cross-curricular literacy is part of this. A balanced reading approach generally incorporates reading skills and **whole language approaches** to becoming a reader; pupils use both top down and bottom up approaches to reading acquisition.

The next activity will have caused you to consider the links between the four modes of English. You may have noted fluency, comprehension, phonics, phonemic awareness or vocabulary as part of reading instruction, identified as those 'with sufficient research to warrant conclusions' by the National Reading Panel in the US but not at the expense of other aspects of reading acquisition (Cassidy et al., 2010: 644). In understanding progression, primary student teachers are learning to identify the most significant aspects of pupils' learning for maximum progress. Progress is not necessarily linear but recursive. It can, for example, be characterised by independence, application, wider or deeper understanding or increased confidence with basic concepts. Each of these may build to the next level of attainment.

Current issues in the pupil vignettes

Look at the selections of next steps for progression taken from the pupil vignettes. Match the selections to wider issues in English progression. The first one has been done for you.

Table 10.3

Pupil	Sample of suggested next steps for progression	Chapter reference	Suggested related pedagogical issue	Notes
Japonica	Uses evidence from the text, extracts key words for note taking, informed selection of various texts for own research, secure reading repertoire	Reading comprehension	Cross-curricular literacy transition between key year groups, reading motivation and reading comprehension	Reading repertoire, note taking and research skills contribute to secondary subject English and secondary English skills across the curriculum A fluent handwriting style is necessary
Analyn	Vocabulary comprehension and expression, including simple idiomatic phrases in conversation	Speaking and listening		
Japonica	Add further detail to description; add dialogue, paragraphs, starts sentences in different ways	Writing composition		
Peter	Vocabulary comprehension, asking for help if unsure	Speaking and listening		
Analyn	Building spoken and read vocabulary, building oral prediction, recall skills and story sequencing skills	Reading comprehension		
John	Increased fluency, recall sequence of main events, uses range of strategies to decode	Reading acquisition		

Reading motivation and reading comprehension

The PIRLS data shows a decline in pupils' attitudes towards reading. Between countries surveyed by the PIRLS, countries with the highest average reading performance scores recorded poor motivations to read. Within countries the more able readers express more positive reading attitude than readers with lower levels of reading comprehension (Twist et al., 2012). In England, pupils are less successful at retrieving and inferring from written text than they are at interpreting, integrating and evaluating it. These findings present questions about the relationship of reading comprehension to reading attitudes.

It is possible to look at reading motivation and reading comprehension from a combination of cognitive, socio-cultural and linguistic perspectives. The purpose of reading is to draw meaning from text for specific purposes. The level of reading comprehension is linked to this purpose. For example academic reading requires a deeper level of synthesis and application in order for students to comprehend and interpret readings with sufficient levels of criticality. Personal reading for pleasure does not make these demands but may require others such as reading stamina for extended novel reading or self-selection skills to choose the 'just right' text in the first instance. Many of these skills are linked to pupils' reading expectations and the value attached to the activity itself (Wigfield and Eccles, 2000). Reading motivation is also part of a much larger debate on reading and literacy engagement as a whole (Guthrie et al. 2012). Both academic and personal readings require different degrees and combinations of cognitive, socio-cultural and linguistic perspectives to aid comprehension.

Research focus

Rewarding reading motivation

Reading motivations grow from the reward of discovery and immersion in relevant text. The Accelerated Reader (AR) is an established commercial tool designed to encourage pupils to read for pleasure. The scheme tracks pupils' progress and personal reading choices from a library. Competitive reading quizzes determine pupils' reading comprehension of the books they have chosen. Initial assessments enable pupils to read books at a suitable level of readability (Renaissance Learning, 2014; Topping, 2014). In 2012 a complementary survey of AR results in the UK looked at reading attitude (Clarke, 2013). 34,910 eight to sixteen year olds participated. Thirty-two per cent of this number said that they used AR. The use of AR was of particular benefit to pupils in secondary schools. Using AR seems to enhance boys' reading attitude. Differences in pupils using AR from different socioeconomic backgrounds were generally not significant. These results highlight the potential of commercial reading reward packages for particular groups of pupils.

Classroom application In the classroom, managing reading motivation and comprehension places a considerable responsibility on class teachers to promote active reading communities. Class teachers and pupils alike benefit from a literature rich environment where all types of text are valued (Cremin et al., 2009). This includes digital and visual literacies such as the use of high quality picture books throughout the primary school years. Interactive talking books online are also useful. The nature and effectiveness of rewards for reading also needs consideration.

Phonics and early reading

The teaching of phonics as part of early reading has been a controversial subject. Part of this controversy has arisen from different emphases on the nature and sequence of strategies required for reading acquisition (Dombey, 2010). Learning to read involves a number of different strategies, including phonics. These include the use of analogy (Goswami and Bryant, 1990), semantic and syntactic (Graham and Kelly, 2008) reading cues and the use of English orthography (Bourassa and Treiman, 2010). In models of the reading process, different emphasis is given to different strategies. For example, in orchestration models (Bussis et al. 1985) all pupils are said to use a mixture of semantic, syntactic, grapho-phonic and phonic cues to strategically decode print.

✍ Research focus

The phonics screening test

In 2012 a statutory phonics screening test was introduced for six year old pupils in England. Pupils taking the phonics screening test are required to read aloud 20 pseudo words and 20 real words. Each word is phonically regular. The screening test is intended to 'make sure that all pupils have learned phonic decoding to an appropriate standard by the age of six' and 'to indentify the children who need extra help' (Department for Education, 2014). A recent study was designed to see if the screening test identified pupils at risk of reading difficulty and how usefully it measured decoding (Duff et al., 2014). Results from the 292 six-year-old pupils who took part in the study suggest that the screening test is a valid measure of phonics skills and that it was capable of identifying pupils at risk of reading difficulty. Teachers in the study were also able to assess phonics progression reliably. Their school-based assessments of pupils' progression through six phonic phases of instruction (Primary National Strategy, 2007; Rose, 2006) related more strongly to measures of reading comprehension, another aspect of reading. The smaller sample size for this study is noted by the authors in respect of its ability to substantiate a national screening process. This research highlights the importance of linking formative and summative assessment in the process of monitoring pupils' phonic progression as part of reading and spelling.

Neuroscience is the study of the brain. The work is usually carried out in a laboratory rather than the classroom or other social contexts. Evidence from studies in neuroscience can provide us with a fascinating insight into how the brain develops and what may underlie effective learning. Cognitive neuroscience examines this link between the physical attributes of the brain and thinking. Neuroscience and cognitive neuroscience use a number of different techniques to measure brain activity. Two of the most familiar are functional Magnetic Resonance Imaging (fMRI), providing electronic images of the brain, and electroencephalography (EEG), which identifies electrical activity produced by the brain. Insights from cognitive neuroscience have looked at infant sensitivity to sound.

Research focus

Detecting onsets and syllables

Studies of infants suggest that they can identify different stress patterns in sound and that some of these patterns relate to understanding word meanings. Some of this research has found significant differences between the ability of dyslexic and non-dyslexic pupils, young early readers and regular readers to identify cues to the stress applied to syllables (Goswami et al. 2002). This research contributes to our understanding of the mechanisms involved in phonological awareness.

Classroom application   In the classroom, the teaching of phonics is part of a range of multisensory methods used to teach pupils to read and spell. This includes teaching phonological awareness leading to phonemic awareness in the early stages of reading acquisition. Planning for phonics progression involves a systematic application of the assess, plan, teach, practise, apply, and review primary teaching cycle (DfES, 2006) in addition to identifying the frequency and duration of discrete phonics teaching sessions for different age groups and pupils' various phonic needs.

Writing

Recent Ofsted reports record a need to improve writing attainment in English primary schools. Their recent reports (Ofsted, 2008, 2011a, 2011b, 2012) contain a number of positive teaching approaches that address this issue. These include:

- writing purposes that include pupils' choices;
- time for extended writing, editing and redrafting;

- modelled, shared and guided writing;
- talk for writing approaches;
- cross-curricular writing;
- explicit marking;
- fluency in spelling, handwriting, sentence construction and word processing.

The list of recommendations illustrates links with reading and speaking and listening as well as highlighting cross-curricular literacy. A common thread amongst these recommendations is the importance of a context for writing. This can be the context of demonstrating composition as in shared, modelled and guided writing. It can also be the context provided by talk and application as in cross-curricular writing. It is very important to incorporate and value the literacy and English experiences of pupils outside of school when considering context. These experiences are part of pupils' social and cultural lives. This includes pupils' experiences of digital and popular culture which may not be acknowledged in school.

✎ Research focus

Toys and writing in the earliest years of primary school

Research from the US has looked at the role of toys and play as part of developing pupils' early writing (Wohlwend, 2009). The study found that girls in the earliest years of primary schooling used Disney dolls to re-enact and reinvent the Disney versions of fairy tales that they had seen and heard at home. The author notes that the toys allowed the girls to remember themes and ideas from how they had already played with them at home. Their Disney dolls helped them to keep meanings constant. The toys provided a bridge between speaking, listening, stories and writing at home and at school.

Classroom application   In the classroom the teaching of writing is part of the dual process of composition and transcription. Ofsted's recommendations indicate the need for regular and extended writing opportunities that have a real purpose and relevancy. The marking of all written work is part of this relevance for pupils' self-assessment of progress and knowledge of how to approach the next piece of writing. Marking provides an opportunity to develop pupils' meta-language. It enables pupils to recognise and describe their own writing processes.

Gender

The relative underachievement of boys in English and literacy has been an issue of international concern for a number of years. Relative to boys' achievement, girls outperform boys in many areas of English. This applies to all social groups. Attainment in English also fluctuates between schools. Here this seems to be more influenced by social circumstances than by gender. The reasons for the underachievement of boys are complex. Key aspects concern the social construction of gender and the nature of the English curriculum itself (DCSF, 2009). Research suggests that there is a link between academic self concept and reading achievement in boys (Chapman et al. 2000). This link has also been found in adolescent boys (Wilheilm and Smith, 2002).

Classroom application   In the classroom, teachers are encouraged to address the English attainment gap by addressing key areas significant for both genders. These may be summarised under four headings, adapted here from advice provided by the former governmental Department for Children, Schools and Families in England (DCSF, 2009).

- Challenge and support work for low ability pupils that builds self-esteem
- Fostering a community of readers in the classroom
- Structuring writing to build pupils' engagement through planning, editing and drafting as well as discussion
- Fostering collaboration and building pupils' personal responsibility for their learning

Many of these recommendations can be addressed through using talk, drama and discussion as a basis for writing preparation and planning via guided reading groups. Reading a range of text provides examples from which to shape and build writing. Guided reading groups need not always be teacher-led. Pupil-led groups can foster reading choice and engagement.

These headings also have implications for the use of digital texts in the classroom. For example, many of the new forms of social media are based on joint construction and collaboration rather than individual written compositions. Reading digital text is frequently an interactive process with online opportunities to interact with authors. Visual texts have increased emphasis. Actively using and evaluating these forms of reading and writing text contributes to bridging the gap between pupils' school and out of school use of language and English skills.

Cross-curricular literacy

Primary teachers are in the fortunate position of being able to teach all subjects. Monitoring progression across different subjects and situations becomes a much easier process because of this holistic approach to teaching and learning. Progression in primary English across the curriculum is underpinned by the pupils' use of language and corresponding literacy skills.

Cross-curricular literacy is also the process of application. Application involves developing subject specific language. Subject specific language is not restricted to technical vocabulary. It includes the language to access the subject too. For example, a term such as *fair* has different connotations and importance for the subjects of science investigations, personal, social and health education and English. Likewise various aspects of English have a greater significance for different subjects. The ability to research, select relevant texts and take notes, for instance, may be more frequently used in the humanities subjects while at primary school. Some aspects of English have a universal cross-curricular importance as in the progression of group discussion and presentation skills.

Classroom application   Planning for cross-curricular literacy is usually a whole school approach. Typically planning is progressive and builds towards an assessment piece of work that presents different aspects of subjects under a common theme (Ofsted, 2012). Useful approaches to cross-curricular literacy that integrate the four modes of English include independent research work, learning in different environments, enquiry-based **Mantle of the Expert** teaching, using good quality children's literature, drama improvisation, integrating analysis of film and literature and thinking skills techniques that encourage discussion and group work such as use of the TASC approach to problem solving (Wallace et al., 2012).

Transitions

The transition between early years' provision to the primary school and between primary and secondary school are key stages in pupils' progression. Making a successful transition relies upon pupils' ability to adapt and to thrive in a new situation. For class teachers and student teachers accommodating the move to a new phase of education means recognising the nature of continuity and progression. Part of this transition involves teachers using pupil data to plan at the right level. Developing pupils' independence in the new school environment and the progression of meta-cognitive skills is also part of this process.

Activity

Recognising emphasis in the English curriculum

Consider the following statements in order of importance for early years, primary or secondary school teachers of English.

- Reading for pleasure is essential for all aspects of English and language development.
- The teaching of literacy is not my main responsibility.
- Choice is key to engaging pupils' interest in the English curriculum.
- Handwriting and presentation are the responsibility of the pupil.
- School library visits are not a feature of English lessons.
- Children should always have the opportunity to experiment with their writing.
- Creative play and investigation build language competency.
- Learning to read and write for increasingly extended periods is a key English skill.
- Learning to spell needs an exploratory element in order to build personal spelling strategies.

This activity will have caused you to consider common aspects of English attainment across different age groups and the particular characteristics of the English curriculum in early years and secondary schooling. For example, play-based learning is a feature of early years. Literary analysis is a feature of secondary school English. You may also have considered baseline features of English attainment that receiving teachers in the next stage of education may require.

Classroom application In the classroom, preparing pupils for transition in primary English means securing key skills and strategies for application within English and across the curriculum. Planning comes from the needs of groups and individuals supported by close observation and recording.

Both the transition to a primary classroom from an early years setting and the transition to secondary school involve a change of teaching emphasis and style. In using books and reading, for example, pupils transferring to secondary school move from the primary school use of books as a stimulus and model for writing and language, to an emphasis on literary analysis. In secondary subject teaching, literacy is seen as a vehicle for delivering the subject whereas in primary teaching individual subjects are seen as a context for developing new language.

A change of teaching style can also have an effect as in the change from mainly play-based and free flow activities in early years to more formal schooling in the primary school. Secondary pupils have many subject specialists in different classrooms, not just one class teacher. This also has an effect. For example, it often requires pupils to apply and consolidate English skills across the curriculum. This can be challenging for their other subject specialist teachers who may not consider themselves to be teachers of literacy and English.

Transition projects can ease the change. For example, an introduction to literary analysis can be supported in the upper primary school by including transition work on a set novel that continues into the first term of the secondary school. Use of familiar picture books and keeping English routines (such as word finding and handwriting practice) work in a similar way between the early years and the primary school. In some schools transition teachers meet. They may work with each other's classes to meet pupils and for their own professional development.

Intervention strategies

Literacy intervention strategies are targeted approaches to teaching that focus on specific educational needs. These educational needs have normally been identified by a series of diagnostic assessments or thorough formative assessment. Intervention teaching happens in addition to regular class work. It may be a short-term intervention that lasts a few days or longer. This distinguishes it from regular classroom differentiation. Examples of interventions may be stretch and challenge work for very able pupils, spelling programmes, handwriting speed and fluency groups, individual **Reading Recovery** work or extra language work for EAL pupils.

Classroom applications   In the classroom, intervention work is frequently, but not exclusively, carried out by teacher assistants or by support teachers such as specialist dyslexia or language support teachers. The class teacher is ultimately responsible for monitoring pupils' responses to intervention so precise liaison with involved staff is crucial. Rotating teaching schedules ensures that the teacher regularly sees the progress of pupils receiving English intervention. If pupils are regularly withdrawn for intervention from lessons, the long-term benefits of doing so need to be carefully considered.

Testing, marking and curricular targets

Testing, marking and curricular targets are part of the assessment of English progression. The current testing focus concerns the type of high stakes statutory testing required by national regulatory bodies. These can be tied to judgements about school performance, teaching and learning as well as pupils' attainment. Marking and curricular targets are based on summative and formative assessments. Curricular targets are those which sit alongside broader lesson objectives. English curricular targets address the skills and knowledge necessary for reading, writing, speaking and listening across the primary school curriculum. Marking pupils' work is one method of showing pupils their progression towards achieving targets, leading to new ones that are jointly constructed. Target setting and marking, like shared lesson objectives, needs to consider the pupils' age and understanding. For example, the youngest children benefit from teachers marking their work with them.

Classroom application   In the classroom, high stakes testing can cause over-preparation, particularly in the run up to the statutory assessment tests. It can result in an imbalanced curriculum. Some statutory assessment requires that teacher assessments are also included. In some cases this involves the evidence from cumulative portfolios of pupils' annotated work to demonstrate progression over a set period of time. Typically, these portfolios of work are externally moderated to check that the work has been assessed correctly. Internal school moderation and moderation with clusters of other schools can also take place. For English, collating portfolios of work across all four modes of English can present a number of administrative challenges. Storage of large amounts of material is one issue. Digital storage is an option, allowing rapid comparison of work for different groups or individuals.

A number of commercial assessment companies produce standardised assessment, baseline assessments and attainment data tracking packages for English. Individual schools will prescribe baselines, standardised assessments and tracking processes in line with the statutory curriculum and regulatory processes.

Working with parents

Working with parents and carers is an essential aspect of primary teaching too large to fully address here. In summary, teachers have a statutory duty to inform parents and carers about their child's progress. By encouraging parents and carers to become actively involved in their child's education, pupils have added support from home. Working with parents also provides opportunities to strengthen the social and cultural context for pupils' use of English inside and outside of school.

Classroom application   Individual school policies and procedures will determine the nature of working with parents and carers. It may be at an individual, class, year group or school level. Working with parents to promote English progression

Activity

Matching features of attainment to classroom approaches to foster progression

Look at the selections of features of attainment taken from the pupil vignettes. Match the selections to examples of classroom approaches that foster progression. The fourth one has been done for you.

Table 10.4

Pupil	Sample of features of attainment	Chapter reference	Examples of classroom approaches to foster progression	Notes
Japonica	**Story ending** *Outside the castle, snow was falling. Inside, the castle, a man cried with sadness. What was he to do? His heart was broken but suddenly, without warning, he lifted his head. His puffy, red eyes opened widely after an amazing idea flashed across his mind. 'That's it, I know,' he shouted and ran into the snow*	Grammar		
Peter	Enjoys favourite books and themes, decodes print, reads high frequency words, uses picture cues, recalls main features of story, uses phonics to decipher unknown words by segmenting phonemes	Reading acquisition		

(Continued)

Pupil	Sample of features of attainment	Chapter reference	Examples of classroom approaches to foster progression	Notes
John	Answers direct questions from an adult and his friends, retells personal events	Speaking and listening	Challenge and support work that builds self-esteem, talk for writing approaches Build opportunities for dialogic talk across the curriculum	Use guided reading to build reading repertoire Use range of digital and multimodal texts. Encourage home school links through notes on book discussion in reading log
Peter	Uses pencil, tripod grip Print script with entry and exit joins attached but letters are not joined Letter size inconsistent, not on line, formation is mostly correct	Handwriting		
Analyn	Uses high frequency words from the first 200 word lists Uses suffixes, ed, s, ing, es, ly Some tense confusions	Spelling		
John	Reads for interest, always reads non-scheme books, favourite author is Dick King-Smith, reads some non-fiction, reads extended simple early novels, beginning to choose humorous poetry, fairy and folk tales	Reading engagement		

has a number of facets. For example, individually, parent meetings and open days are an opportunity to share the pupil's targets and discuss progress. The daily reading home school log and homework journal also serve this purpose. General English or literacy meetings are an opportunity for teachers to describe an aspect of classroom work and to receive feedback. Parent helpers receive an insight into classroom practice and opportunities to contribute such as through storytelling.

Features of progression

Progression in primary English is a recursive process. Pupils need opportunities to consolidate their learning before moving to the next stage of development. The five headings from Chapter 1 provide headings to assist in exemplifying aspects of progression in English as part of the teaching cycle: assess, plan, teach, practise, apply and review (National Primary Strategy, 2006).

The activity in Table 10.5 will have caused you to separate a number of different aspects of English attainment. The features you have separated will have a core of consistent attainment for all pupils. Looking at attainment like this allows for personalisation according to individual, group, class or school priorities.

Summary of chapter

In this chapter some current issues in primary English have been discussed. Each issue has been related to the primary classroom and to work samples taken from the pupil vignettes. The recursive nature of progression has been discussed. This chapter has emphasised your role in continuing professional development beyond initial teacher training and the probationary period of class teaching.

 Self-assessment

1. Write a pen portrait of one of the vignette pupils for the child's next class teacher.
2. Write a list of ten key English knowledge points and skills in preparation for secondary school transfer or for transfer from early years to primary education.

Looking at features of progression

Look at the examples of attainment in English. Write further examples of development, clarity, security, implicit and explicit learning for each example. Some sections have been completed for you.

Table 10.5

Examples of English attainment	Development	Clarity	Security	Implicit learning	Explicit learning
Builds on points made by others in group discussion			Builds on points made by others in discussion across the curriculum		
Relates what has just been read in a logical order	Consistently recalls what has been read with familiar and unfamiliar text				
Rehearses a sentence orally before writing and reads it back after it has been written					Rehearses with peer or teacher
Describes own reading preferences	Actively seeks reading recommendations			Enjoys books for pleasure	
Use commas in a sentence	Evaluates the use of commas in a range of unseen texts	Use commas in different ways to alter the meaning of a sentence	Use commas to make the sentence make sense		

Annotated further reading

Hardiman, M. (2012) *The Brain-targeted Teaching Model for 21st Century Schools*. Thousand Oaks: Corwin.
This book applies common findings from cognitive neuroscience research to the classroom context. It describes a clear teaching framework for the use of these ideas in the classroom.

Howe, A. and Richards, V. (Eds) (2011) *Bridging the Transition from Primary to Secondary School*. London: David Fulton.
This book provides a comprehensive guide to the issues surrounding pupils' transfer to secondary school. It includes useful chapters on reading choices and global citizenship and suggestions for curriculum transition projects.

DfE and ESARD (2012) *The Research Evidence on 'Writing'*. London: Education Standards Analysis and Research Division.
This report summarises international and national research evidence on writing in England.

Further resources

The website www.voiceofliteracy.org provides a regular series of recent podcasts from leading literacy researchers based in the USA.

The website www.literacytrust.org.uk provides information to support understanding of the gender gap in English and literacy and a useful *English Curriculum Review and Planning Tool* for auditing student teachers' subject knowledge in English. Periodic overviews of national literacy issues are produced.

The Talk for Writing website provides a range of teaching resources for primary and secondary writing: www.talk4writing.co.uk/

The drama-based Mantle of the Expert techniques created by Dorothy Heathcote support enquiry-based cross-curricular learning. Details can be found at: www. mantleoftheexpert.com/

References

Bourassa, D. and Treiman, R. (2010) Linguistic foundations of spelling development. In D. Wyse, R. Andrews and J. Hoffman (Eds), *The Routledge International Handbook of English Language and Literacy Teaching*. Abingdon: Routledge.
Bussis, A. M., Chittenden, E. A., Amarel, M. and Klausner, E. (1985) *Inquiry into Meaning: An Investigation of Learning to Read*: Hillsdale, NJ: Erlbaum.
Cassidy, J., Montalvo-Valadez, C. and Garrett, S. D. (2010) Literacy trends and issues: A look at the five pillars and the cement that supports them. *The Reading Teacher*, 63, 644–655.

Cassidy, J. and Ortlieb, E. (2011) Literacy: The first decade of the new millennium. *Reading Horizons*, 51 (2), 93–102.

Cassidy, J. and Ortlieb, E. (2013) What was hot (and not) in literacy: What we can learn. *Journal of Adolescent and Adult Literacy*, 57, 21–29.

Chapman, J. W., Tumner, W. E. and Prochnow, J. E. (2000) Early reading-related skills and performance, reading self concept and the development of academic self concept: A longitudinal study. *Journal of Educational Psychology*, 92, 703–708. doi:10.1037//0022–0663.92.4.703

Clarke, C. (2013) *Accelerated Reader and Young People's Reading*. London: National Literacy Trust.

Cremin, T., Mottram, M., Powell, F. and Safford, K. (2009) Teachers as readers: Building communities of readers. *Literacy*, 43, 11–19.

DCSF (2009) *Gender Issues in School: What Works to Improve Achievement for Boys and Girls* (DCSF 00601–2009BKT-EN).

DfES (2006) *Primary National Strategy: Primary Framework for Literacy and Mathematics*. London: DfES.

Department for Education (2014) *Statutory Phonics Screening Check*. London: DFE. Available at: www.gov.uk/government/policies/reforming-qualifications-and-the-curriculum-to-better-prepare-pupils-for-life-after-school/supporting-pages/statutory-phonics-screening-check

Dombey, H. (2010) *Teaching Reading: What the Evidence Says*. Leicester: United Kingdom Literacy Association.

Duff, F. J., Mengoni, S. E., Bailey, A., M. and Snowling, M. J. (2014) Validity and sensitivity of the phonics screening check: Implications for practice. *Journal of Research in Reading, Online*, 1–15. doi:DOI:10.1111/1467–9817.12029

Goswami, U. and Bryant, P. (1990) *Phonological Skills and Learning to Read*. Hillsdale, NJ: Lawrence Erlbaum.

Goswami, U., Thomson, J., Richardson, U., Stainthorp, R., Hughes, D., Rosen, S., et al. (2002). *Amplitude Envelope Onsets and Developmental Dyslexia: A New Hypothesis*. Paper presented at the Proceedings of the National Academy of Sciences.

Graham, J. and Kelly, A. (2008) *Reading Under Control* (3rd edn). London: David Fulton.

Guthrie, J. T., Wigfield, A. and You, W. (2012) Instructional contexts for engagement and achievement in reading. In S. L. Christenson, A. L. Reschly and C. Wylie (Eds), *Handbook of Research on Student Engagement*. pp. 601–634. doi:10.1007/978–1–4614–2018–7_29

Mullis, I. V. S., Martin, M. O., Foy, P. and Drucker, K. T. (2012) *PIRLS 2011 International Results in Reading*. Chestnut Hill, MA: TIMSS and PIRLS International Study Center, Boston College.

National Literacy Trust (2009) *What's Hot, What's Not 2009*. Available at: www.nationalliteracytrust.org.uk/research

National Primary Strategy (2006) *Excellence and Enjoyment: Learning and Teaching in the Primary Years*. (Ref: 0521–2004). London: DFES.

Ofsted (2008) *English at the Crossroads: An Evaluation of English in Primary and Secondary Schools 2005/2008*. (080247). London: Ofsted.

Ofsted (2011a) *Excellence in English: What We Can Learn from 12 Outstanding Schools*. London: Ofsted. Available at: www.ofsted.gov.uk.

Ofsted (2011b) *Removing the Barriers to Literacy.* (190237). London: Ofsted. Available at: www.ofsted.gov.uk.

Ofsted (2012) *Moving English Forward: Action to Raise Standards in English* (110118). London: Ofsted.

Primary National Strategy (2006) *Primary National Strategy.* Available at: www. educationengland.org.uk/documents/pdfs/2006-primary-national-strategy.pdf

Primary National Strategy (2007) *Letters and Sounds: Principles and Practice of High Quality Phonics.* (00281–2007BKT-EN). London: Primary National Strategy.

Renaissance Learning (2014) *What are Kids Reading? The Book Reading Habits of Students in American Schools.* Wisconson Rapids, WI: Renaissance Learning.

Rose, J. (2006) *Independent Review of Early Reading: Final Report.* London: Department for Education and Science.

Teen, N. P. (2003) The Singaporean school and the school excellence model. *Educational research for policy and practice,* 2, 27–39.

Topping, K. (2014) *What Kids are Reading: The Book Reading Habits of Students in British Schools.* London: Renaissance Learning.

Twist, L., Sizmur, L., Bartett, S. and Lynn, L. (2012) *PIRLS 2011 Reading Achievement in England.* (DFE- RB262). London: DFE.

Wallace, B., Bernardelli, A., Molyneaux, C. and Farrell, C. (2012) TASC: Thinking actively in a social context. A universal problem-solving process. A powerful tool to promote differentiated learning experiences. *Gifted Education International,* 28, 58–83. doi:10.1177/0261429411427645

Wigfield, A. and Eccles, J. S. (2000) Expectancy-value theory of achievement motivation. *Contemporary Educational Psychology,* 25, 68–81.

Wilheilm, J. D. and Smith, M. W. (2002) *Reading Don't Fix no Chevys: Literacy in the Lives of Young Men.* Boise, NJ: Heinemann.

Wohlwend, K. (2009) Damsels in discourse: Girls consuming and producing identity texts through Disney princess play. *Reading Research Quarterly,* 44, 57–84.

SELF-ASSESSMENT ANSWERS

Use of multimodal, digital and paper based text is implied in all of these model answers.

Chapter 1: What do we mean by progression in primary English?

1. Provide at least two reasons why behaviourism and nativism cannot be complete explanations of how children acquire language.

Reasons may include the following:

- *Behaviourism does not give an explanation of how children acquire language that they have not heard.*
- *Nativism does not fully address the conversational interaction necessary for language acquisition.*
- *Nativism does not fully address the role of parents and carers in the development of children's language.*

2. List three examples of different types of primary English assessment.

Examples include: diagnostic reading assessments, initial screening assessments for dyslexia, standardised reading tests of reading accuracy and language comprehension, miscue analysis, standardised spelling assessments, spelling error analyses, handwriting speed and fluency assessments, formative portfolios of annotated writing, reading attitude surveys.

3. List one classroom example of English progression characterised by two of the following: development, clarity, security, implicit or explicit learning.

The following are illustrative examples.

- *Development: pupil's reading age rises on a standardised reading assessment.*
- *Clarity: pupil consistently edits written work to use range of connectives according to the purpose for writing.*
- *Security: pupil takes turns and actively listens in all group discussions.*
- *Implicit learning: pupil switches between standard and non-standard English forms in speech.*
- *Explicit learning: pupil uses physical word banks, punctuation or connectives prompt sheets to edit own writing.*

Chapter 2: Speaking and listening

1. List the four components of language

Phonemes, morphemes, syntax and pragmatics.

2. Provide at least three reasons why the pragmatic use of language is emphasised in the primary classroom.

The following are illustrative examples. Pragmatics develops active listening, non-verbal language, turn-taking, ability to adapt speech for different purposes, encourages the use of Standard and non-Standard English, inference skills, conversation and group discussion skills.

3. List and justify three items that you consider important features or a suggested next step for progression in speaking and listening. Choose items for the oldest, mid-range and youngest pupils in the primary school.

The following are illustrative examples.

- *Youngest: turn taking sets basic rules for conversation. It sits alongside an ability to speak full sentences audibly.*
- *Mid-range: demonstrating empathy with the speaker allows for active listening skills.*

- *Oldest: consistently adapt language and body language for different audiences and for effect. This allows for a deliberate selection of vocabulary and intonation.*

Chapter 3: English as an additional language

1. List and justify three items that you consider important features or a suggested next step for progression in learning English as a second language for communication and learning. Choose items for elementary, intermediate and advanced English language learning pupils in the primary school. Look at the NALDIC and older Hester descriptors to help you.

This task is designed to encourage reflection on the types of language used in BICS and CALP communication and the effect of different social circumstances for each EAL child. The Hester scales note that elementary users of English will be developing language for communication and for meeting immediate social needs such as following routines, requesting basic needs and developing a labelling vocabulary. Intermediate users of English will be more able to hold conversations with their peers and be developing a wider vocabulary including some success with tenses. They may understand more than they can express. Advanced users of English have begun to master CALP through using English books and through writing English with increasing confidence. They are confident to use each language.

Chapter 4: Reading acquisition

1. Compare and contrast the elements of psycholinguistic, cognitive and socio-cultural approaches to reading.

The three approaches to reading differ in their conceptions of how reading takes place. Cognitive approaches are essentially processing models that address reading acquisition through the skills necessary to read words. Psycholinguistic and socio-cultural approaches prioritise the role of language, readers and their circumstances in the reading process. Although different in their techniques each approach develops the key skills of reading and language comprehension and decoding print. Classroom techniques for assessment and the teaching of reading will look different but the provision of a literature rich environment that builds a community of readers is accepted practice for each approach.

2. List the advantages and disadvantages of summative and formative assessments for monitoring daily reading progression.

Choosing any assessment is closely linked to its purpose and the audience for whom the results are represented. The advantages and disadvantages of it will link to this. For example:

- *high stakes standardised summative assessment can cause curriculum imbalance;*
- *summative assessments provide a baseline for classroom practice;*
- *cumulative formative assessment feeds into the assess, plan, teach, practise, apply, and review cycle;*
- *pupil self-assessment is empowering and formative.*

3. List and justify three items that you consider important features of progression or a suggested next step in learning to read. Choose items for the oldest, mid-range and youngest pupils in the primary school.

The following are illustrative examples with an emphasis on word recognition skills.

- *Youngest: fluent reading through rapid word recognition linking to vocabulary development and comprehension, pupils may use a mix of reading strategies that include phonics.*
- *Mid-range: consistent use of a range of strategies to decode print builds on syntactic, grapho-phonic and semantic skills.*
- *Oldest: consistent identification of unknown and key vocabulary before, during and after reading builds into a clear summary of what has been read, may return to phonics with unknown vocabulary out of context.*

Chapter 5: Reading comprehension

1. List and justify three items that you consider important features or next steps for progression in reading comprehension. Choose items for the oldest, mid-range and youngest pupils in the primary school.

The following are illustrative examples with an emphasis on developing literal, inferential and evaluative comprehension.

- *Youngest: listening to stories for pleasure, reading and re-reading favourite books helps to secure concepts about print and the structure of narratives as well as fostering a love of reading. Prediction, recall and sequencing skills are developed through familiar books.*
- *Mid-range: using a range of digital and paper based texts to read between the lines and make connections between ideas in small parts of a text. Pupils use inference in ideas from text and the pupil's experiences, including some links to what has been read elsewhere.*

- *Oldest: reads like a writer, recognises the way that words and sentences are chosen to interest the reader.*

2. Draw Venn diagrams to show the connections between reading acquisition and reading comprehension strategies and the factors that influence their progression.

This task is designed to encourage you to reflect on key skills and conditions for reading comprehension and reading acquisition from across Chapters 4 and 5. Illustrative examples of influences and connections are listed below.

Progression in reading acquisition and comprehension is influenced by a literature rich community of readers, systematic development of a reading repertoire, word reading skills, phonics, opportunities to build reading fluency and reading stamina, availability of reading materials at home and at school.

Acquisition and comprehension are connected by vocabulary, active reading for meaning with a range of reading strategies, the ability to transfer skills across a range of texts, phonics and word reading strategies and reading fluency.

Chapter 6: Reading engagement

1. List and justify three items that you consider important features or tipping points of progression in reading engagement. Choose items for the oldest, mid-range and youngest pupils in the primary school.

The following are illustrative examples with an emphasis on developing independent and extended reading for academic, social and personal purposes.

- *Youngest: choose books for own pleasure and have favourites. Enjoy listening to stories, songs and rhymes. This builds motivation to read for interest as well as pleasure. Use of stories, songs and rhymes builds phonological awareness and knowledge of narrative structure.*
- *Mid-range: choose a range of texts for their own pleasure and/or given purpose. Be familiar with selecting text from a library and from online sources. Know favourite books and authors. Discuss favourite reading with peers. Swap reading material with reading friends.*
- *Oldest: know favourite books, authors and genres. Established, growing repertoire. Read extended texts consistently. Use book recommendations. Write book reviews for pleasure. Readily take up reading challenges to read unfamiliar authors and genres. Discuss reading with peers. Use mixture of online and paper-based materials for research.*

2. Draw Venn diagrams to show the connections between reading acquisition, reading comprehension strategies and reading engagement and factors that influence their progression.

This task is designed to encourage you to reflect on key skills and knowledge required to promote reading engagement as part of reading acquisition. Necessarily, this is influenced by a literature rich environment and an active community of readers. Reading engagement is connected to reading purpose, practise and stamina which build fluency, word recognition and comprehension skills.

3. Write a definition of an effective reader for the oldest, mid-range and youngest pupil in the primary school. Note the similarities and differences between them.

Answers to this question are influenced by your perception of what it means to be a reader. This will necessarily change as the reading demands of pupils' social, cultural and school communities alter and your classroom teaching experience grows. The following are illustrative examples built on the premise of encouraging pupils to become life-long readers.

- *An effective reader in the youngest part of primary schooling loves books, rhymes, song and listening to stories. They can decode using an increasing range of strategies that include phonics. They read for meaning.*
- *An effective reader in the mid-range part of the primary school loves to read and has a reading repertoire. They are confident to read, understand and interpret a range of fiction and non-fiction texts and to select the 'just right', book for their own reading pleasure. They can find information and present it in different ways. Reading stamina is developing.*
- *An effective reader in the upper part of the primary school loves to read and has an established reading repertoire. They are confident to read, understand and interpret a range of fiction and non-fiction texts and to give and try reading recommendations. They can research. They can consistently read with a writer's eye. They have reading stamina.*

Chapter 7: Writing composition

1. List and justify three items that you consider important features of or suggested next steps for progression in writing composition. Choose items for the oldest, mid-range and youngest pupils in the primary school.

The following are illustrative examples with an emphasis on developing independent and extended writing for academic, social and personal purposes.

- *Youngest: know that print carries meaning, know a range of stories that support ability to recall and write simple stories and recounts, putting ideas together. Narrative understanding is an important aspect of early writing composition.*

- *Mid-range: structure writing into recognisable parts, be able to edit writing, write a range of generic structures. Editing writing develops the process of writing like a reader, developing writing for an audience and purpose.*
- *Oldest: redraft writing for content as well as transcription. Write a range of text forms. Use language and sentence structures to affect an identified audience and purpose for writing. These develop extended, short and sustained writing skills, all necessary for secondary school.*

2. List linguistic, socio-cultural and cognitive perspectives of writing composition.

This task is designed to develop awareness of the range of influences of pupils' motivation and engagement in writing composition. Look at the similarities between them. Linguistic perspectives include pupils' breadth of vocabulary, knowledge of text structure and genres, spoken and written grammar, choosing and using language (register) for audience and purpose. Cognitive perspectives look at information processing areas such as pupils' oral and written comprehension of language, storage and retrieval of information in the memory and problem solving approaches to composition. Socio-cultural perspectives include the pupils' school, community and culture as well as the broader influences from the media. The type, place and value of texts within a community are part of this area.

3. List linguistic, socio-cultural and cognitive aspects of writing composition

Linguistic aspects include pupils' use of implicit and explicit grammar and non-fiction and narrative structures and their range of vocabulary. Cognitive aspects include the use of meta-cognitive writing tools such as writing frames, sentence stems and early primary writing tools such as 'rainbow writing', where pupils trace over highlighted print that they have dictated to an adult. Socio-cultural aspects of writing composition link to the development of pupils' identities as readers, writers, speakers and listeners. Relevant contexts for writing composition serve to promote writing engagement and serve as a springboard from which to broaden pupils' reasons to write.

Chapter 8: Grammar

1. List and justify three items that you consider important features or next steps for progression in written grammar. Choose items for the oldest, mid-range and youngest pupils in the primary school.

This task is designed to illustrate the cumulative and recursive nature of grammar progression. The examples below track selected aspects of sentence writing skills to demonstrate how reading, composition and speaking and listening skills contribute to its progression.

- *Youngest: construct a descriptive sentence orally before writing, read back what has been written, use a full stop and a capital letter to demarcate the sentence, use commas in a list, read with intonation and growing fluency, experiment with sentence types, write simple and compound sentences.*
- *Mid-range: construct a descriptive sentence orally before writing, use a range of vocabulary, edit what has been written, use a full stop and capital letters to demarcate a sentence, use capital letters for proper nouns, use commas to separate parts of a sentence and to alter the meaning, use different connectives to join and build sentence sections and expanded phrases to show shades of meaning, use all sentence structures.*
- *Oldest: construct descriptive sentences planned for effect, edit and redraft what has been written, use a full range of punctuation to demarcate the sentence and to clarify meaning, accurately use a full range of connectives according to the purpose of the sentence and for the type of text as a whole, write the full range of sentence types and structures.*

2. List linguistic, socio-cultural and cognitive perspectives on written grammar.

This task is designed to clarify the three main types of grammatical study:

Linguistic perspectives of grammar look at phonics, phonological awareness, morphology, syntax and semantics. Socio-cultural perspectives of grammar look at language variation, including non-Standard and Standard English based on the pupils' school, community and culture as well as the broader influences from the media. The effect of context on meaning is part of this area and includes the development of genre. Cognitive perspectives of grammar address how language and grammar are acquired and processed through the four modes of English. They include pupils' oral and written comprehension of language, storage and retrieval of information in the memory and problem solving approaches to using grammar.

3. Describe contrasting and comparable elements of written grammar in examples of digital and multimodal texts.

This task is designed to encourage reflection on the reading and writing demands of different types of text. Three illustrative examples are given here:

Interactive talking books that combine reading e-books with comprehension provide immediate and accessible pupil feedback and audio effects. Some schemes automatically provide ability based e-books based on the pupils' responses. Pupils navigate the book with on-screen icons. Similar paper-based material is available without built-in feedback. Paper-based reading can be closely linked to modelled and shared writing. The navigation and self-selection of the text is different in both types of books.

Films provide visual opportunities to look at structure and coherence through elements such as characterisation, screen shots and colour. Film can serve as an introduction to looking at cohesion and coherence in written text.

Wordless picture books for all primary ages are a vehicle for developing pupils' vocabulary without the presence of the author's words. Picture books provide opportunities for multiple interpretations of layers of meaning within a range of genres. Oral work from picture books provides a vehicle for a range of writing work.

Chapter 9: Spelling and handwriting

1. List and justify three items that you consider important features or next steps for progression in spelling or handwriting. Choose items for the oldest, mid-range and youngest pupils in the primary school.

This task is designed to allow you to reflect on the connections between spelling and handwriting and to consider their links to the four modes of English. Illustrative examples are:

Youngest: consistent letter formation in the early stages of writing promotes fluency, combined with application of phonics to reading and spelling patterns in words.

Mid-range: modelling consistent strategies for self-editing of transcription skills that include spelling, promotes pupils' awareness of the audience and purpose for writing and promotes the presentation of final written drafts.

Oldest: looking at the etymology of words, and root words through word investigations promotes an interest in the construction and nature of words. It develops pupils' vocabulary.

2. Relate linguistic, socio-cultural or cognitive research perspectives to common examples of classroom practice in the teaching of handwriting or spelling.

This task is designed to illustrate multisensory teaching.

Linguistic perspectives of spelling look at phonics, phonological awareness, and morphology. Graded daily spelling foci that concentrate on specific phonics or morphemes lead to cumulative weekly spelling tests. Cognitive perspectives address spelling acquisition and processing. Class work to promote pupils' spelling strategies is relevant here. Socio-cultural perspectives look at word games, word play and the nature and function of spelling in different contexts.

3. List evidence for the importance of monitoring handwriting and spelling as part of writing composition; include digital and multimodal texts.

This activity is designed to encourage you to reflect on the importance of spelling and handwriting skills in a word processing and digital age of technology.

Monitoring the use of different written presentation skills and styles, including word processing, provides a range of evidence for pupils' editing and spelling self-correction skills. Online and paper based dictionary forms are part of this.

Analysis of pupils' manual handwritten 'try out', spelling note pads in the classroom shows details of pupils' exploratory attempts at spelling.

Monitoring regular handwriting practice for itself allows teachers to observe pupils' handwriting in action and their written results. Both provide information about letter formation, fluency and writing speed. Written spelling dictations with older pupils are another technique.

Chapter 10: Looking forward

1. Write a pen portrait of one of the vignette pupils for the child's next class teacher.

Model examples of this activity appear in Chapter 1. Pen portraits are necessarily accompanied by evidence of pupils' work and hard copies of summative and diagnostic assessments. Data statistics by themselves do not provide sufficient detail with which to monitor progression for the primary teacher.

2. Write a list of ten key English knowledge points and skills in preparation for secondary school transfer or for transfer from early years to primary education.

The following are illustrative examples of generic points to consider before transfer. Individual, local and national priorities will add to these lists.

Early years to primary
 1. *Specialist language and literacy and related special educational needs*
 2. *Details of pupils with EAL*
 3. *Details of stage of phonic and word reading acquisition*
 4. *Standardised test data*
 5. *Cumulative English portfolio of work*
 6. *Reading book level*
 7. *Favourite reading or book listening choices*
 8. *Pencil control and eye hand coordination*
 9. *Left or right handedness*
 10. *Copy of latest home school reading or sharing books log*

Primary to secondary
 1. *Specialist language and literacy and related special educational needs*
 2. *Details of pupils with EAL*

3. *Details of stage of phonic and word reading acquisition and preferred spelling strategies*
4. *Standardised test data*
5. *Examples of recent written work across subject areas*
6. *Recent reading attitudes and interest survey*
7. *Left or right handedness*
8. *Details of whether the pupil has used biro, ink or only pencil*
9. *Details of pupils' favourite authors and genres, past and present*
10. *Pupils' own English self-assessed goals for secondary school*

PHOTOCOPIABLE RECORDING SHEETS

Individual miscue analysis recording sheet for reading

Examples of points for observing reading behaviour

What reading strategies are used? [Semantic, syntactic, phonic, grapho-phonic] Can the pupil read silently as well as aloud? Does the pupil understand what has been read? Are there any vocabulary comprehension difficulties? Are there any consistent phoneme errors? Does the pupil use visual information to make meaning? How does the pupil use evidence to support prediction? Can the pupil summarise what has been read?

Name		
Date		
Level of reading attainment	Easy text (over 95% correct) / **Instructional text (90–95% correct)** / Hard text (below 95% correct) / Fluency	

Word in the text	What the pupil read	Self correction	Strategy keeps meaning of the text	Strategy loses meaning of the text	Hesitation	Substitution	Omission or refusal	Insertions	Repetition	Reads high frequency words	Reverses letters or words	Segments phonemes and re-blends	Segments syllables and re-blends	Uses onset and rime	Reads back and on in the text, uses oral language to predict	Uses pictures	Tracks print with finger	Teacher gives the word or assists	Reads with intonation	Recalls and asks questions about the text	Makes predictions about the text, recalls similar text	Other
Totals																						

Title of book

Notes and evaluation

Individual spelling analysis recording sheet [Source: Adapted and reprinted with permission from First Steps Spelling Resource Book © Department of Education, Western Australia, 2001]

Name Date	Level of spelling attainment	Source and subject	Correct word	Spelling attempt	Phonemically plausible	Alphabet error	Phonemic error	Morphemic error	Orthographic error	High frequency word error	Homophone error	Unlikely spelling	Other

Guided group reading recording sheet

Lesson Objective						Success criteria		
Group		Strategies for understanding (grapho-phonic, syntactic, semantic)						
Date	Level of reading attainment	Accuracy in decoding		Fluency	Literal	Vocabulary	Inferential	Evaluative	Achieved, not achieved, partially achieved
Name								
Text or book title		Notes and evaluation						

Guided writing group recording sheet

Lesson Objective							
Group							
Date			Success Criteria				
Name	Level of writing attainment	Structure focus	Sentence and punctuation focus	Vocabulary focus	Spelling focus	Handwriting focus	Other	Achieved, not achieved, partially achieved
Context for writing			Notes and evaluation					

Speaking and listening recording sheet

Lesson Objective									
Group			Success Criteria						
Date									
Name	Level of speaking and listening attainment	Listening	Vocabulary	Group discussion	Question and answer skills	Presentation	Choice of Standard or non-Standard English as appropriate	Other	Achieved, not achieved, partially achieved
Context for speaking and listening			Notes and evaluation						

GLOSSARY

Analogies are used to explain something by comparing it to another.

Analytic phonics segments parts of words and looks for common letter patterns.

Automaticity describes pupils' level of rapid word reading.

Balanced approaches are those which use a mix or techniques and philosophies to meet pupils' English needs.

Blends are groups of letters where each letter sound can be heard.

Cohesion refers to the sense of a whole piece of text through words or structure. Examples of cohesive links are conjunctions, pronouns and using synonyms to avoid repetition.

Complex sentences have one chief clause and one or more subordinate clauses.

Compound sentences have at least two clauses joined by a simple connective which could stand alone.

Concepts about print was a term coined by Marie Clay. Her 'Concepts about print' test looks at pupils' familiarity with aspects of the book such as reading left to right and understanding the purpose of punctuation.

Coordinating conjunctions link equal parts of a sentence.

Decode means to be able to decipher the printed word. Decoding is possible without comprehension.

Determiners are used with a noun or noun phrase. Examples include a, the, this, some, its.

Fluency describes the smoothness with which pupils read.

Fronted adverbials are an example of a type of word, clause or phrase that comes before the verb, or clause, often followed by a comma.

Graphemes are the written shapes of phonemes.

Grapheme-phoneme correspondence is the ability to link the sound to written grapheme forms of the phoneme.

High frequency sight words are words most frequently read in the early stages of reading.

Homophones are words that sound the same but have different spellings and meanings.

Hot seating describes a drama activity. Pupils in role are questioned.

Instructional text describes a level of text difficulty. The terms and percentages for instructional, hard and easy text difficulty were devised by Marie Clay.

Lexical terms refer to the use of words and language.

Listening comprehension is the language pupils can hear and understand.

Mantle of the Expert teaching is a drama, enquiry-based and cross-curricular approach to teaching that involves pupils working to solve real life problems. It was developed by Dorothy Heathcote.

Miscue analysis is a diagnostic procedure for identifying pupils' reading strategies to decode and comprehend print. Teachers mark a copy of the text while the pupil is reading to collate semantic, syntactic and grapho-phonic reading strategies and combinations of each. The level of self correction is important because this illustrates pupils' reading for meaning. The term was coined by Kenneth Goodman.

Morphemes are the smallest units of meaning in a language.

Onsets are the first consonant phoneme in a word before a vowel: <u>Ch</u> (op)_

Orthographic (systems) are the spelling aspects of a language.

Phonemes are the smallest units of sound in a language.

Phonics is a general term for the process of reading and articulating speech sounds by linking sounds (phonemes) to letter (graphemes).

Phonological awareness is the ability to discriminate sounds in speech.

Prefixes are morphemes added to the beginning of words.

Reading Recovery is an individual reading intervention designed to boost pupils' reading fluency. Reading Recovery teachers are specifically trained.

Reading strategies are adopted by pupils to decipher print. According to psycholinguistic approaches they may be semantic, syntactic, or grapho-phonic.

Received Pronunciation describes a formal form of pronunciation and accent for British speakers. It used to be called BBC English because this pronunciation was historically used by BBC announcers.

Relative clauses are often linked to the main clause with that, who, what, which, and where and why.

Rimes are the vowel and final phoneme in a word: (ch) <u>op</u>

Running records are simple forms of miscue analysis.

Segment refers to the process of separating the phonemes in a word.

Simple sentences have one clause, one subject and a verb.

Standard English is the language given status in formal communications. It is taught to pupils with English as foreign language. It can be spoken with any accent.

Subordinating conjunctions connect subordinate clauses to a main clause. They have specific purposes and can alter the meaning of a sentence.

Suffixes are morphemes added to the ends of words.

Synthetic phonics segments and blends phonemes to make words.

Whole Language theory approaches to reading embrace the teaching of reading as a whole process in itself without breaking it down into its separate parts. Whole language teachers often advocate the use of non-scheme reading books. Reading engagement is a focal point.

INDEX